LOOK BEFORE YOU WATCH!

Before you switch on that TV set or go out to the stadium to watch your favorite pro football team in action, you owe yourself a long look at **Pro Football 1977.** No other book gives you more vital information, exciting features and dramatic action photographs. Here is all you need to know to follow the action, including:

- Total team-by-team coverage and analysis— team statistics, roster, performance quotient rating system, depth chart, schedule, predictions

- Player draft selections

- Complete statistical reference section

- All-Star action photos

- Special features on great players and moments of 1976, including Super Bowl XI, Walter Payton, O.J. Simpson, Bert Jones, and the versatile champions, the Oakland Raiders.

All of this in
PRO FOOTBALL 1977.
A Ballantine Original

Don't miss the other exciting books in this series
published by Ballantine Books:

MAJOR LEAGUE BASEBALL 1977
PRO BASKETBALL 1977-78
HOCKEY 1977-78

available at your local bookstore

PRO
FOOTBALL
1977

in association with
Talisman Books, Inc.

illustrated

BALLANTINE BOOKS • NEW YORK

Published in the United States by Ballantine Books, a division of Random House, Inc., New York, and simultaneously in Canada by Ballantine Books of Canada, Ltd., Toronto, Canada.

ISBN 0-345-25822-3

Manufactured in the United States of America

First Edition: September 1977

CREDITS:

Writing by Larry Felser and Dave Klein.

Cover photograph of O.J. Simpson of the Buffalo Bills by George Gojkovich.

Inside photos by Vernon J. Biever, Malcolm W. Emmons, Jerry Binder, George Gojkovich, Nate Fine, Thomas J. Croke, and Henry M. Barr Studios.

Contents

ALL-STARS IN ACTION

THE NATIONAL CONFERENCE

Eastern Division

Central Division

Western Division

THE AMERICAN CONFERENCE

Eastern Division

Central Division

Western Division

SUPER FEATURES

HALL OF RECORDS

NATIONAL FOOTBALL CONFERENCE

Whatever you want to know about each of the 14 teams in the National Conference is available in the next 112 pages. The complete team-by-team rundown will prepare you to follow your favorite club and scout its rivals through the 1977 season.

The analysis of each NFC team takes this shape: First, the club's strengths and weaknesses are examined in an in-depth study; that is followed by the important statistics of the team and its players for the 1976 season and the 1977 schedule; then comes a detailed roster of veteran personnel—with height, weight, age as of August 31, years of pro experience and college shown for each player; incorporated into this roster are our Performance Quotient ratings for every department on offense and defense, plus kickers; this is followed by a depth chart showing the team's starting and reserve players at each position; lastly, the club's 1977 draftees are listed, along with a Performance Quotient rating of these youngsters.

These are the data our experts have considered when making their predictions for each team. The club's tangible strengths and weaknesses, as detailed in our Performance Quotients, were evaluated, as were the intangibles that can make a team perform even better—or worse—than one would expect it to.

Here is how the Performance Quotients are set up: Every area is given a rating and an appraisal summary. On offense, rated categories are quarterbacks, running backs, receivers, interior linemen, and kickers; on defense, the departments are front linemen, linebackers, cornerbacks, and safeties. (The rookies are also rated, as we said.) The rating system is based on a scale of 1 to 5. A category rated 1 is the best or tied for the best in the conference; a rating of 2 stands for excellent; 3 equals good; 4 is fair; and 5 is poor. By adding up the ratings of each team's various units, you will be able to match the strength of one team against the capability of any other.

The teams are arranged according to the order in which we predict they will complete regular-season play. Here's what our experts envision for the postseason playoffs: The divisional winners will be the Dallas Cowboys in the East, the Minnesota Vikings in the Central and the Los Angeles Rams in the West. The wild-card team that we believe will qualify for the playoffs is the St. Louis Cardinals. And who will be the National Conference champion? We pick the newly strengthened Eastern champions, the Dallas Cowboys, to defend their NFC crown. To check out our selection of the AFC team that will attempt to beat the Cowboys, see the American Conference section that begins on page 115.

DALLAS COWBOYS

Prediction: First

The only thing that kept Dallas from a trip to the Super Bowl last time around was the lack of a speed back with game-breaking potential.

Fret no longer, Cowboy fans. Dallas found its pigeon up in Seattle and traded away its first-round selection and three draft picks in the second round for Seattle's choice in the first round.

Since Seattle was the second team to pick, and since Tampa Bay had decided months earlier to take USC fullback Ricky Bell, the Cowboys found what they needed: Tony Dorsett.

The rest of the NFC Eastern teams, acting as one, mumbled "we are not amused" just before slashing their wrists.

Okay, so the Cowboys now have the best runner to come zipping out of college since O.J. Hertz. They have a veteran unit on the offensive line, the conference's top wide receiver, a first-rate tight end and a defense that would rather shoot first and then ask questions.

What can stop Dallas now? Short of emergency legislation, not a hell of a lot.

The quarterback is Roger Staubach, who had some hand injuries last season but still played heroically, if not as well as he might have normally. The fullback figures to be Robert Newhouse, although Scott Laidlaw or second-year man Jim Jensen (6-3, 230) may muscle their way to the front.

Other runners include Doug Dennison, the best of the reserves, who, elsewhere, might be a starter, and such as former No. 1 draft pick Charles Young, veteran Preston Pearson, both of whose days might be numbered in Dallas, and 1976 third-round choice John Smith, who missed last season because of a foot injury. Talk about your abundance of riches.

Danny White is a brilliant young quarterback who'll get more work and who, as Staubach was before him, is clearly being groomed for stardom. Rookie Glenn Carano, perhaps the pick of the college QBs, is on the roster now, too.

The offensive line is peopled by former All-Pro types, though most of them are beyond that now and the unit is a potential trouble spot. Tackles will be Ralph Neely and Rayfield Wright, guards Blaine Nye and either Herbert Scott or Burton Lawless, and center John Fitzgerald. Youngsters such as Pat Donovan, Tom Rafferty, Jim Eidson, Kyle Davis and rookie Val Belcher may be of help.

Billy Joe DuPree, who catches well and blocks even better, is the tight end.

Wide receivers are led by Drew Pearson, the NFC's leader last year with 58 receptions for 806 yards. He will team with either Golden Richards or Butch Johnson, although Percy Howard, who missed 1976 with an uncooperative knee and had off-season surgery, and rookie Tony Hill will push.

But the offense will be Dorsett, the kind of runner the perennially strong Cowboys have never possessed.

And that should make matters even easier for a violently good defense.

There is some lack of depth on the front line, but the starters range from quite good to outstanding.

The ends are Harvey Martin and Ed "Too Tall" Jones. The tackles are Larry Cole and Jethro Pugh. Cole is not an All-Star and Pugh (33) is getting old. Behind them are Greg Schaum and Bill Gregory, with rookies David Stalls and Andy Frederick in reserve.

The linebacking area is where the Cowboys excel, despite the retirement of Lee Roy Jordan, which puts 6-2, 228-pound Bob Breunig in the middle, his natural location. Budding superstar Randy White is 6-4, 240 and about to depress running backs from the strongside slot, while veteran D.D. Lewis may not be able to fight off Thomas Henderson, the fastest man on the team at 6-2, 223.

Cornerbacks figure to be 35-year-old Mel Renfro and younger Benny Barnes—at least for a while. But Renfro has a knee problem and at his age he seems better suited to be a quality reserve. That will make a starter out of Mark Washington. Cliff Harris is an All-Pro free safety and Charley Waters played well at strong safety. There is a young, strong, third-year man, 6-4, 210-pound Randy Hughes, who can play free safety and wants to desperately. Other reserves are Aaron Kyle, last year's No. 1 pick, and converted WR Beasley Reece.

The secondary isn't among the conference's most adept, but as has been proved over and over again, the quality of the secondary is directly tied to the effectiveness of the pass rush and the movement of the linebackers.

In this case, the Dallas secondary is at least as good as it has to be.

1976 RECORD (11-4)

27	Philadelphia	7	9	New York Giants		3
24	New Orleans	6	17	Buffalo		10
30	Baltimore	27	10	Atlanta		17
28	Seattle	13	19	St. Louis		14
24	New York Giants	14	26	Philadelphia		7
17	St. Louis	21	14	Washington		27
31	Chicago	21		(Playoff)		
20	Washington	7	12	Los Angeles		14

PASSING

	Atts	Comps	Yds	Lgst	TDs	Ints	Pct
Staubach	369	208	2715	53	14	11	56.4
D. White	20	13	213	56	2	2	65.0

SCORING

	TDs	PATs	FGs	Total
Herrera	0	34	18	88
D. Pearson	7	0	0	42
Dennison	6	0	0	36
Laidlaw	4	0	0	24
Four tied with	3	0	0	18

RUSHING

	Atts	Yds	TDs	Lgst	Avg
Dennison	153	542	6	14	3.5
Newhouse	116	450	3	24	3.9
Laidlaw	94	424	3	28	4.5
P. Pearson	68	233	1	21	3.4
Young	48	208	0	24	4.3
Staubach	43	184	3	18	4.3

RECEIVING

	Recs	Yds	TDs	Lgst	Avg
D. Pearson	58†	806	6	40	13.9
DuPree	42	680	2	38	16.2
Laidlaw	38	325	1	26	8.6
P. Pearson	23	316	2	30	13.7
Richards	19	414	3	56	21.8
Newhouse	15	86	0	16	5.7

INTERCEPTIONS

	Ints	Yds	TDs	Lgst	Avg
Washington	4	49	0	22	12.3
Harris	3	32	0	29	10.7
Renfro	3	23	0	23	7.7
Waters	3	6	0	5	2.0

SYMBOL †—Conference leader

1977 SCHEDULE

Home: Sept. 25—New York Giants; Oct. 2—Tampa Bay; Oct. 16—Washington; Oct. 30—Detroit; Nov. 14—St. Louis; Dec. 4—Philadelphia; Dec. 18—Denver.

Away: Sept. 18—Minnesota; Oct. 9—St. Louis; Oct. 23—Philadelphia; Nov. 6—New York Giants; Nov. 20—Pittsburgh; Nov. 27—Washington; Dec. 12—San Francisco.

OFFENSE

QUARTERBACKS	Ht	Wt	Age	Exp	College
Staubach, Roger	6-3	197	35	9	Navy
White, Danny	6-2	180	25	2	Arizona State

Staubach had injury problems in '76, but is healed and still brilliant. White may be the best young sub in the league. PERF. QT.: 2.

RUNNING BACKS	Ht	Wt	Age	Exp	College
Newhouse, Robert	5-10	205	27	6	Houston
Dennison, Doug	5-11	208	25	4	Kutztown State
Laidlaw, Scott	6-0	206	24	3	Stanford
Pearson, Preston	6-1	208	32	11	Illinois
Jensen, Jim	6-3	230	23	2	Iowa
Young, Charles	6-1	220	24	4	North Carolina St.
Smith, John	5-11	186	23	1	Boise State

Newhouse had an off-year last season but has power to the inside and blocks. Dennison, sometimes erratic, has flashy speed and works hard. Laidlaw may challenge for a regular job; he can run, block, catch. Pearson may be near the end of the line but still uses his head. Young has been a disappointment but is young enough to keep. Jensen has size and power, can surprise. Smith missed his rookie year, 1976, with a foot injury. He is worth a look. PERF. QT.: 3.

RECEIVERS	Ht	Wt	Age	Exp	College
Pearson, Drew (W)	6-0	185	25	6	Tulsa
Richards, Golden (W)	6-0	190	26	5	Hawaii
DuPree, Billy Joe (T)	6-4	230	27	5	Michigan State
Johnson, Butch (W)	6-1	187	23	2	Cal-Riverside
Howard, Percy (W)	6-4	215	25	2	Austin Peay
Saldi, Jay (T)	6-3	225	23	2	South Carolina

(W)—Wide Receiver   (T)—Tight End

Pearson may be as good as any wide receiver in the NFC. Richards has speed and makes big catches but is too unpredictable. DuPree took over when Jean Fugett left and turned into a wonderful surprise. Howard may have a shot at Richards' job if his knee recovers. Johnson has the ability to start. He returns kicks, too. Saldi is the only reserve tight end, and the Cowboys are looking to improve here. PERF. QT.: 2.

INTERIOR LINEMEN	Ht	Wt	Age	Exp	College
Wright, Rayfield (T)	6-6	255	32	11	Fort Valley State
Neely, Ralph (T)	6-6	255	33	13	Oklahoma
Nye, Blaine (G)	6-4	255	31	10	Stanford
Scott, Herbert (G)	6-2	250	24	3	Virginia Union

INTERIOR LINEMEN (Contd.)	Ht	Wt	Age	Exp	College
Fitzgerald, John (C)	6-5	252	29	7	Boston College
Lawless, Burton (G)	6-4	250	23	3	Florida
Donovan, Pat (T)	6-4	250	24	3	Stanford
Eidson, Jim (C-G)	6-3	264	23	2	Mississippi State
Davis, Kyle (C)	6-4	245	24	2	Oklahoma
Rafferty, Tom (G)	6-3	250	23	2	Penn State

(T)—Tackle   (G)—Guard   (C)—Center

Wright slipped a bit in '76 but still ranks as one of the top tackles. Neely may need some relief but probably won't be replaced as a starter this year. Nye remains the team's top lineman despite his retirement talk. Scott seems in line for a regular job, but he'll have to improve to be a top-level guard. Fitzgerald is one of the top centers, and young enough to stay there. Lawless will be Scott's challenger, and he could win the job. Donovan has spent two years as a reserve; if Neely falters, the youngster is in. As a rookie, Eidson showed versatility, which the Cowboys always seek. Davis, a promising youngster, missed all of '76 with an injury. Rafferty will have to hustle to stick. PERF. QT.: 2.

KICKERS	Ht	Wt	Age	Exp	College
Herrera, Efren (Pk)	5-9	190	26	4	UCLA
White, Danny (P)	6-2	180	25	2	Arizona State

(Pk)—Placekicker   (P)—Punter

Herrera had a top-flight year and surprised Coach Landry. White is a valuable punter with potential to improve. PERF. QT.: 2.

DEFENSE

FRONT LINEMEN	Ht	Wt	Age	Exp	College
Martin, Harvey (E)	6-5	252	26	5	East Texas State
Jones, Ed (E)	6-9	265	26	4	Tennessee State
Pugh, Jethro (T)	6-6	248	33	13	Elizabeth City (N.C.)
Cole, Larry (T)	6-5	250	30	10	Hawaii
Gregory, Bill (T)	6-5	252	27	7	Wisconsin
Schaum, Greg (E)	6-4	246	23	2	Michigan State

(E)—End   (T)—Tackle

Martin may already be one of the best ends in the league and he's only 26. Jones is effective, though not the superstar he was supposed to be. Pugh is aging and may find some new faces around wanting his job. Cole, once an end, is satisfactory inside but not near All-Pro grade. Gregory has been around six years without winning a regular job. Schaum will have to improve considerably to stay. PERF. QT.: 2.

LINEBACKERS	Ht	Wt	Age	Exp	College
Lewis, D. D. (O)	6-1	215	31	9	Mississippi State
White, Randy (O-M)	6-4	240	24	3	Maryland
Breunig, Bob (M)	6-2	228	24	3	Arizona State
Henderson, Thomas (O)	6-2	223	24	3	Langston
Hegman, Mike (O)	6-1	221	24	2	Tennessee State
Cook, Leroy (O)	6-2	225	23	1	Alabama

(O)—Outside Linebacker   (M)—Middle Linebacker

Lee Roy Jordan's retirement moves Breunig to the middle from the strong-side and opens a place for White, who is on the verge of superstardom. Lewis will compete with Henderson for the weak-side job, and Insiders expect Henderson to win. Hegman is simply a reserve. Cook, drafted last year as a DE, was hurt, and is now a hot-shot prospect here—as if one is needed! PERF. QT.: 1.

CORNERBACKS	Ht	Wt	Age	Exp	College
Renfro, Mel	6-0	190	35	14	Oregon
Barnes, Benny	6-1	190	25	6	Stanford
Washington, Mark	5-11	186	29	8	Morgan State
Reece, Beasley	6-1	186	23	2	North Texas State
Kyle, Aaron	5-10	181	23	2	Wyoming

Renfro is old enough to think about retiring, or sitting. Washington played well when given the chance and should be Mel's inheritor. Barnes figures to retain the left corner job. Reece showed quickness as a rookie and doubles as a wide receiver. Kyle, 1976's No. 1 pick, was mildly disappointing. PERF. QT.: 3.

SAFETIES	Ht	Wt	Age	Exp	College
Waters, Charlie (S)	6-2	195	28	8	Clemson
Harris, Cliff (W)	6-1	190	28	8	Ouachita
Hughes, Randy (W)	6-4	210	24	3	Oklahoma

(S)—Strong-side   (W)—Weak-side or "Free" Safety

Waters is a Pro Bowler; he finally upheld Landry's patience. Harris is the best free safety in the league. Hughes could start for most other teams. Cornerback Barnes backs Waters. PERF. QT.: 1.

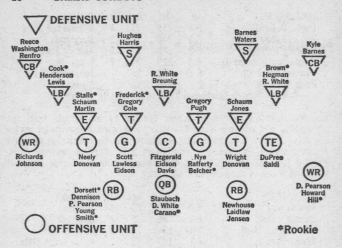

DEFENSIVE UNIT

Reece
Washington
Renfro
CB

Cook*
Henderson
Lewis
LB

Hughes
Harris
S

Stalls*
Schaum
Martin
E

Frederick*
Gregory
Cole
T

R. White
Breunig
LB

Gregory
Pugh
T

Schaum
Jones
E

Barnes
Waters
S

Brown*
Hegman
R. White
LB

Kyle
Barnes
CB

WR
Richards
Johnson

T
Neely
Donovan

G
Scott
Lawless
Eidson

C
Fitzgerald
Eidson
Davis

G
Nye
Rafferty
Belcher*

T
Wright
Donovan

TE
DuPree
Saldi

Dorsett* RB
Dennison
P. Pearson
Young
Smith*

QB
Staubach
D. White
Carano*

RB
Newhouse
Laidlaw
Jensen

D. Pearson
Howard
Hill*
WR

OFFENSIVE UNIT

*Rookie

1977 DRAFT SELECTIONS

1	Dorsett, Tony	RB	5-11	192	Pittsburgh
2	Carano, Glenn	QB	6-3	197	Nevada-Las Vegas
3A	Hill, Tony	WR	6-3	193	Stanford
3B	Belcher, Val	G	6-3	252	Houston
4	Brown, Guy	LB	6-4	220	Houston
5	Frederick, Andy	DT	6-7	250	New Mexico
6	Cooper, Jim	T	6-5	262	Temple
7	Stalls, David	DE	6-4	240	Northern Colorado
8A	Cleveland, Al	DE	6-5	245	Pacific
8B	Williams, Fred	RB	5-11	194	Arizona State
9	Cantrell, Mark	C	6-3	246	North Carolina
10	DeBerg, Steve	QB	6-3	190	San Jose State
11	Wardlow, Don	TE	6-3	231	Washington
12	Peters, Greg	G	6-5	250	California

Few teams are as smart as Dallas, and this draft proves it. Dorsett will take the Cowboys to the Super Bowl; he supplies, in a maximum sense, the only ingredient the team lacked. Then they picked Carano, to some minds the best QB in the draft, and he'll be ready to challenge White in a year. Hill should have a chance (at Richards' spot) and Belcher may upgrade the depth on the offensive line. Frederick, massive and quick, and Stalls may push the defensive line reserves. Keep an eye on Peters, the final pick. He was rated highly by some. PERF. QT.: 1.

ST. LOUIS CARDINALS

Prediction: Second

The best offensive line in the business and two of the most dangerous wide receivers pool their unique talents to protect and display the ability of quarterback Jim Hart, who can also hand off to one of the most explosive runners in the business.

And so it is that the St. Louis Cardinals conduct business.

The line is anchored by All-Pro guard Conrad "Dirty" Dobler and All-Pro tackle Dan Dierdorf, though center Tom Banks was also in the Pro Bowl last time around and guard Bob Young is possibly the most underrated lineman in the NFC, while tackle Roger Finnie is much more than competent.

They protect Hart, the 33-year-old quarterback, and when Hart chooses not to pass to Mel Gray and Ike Harris, he can deposit the ball into the tummy of Terry Metcalf and move aside—quickly. There is also fullback Jim Otis, nobody's All-Pro but one of the most consistent producers around.

Add all that up and include tight end J.V. Cain, who has deep-threat potential and, in fact, has played wide receiver, and the overall effect is a startlingly effective offense.

It has to be. The defense isn't all that good. And

this season, with the retirements of linebacker Larry Stallings and tackle Bob Rowe and the defections of All-Pro cornerback Norm Thompson to Baltimore and linebacker Greg Hartle to Washington, there will be more problems than ever.

Clearly, the offense has large swatches of work cut out for it.

The defense that Coach Don Coryell ("if you can score 30 points a game, any defense is a good one") will field should include a front line of ends John Zook and Ron Yankowski; tackles Mike Dawson and Leo Brooks.

Zook came from Atlanta last season and was solid. Yankowski seems to fight off all challengers and should do so again. Dawson was the No. 1 pick a year ago and showed huge talent. Brooks is the quiet man, but he doesn't allow much to get through.

Reserves up front include Bob Bell, Charlie Davis and Walt Patulski, all of whom have been starters (Patulski missed last season with a knee injury) and rookie Ernest Lee, who should have enough to beat out journeyman Steve Okoniewski.

The revamped linebacking corps should line up with Tim Kearney in the middle, flanked by Mark Arneson and Al Beauchamp. Kurt Allerman, the second-round draft choice, will fight for a job. Steve Neils, Ray White, Mike McGraw and rookie Andy Spiva compete for reserve spots.

Two trades brought help to the secondary. Perry Smith (from Green Bay) should take over for Thompson and team with All-Pro Roger Wehrli. Neal Craig, from Cleveland, will back up strong safety Ken Reaves. Free safety Mike Sensibaugh will have Clarence Duren behind him.

But the offense is what makes this team click.

Dierdorf is the best tackle in the NFC, and one of the very best in the league. Dobler gets a lot of gimmicky publicity but remains a competent performer anyway. The line is further secured with such valuable reserves as 6-6, 270-pound tackle Brad Oates, a rookie last year; center Tom Brahaney, who used to start; guard-tackle Hank Allison; and guard Keith Wortman, whose place on the roster is not secure.

The problem in previous seasons has been a lack of depth behind Hart. But Coryell corrected that in the first round of the draft, taking hot-shot Missouri quarterback Steve Pisarkiewicz, who figures to be the Cards' quarterback of the future.

Running back depth is good, with Steve Jones, Jerry Latin, Wayne Morris and the No. 2 pick, George Franklin, the 6-3, 225-pound fullback from Texas A&I who can also play wide receiver.

Even the receiving corps is well insured, with Gary Hammond, Pat Tilley and Mel Baker the wide reserves and old pro Jackie Smith the second tight end. It may be time for Smith to retire, but not until a competent replacement is found.

The only problem related to the offense concerns punting. Before training camp it was still Terry Joyce's job, but it doesn't figure to be by the time the season opens. The placekicking, on the other hand (foot?), is well protected by veteran Jim Bakken, who has the best pressure-kicking record in the game and seems near his peak at age 36.

With Hart and Metcalf, Otis and Gray, Harris and Cain and that nearly impregnable offensive line, it should be another season of buckets of yards and bushels of points.

And the defense, as always, will be good enough.

1976 RECORD (10-4)

30	Seattle	24	23	San Francisco (OT)		20
29	Green Bay	0	17	Philadelphia		14
24	San Diego	43	30	Los Angeles		28
27	New York Giants	21	10	Washington		16
33	Philadelphia	14	14	Dallas		19
21	Dallas	17	24	Baltimore		17
10	Washington	20	17	New York Giants		14

PASSING

	Atts	Comps	Yds	Lgst	TDs	Ints	Pct
Hart	388	218	2946	77	18†	13	56.2

SCORING

	TDs	PATs	FGs	Total
Bakken	0	33	20	93
Jones	9	0	0	54
Metcalf	7	0	0	42
Cain	5	0	0	30
Gray	5	0	0	30
Morris	4	0	0	24

RUSHING

	Atts	Yds	TDs	Lgst	Avg
Otis	233	891	2	23	3.8
Metcalf	134	537	3	36	4.0
Jones	113	451	8	19	4.0
Morris	64	292	3	27	4.6
Latin	25	115	1	26	4.6

RECEIVING

	Recs	Yds	TDs	Lgst	Avg
Harris	52	782	1	40	15.0
Gray	36	686	5	77	19.1
Metcalf	33	388	4	48	11.8
Jones	29	152	1	15	5.2
Tilley	26	407	1	45	15.7
Cain	26	400	5	34	15.4

INTERCEPTIONS

	Ints	Yds	TDs	Lgst	Avg
Thompson**	4	83	0	38	20.8
Sensibaugh	4	60	1	35	15.0
Wehrli	4	31	0	26	7.8
Reaves	2	41	0	25	20.5
White	2	20	0	16	10.0

SYMBOLS **—Departed via option playout
         †—Conference leader

1977 SCHEDULE

Home: Sept. 25—Chicago; Oct. 9—Dallas; Oct. 23—New Orleans; Oct. 31—New York Giants; Nov. 20—Philadelphia; Nov. 24—Miami; Dec. 10—Washington.

Away: Sept. 18—Denver; Oct. 2—Washington; Oct. 16—Philadelphia; Nov. 6—Minnesota; Nov. 14—Dallas; Dec. 4—New York Giants; Dec. 18—Tampa Bay.

OFFENSE

QUARTERBACKS	Ht	Wt	Age	Exp	College
Hart, Jim	6-1	210	33	12	Southern Illinois
Donckers, Bill	6-1	205	26	2	San Diego State

Hart shows no signs of aging and loves Coach Coryell's big-pass offense. Donckers has no future. PERF. QT.: 2.

RUNNING BACKS	Ht	Wt	Age	Exp	College
Otis, Jim	6-0	225	29	8	Ohio State
Metcalf, Terry	5-10	185	25	5	Long Beach State
Jones, Steve	6-0	200	26	5	Duke
Latin, Jerry	5-10	190	24	3	Northern Illinois
Morris, Wayne	6-0	200	23	2	Southern Methodist

Otis doesn't do anything right but he makes big yardage, big plays. Metcalf is one of the NFL's most exciting runners if he isn't sulking. Jones proved to be dependable workhorse who can run, catch, block. Latin could develop into a top-flight back. Morris showed enough as a rookie to warrant further chances. PERF. QT.: 2.

RECEIVERS	Ht	Wt	Age	Exp	College
Gray, Mel (W)	5-9	175	28	7	Missouri
Harris, Ike (W)	6-3	205	24	3	Iowa State
Cain, J. V. (T)	6-4	225	26	4	Colorado
Tilley, Pat (W)	5-10	175	24	2	Louisiana Tech
Smith, Jackie (T)	6-4	230	37	15	N.W. Louisiana
Hammond, Gary (W)	5-11	185	28	5	Southern Methodist
Baker, Mel (W)	6-0	190	27	4	Texas Southern

(W)—Wide Receiver   (T)—Tight End

Gray strikes from anywhere and is almost impossible to defend. Harris became a reliable, quality receiver and has good size, too. Cain has the speed of a wide receiver, the size and strength of a tight end. Tilley was a rookie with good speed but can't crack this lineup. Smith is at the end of the road and may well announce his retirement if a replacement can be found. Hammond is a versatile performer. Baker can't cut it against this level of competition. PERF. QT.: 1.

INTERIOR LINEMEN	Ht	Wt	Age	Exp	College
Dierdorf, Dan (T)	6-3	280	28	7	Michigan
Finnie, Roger (T)	6-3	250	31	9	Florida A&M
Dobler, Conrad (G)	6-3	255	26	6	Wyoming
Young, Bob (G)	6-1	270	34	12	Howard Payne
Banks, Tom (C)	6-2	245	29	6	Auburn
Oates, Brad (T)	6-6	270	23	2	Brigham Young

INTERIOR LINEMEN (Contd.)	Ht	Wt	Age	Exp	College
Allison, Hank (G-T)	6-3	255	30	5	San Diego State
Brahaney, Tom (C)	6-2	250	25	5	Oklahoma
Wortman, Keith (G)	6-2	250	27	6	Nebraska

(T)—Tackle   (G)—Guard   (C)—Center

Dierdorf—absolutely—is the best (and heaviest) tackle in the NFC. Finnie continues to amaze the experts—and the Jets, who cut him. Dobler may be over-publicized, but he isn't over-rated as a pro. Young is more consistent and much quieter, but he gets his job done. Banks is another anonymous performer who makes the holes open up. Oates has the potential, and certainly the size, to be a good one. Allison hasn't developed into the kind of player he was supposed to be. Brahaney proved he can play when he filled in for Banks two years ago. Wortman doesn't have much chance here. PERF. QT.: 1.

KICKERS	Ht	Wt	Age	Exp	College
Bakken, Jim (Pk)	6-0	200	36	16	Wisconsin
Joyce, Terry (P)	6-6	230	23	2	Missouri Southern

(Pk)—Placekicker   (P)—Punter

Bakken seldom misses the pressure field goal, which is what counts. Joyce is a definite handicap. PERF. QT.: 3.

DEFENSE

FRONT LINEMEN	Ht	Wt	Age	Exp	College
Zook, John (E)	6-5	250	29	9	Kansas
Yankowski, Ron (E)	6-5	250	30	7	Kansas State
Brooks, Leo (T)	6-6	240	29	8	Texas
Dawson, Mike (T)	6-4	270	23	2	Arizona
Bell, Bob (E)	6-4	250	29	7	Cincinnati
Davis, Charlie (T)	6-2	265	25	4	Texas Christian
Patulski, Walt (E)	6-6	260	27	5	Notre Dame
Okoniewski, Steve (T)	6-3	255	28	6	Montana

(E)—End   (T)—Tackle

Zook was expensive when he came from Atlanta, but proved worth it. Yankowski somehow meets the challenges and keeps starting. Brooks is a quiet performer but repeatedly makes good grades. Dawson emerged as a smart No. 1 draft pick; he should get better with experience. Bell lost his job to Zook, and this year could lose his roster spot. Davis thrives because of his quickness. Patulski came from Buffalo, injured his knee and sat out the season. He has never lived up to his notices. Okoniewski will be surprised if he stays. PERF. QT.: 3.

LINEBACKERS	Ht	Wt	Age	Exp	College
Arneson, Mark (O)	6-2	220	27	6	Arizona
Beauchamp, Al (O)	6-2	235	33	10	Southern
Kearney, Tim (M)	6-2	230	26	6	Northern Michigan
White, Ray (M)	6-2	220	28	5	Syracuse
Neils, Steve (O)	6-2	215	26	4	Minnesota
McGraw, Mike (O)	6-2	215	23	2	Wyoming

(O)—Outside Linebacker   (M)—Middle Linebacker

Arneson has developed into a steady linebacker with intelligence. Beauchamp hits hard, moves well, but may be threatened by the calendar. Kearney isn't the answer in the middle, but Greg Hartle is gone. White could win a job, but if he does it will be due to weaknesses on the unit. Neils may still live up to his promise. McGraw showed enough as rookie to raise a few eyebrows. PERF. QT.: 4.

CORNERBACKS	Ht	Wt	Age	Exp	College
Wehrli, Roger	6-0	190	29	9	Missouri
Smith, Perry	6-1	195	26	5	Colorado State
Crump, Dwayne	5-11	180	27	5	Fresno State
Nelson, Lee	5-10	185	23	2	Florida State

Wehrli is still as good as any in the league; no one throws at him. Smith, from Green Bay, is a competent defender who will replace Norm Thompson, departed to the Colts. Nelson may develop in a reserve capacity. Crump just can't do it consistently. PERF. QT.: 3.

SAFETIES	Ht	Wt	Age	Exp	College
Reaves, Ken (S)	6-3	210	32	12	Norfolk State
Sensibaugh, Mike (W)	5-11	190	28	7	Ohio State
Duren, Clarence (W-S)	6-1	190	26	5	California
Craig, Neal (S)	6-1	190	29	7	Fisk
Severson, Jeff (W)	6-1	185	27	6	Long Beach State

(S)—Strong-side   (W)—Weak-side or "Free" Safety

Reaves hasn't slipped much and now enjoys the wisdom of experience. Sensibaugh turned into a surprise when acquired from the Chiefs. Duren is a valuable reserve who can play if injury dictates. Craig, from Cleveland, can't do more than spot duty. Severson is a mediocre performer at best. PERF. QT.: 3.

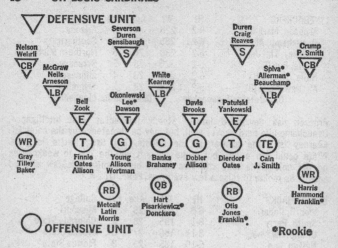

DEFENSIVE UNIT

Nelson Wehrll		Severson Duren Sensibaugh					Duren Craig Reaves		Crump P. Smith

CB — McGraw Neils Arneson (LB) — White Kearney (LB) — Spiva* Allerman Beauchamp (LB) — CB

Bell Zook (E) — Okoniewski Lee* Dawson (T) — Davis Brooks (T) — Patulski Yankowski (E)

WR	T	G	C	G	T	TE	
Gray Tilley Baker	Finnie Oates Allison	Young Allison Wortman	Banks Brahaney	Dobler Allison	Dierdorf Oates	Cain J. Smith	WR — Harris Hammond Franklin*

RB — Metcalf Latin Morris

QB — Hart Pisarkiewicz* Donckers

RB — Otis Jones Franklin*

OFFENSIVE UNIT

*Rookie

1977 DRAFT SELECTIONS

1	Pisarkiewicz, Steve	QB	6-2	205	Missouri
2	Franklin, George	RB-WR	6-3	225	Texas A&I
3A	Allerman, Kurt	LB	6-3	220	Penn State
*3B	Middleton, Terdell	RB	6-0	191	Memphis State
4	No Choice				
5A	Lee, Ernest	DT	6-4	250	Texas
5B	Spiva, Andy	LB	6-2	220	Tennessee
6	No Choice				
7	No Choice				
8	Williams, Eric	LB	6-2	215	So. California
9	Jackson, Johnny	DT	6-5	260	Southern
10	LeJay, Jim	WR	6-0	189	San Jose State
11	Lee, Greg	DB	5-11	180	Western Illinois
12	Fenlaw, Rick	LB	6-2	220	Texas

*—Traded to Green Bay

Pisarkiewicz was a wise, much-needed pick. He should become the heir apparent to Hart's starting job. Franklin can play fullback or a wide receiver; he has the tools. Allerman may instantly replace the retired Stallings and the aging Beauchamp. Middleton was traded for Perry Smith of Green Bay moments after he was selected by the Cardinals. Lee has some potential, but he's raw and may need time. Spiva is for further depth but may not be able to handle the task. **PERF. QT.: 2.**

NEW YORK GIANTS

Prediction: Third

The Giants find themselves in an interesting position. They have a sound, young, improving defense. They have a head coach, John McVay, who is starting his first full season and who is generally respected by the squad. They have their new stadium in the New Jersey meadows for a full season and they have an easier schedule—though not by much—than last year.

But they don't have a quarterback.

Well, that's not strictly accurate. They do have a quarterback, several of them, in fact. But having traded away Craig Morton (regrettable but necessary), they left themselves without a regular at the position. At the moment, the job is probably Steve Ramsey's. He came from Denver for Morton. But Dennis Shaw has made great strides and should get a long look. And in McVay's plans for the future is the name Jerry Golsteyn. No one else.

Golsteyn was a rookie last summer, a No. 12 pick who suddenly looked like the pearl of the draft. Then he stepped into a hole the week before the season started and needed knee surgery. Now he's back. It is of great excitement to McVay.

Fullback Larry Csonka is back, too, fully recovered from a knee operation. He'll team with either Doug

Kotar or Gordon Bell in the backfield, while Marsh White, Bob Hammond and Larry Watkins vie for relief spots. Only White is sure to make it.

The tight end is Bob Tucker, which isn't bad at all. Behind him is Gary Shirk, which has to change. Rookie Al Dixon should send Shirk home.

Another gaping vacancy was at wide receiver, and the Giants have taken steps to correct that, too. They drafted, on the second round, 6-2, 208-pound Johnny Perkins of Abilene Christian. He should start, beating out Ray Rhodes. Ed Marshall, who joined the team as a free agent late last season, will probably win the other spot after a challenge from free agent Don Zimmerman and last year's rookie free agent, Jimmy Robinson. Walker Gillette may not get out of camp. Rookie Emery Moorehead (the pearl of this year's draft?) bears watching.

The front line was another problem, simply because too few of the regulars played well. The present lineup has Tom Mullen and Doug Van Horn at tackles, Al Simpson and John Hicks at guards, Karl Chandler at center. Hicks must get better, Simpson must continue to improve and Van Horn must be beaten out.

Ron Mikolajczyk, Mike Gibbons, and rookies Mike Vaughan (285 pounds) and Bob Jordan will provide tackle competition, while Bill Ellenbogen wants one guard spot and could take it. He filled in nicely for Hicks on several occasions last season.

The defense is a-building, as they say. The front four should start out as ends Jack Gregory and George Martin, tackles Troy Archer and John Mendenhall. But the No. 1 draft pick was Gary Jeter of USC, 6-4 and 265, and he must start. His presence may free Mendenhall to be used as trading material, or could shift Archer to end if Gregory's knee (no operation) hasn't come around.

Archer was the No. 1 pick last year and played like it. Martin continued to improve and he's only 24.

Linebacking might be the best area of all. In the middle is Harry Carson, a 6-2, 235-pound converted DE who was a No. 4 pick last year and who took command before the season was half over. He has incredible potential and unusual strength. Brad Van Pelt on the strong-side finally played up to Pro Bowl caliber. He's 6-5, 235 and should be around for a long time. Brian Kelley moved to the weak-side to make room for Carson and liked it, as the coaches liked his play. The leading reserve is another soph, Dan Lloyd, who made noises as though he must become a starter.

Strong safety Robert Giblin moves up to linebacker, joining Brad Cousino and Bob Schmit on the depth chart.

The secondary is so-so at the moment, but could be better if several injuries are healed. The projected corners are Bill Bryant, a free agent (WFL) rookie last year, and Bobby Brooks, who missed most of the season with a knee. Veteran backup Charlie Ford missed it, too, and must be fully recovered to have any chance to stick this year.

Clyde Powers is the strong safety and Jim Stienke, if he isn't needed at corner, will be the free safety. Rick Volk, the old Baltimore veteran, joined up after the season started and played well.

But no matter the improvement on defense, the Giants' overriding problem is still quarterback. If McVay gets an affirmative answer from Golsteyn's performance, this could be a surprise team. But for a non-regular quarterback to take over and star immediately would be a surprise of major proportions.

1976 RECORD (3-11)

17	Washington	19	0	Philadelphia		10
7	Philadelphia	20	3	Dallas		9
10	Los Angeles	24	12	Washington		9
21	St. Louis	27	13	Denver		14
14	Dallas	24	28	Seattle		16
7	Minnesota	24	24	Detroit		10
0	Pittsburgh	27	14	St. Louis		17

PASSING

	Atts	Comps	Yds	Lgst	TDs	Ints	Pct
Morton**	284	153	1865	63	9	20	53.9
Snead	42	22	239	31	0	4	52.4

SCORING

	TDs	PATs	FGs	Total
Danelo	0	20	8	44
Csonka	4	0	0	24
Kotar	3	0	0	18
Marshall	3	0	0	18
Bell	2	0	0	12
Gillette	2	0	0	12

RUSHING

	Atts	Yds	TDs	Lgst	Avg
Kotar	185	731	3	24	4.0
Csonka	160	569	4	13	3.6
Bell	67	233	2	26	3.5
White	69	223	1	29	3.2
Watkins	26	96	1	13	3.7

RECEIVING

	Recs	Yds	TDs	Lgst	Avg
Tucker	42	498	1	39	11.9
Kotar	36	319	0	30	8.9
Bell	25	198	0	20	7.9
Robinson	18	249	1	30	13.8
Rhodes	16	305	1	63	19.1
Gillette	16	263	2	62	16.4

INTERCEPTIONS

	Ints	Yds	TDs	Lgst	Avg
Volk	2	14	0	11	7.0
Van Pelt	2	13	0	7	6.5
Stienke	2	0	0	0	0.0

SYMBOL **—Traded

1977 SCHEDULE

Home: Sept. 18—Washington; Oct. 9—Philadelphia; Oct. 16—San Francisco; Nov. 6—Dallas; Nov. 20—Cleveland; Dec. 4—St. Louis; Dec. 18—Chicago.

Away: Sept. 25—Dallas; Oct. 2—Atlanta; Oct. 23—Washington; Oct. 31—St. Louis; Nov. 13—Tampa Bay; Nov. 27—Cincinnati; Dec. 11—Philadelphia.

OFFENSE

QUARTERBACKS	Ht	Wt	Age	Exp	College
Ramsey, Steve	6-2	210	29	8	North Texas State
Golsteyn, Jerry	6-4	208	23	1	Northern Illinois
Shaw, Dennis	6-3	210	30	8	San Diego State

The game plan calls for Golsteyn to be the regular in a short while. Ramsey, obtained from Denver for Craig Morton, is a mediocre veteran. Shaw may challenge for the early lead. PERF. QT.: 4.

RUNNING BACKS	Ht	Wt	Age	Exp	College
Csonka, Larry	6-3	235	30	9	Syracuse
Kotar, Doug	5-11	205	26	4	Kentucky
Bell, Gordon	5-9	180	23	2	Michigan
White, Marsh	6-2	220	24	3	Arkansas
Watkins, Larry	6-2	230	30	9	Alcorn State
Hammond, Bob	5-10	170	25	2	Morgan State

Csonka says he's fully healed from knee surgery; he might be, since speed was never his forte. Kotar does everything well and is a quiet but respected back. Bell has the flash and fire, but maybe not enough poise. White has lived off his potential for two years now. Watkins doesn't do badly when he gets a chance, and he's able. Hammond should leave the premises quickly. PERF. QT.: 3.

RECEIVERS	Ht	Wt	Age	Exp	College
Marshall, Ed (W)	6-5	200	29	2	Cameron State
Rhodes, Ray (W)	5-11	185	26	4	Tulsa
Tucker, Bob (T)	6-3	230	32	8	Bloomsburg State
Robinson, Jimmy (W)	5-9	170	24	2	Georgia Tech
Zimmerman, Don (W)	6-3	195	28	5	N.E. Louisiana
Shirk, Gary (T)	6-1	220	27	2	Morehead State
Gillette, Walker (W)	6-5	200	30	8	Richmond

(W)—Wide Receiver   (T)—Tight End

Marshall saved the day in the latter part of last season but isn't consistent. Rhodes has been a three-year bust and may move to cornerback now. Tucker is still among the best tight ends in the league when he's thrown to. Robinson has lots of heart, lots of speed, some moves and little height. Zimmerman, as a free agent, could challenge for a starting position. Shirk made the team because there weren't any other tight ends around. Gillette was never sharp. PERF. QT.: 3.

INTERIOR LINEMEN	Ht	Wt	Age	Exp	College
Mullen, Tom (T)	6-3	250	25	4	S.W. Missouri State
Van Horn, Doug (T)	6-3	245	33	11	Ohio State

INTERIOR LINEMEN (Contd.)	Ht	Wt	Age	Exp	College
Simpson, Al (G)	6-5	255	26	3	Colorado State
Hicks, John (G)	6-2	258	26	4	Ohio State
Chandler, Karl (C)	6-5	250	25	4	Princeton
Hill, Ralph (C)	6-1	245	27	2	Florida A&M
Mikolajczyk, Ron (T)	6-3	275	27	2	Tampa
Ellenbogen, Bill (G)	6-5	255	26	2	Virginia Tech
Gibbons, Mike (T)	6-4	262	26	2	S.W. Oklahoma State

(T)—Tackle   (G)—Guard   (C)—Center

Mullen may be the best lineman on the team, and his torn knee has mended. Van Horn is facing the reality of age, but he can hang on as a reserve. Simpson has a world of potential but not too many blue ribbons. Hicks has been a disappointment and has been subject to trade rumors. Chandler will retain the center's job if he isn't shifted to guard. Hill is to short for this league, but he plays with verve to try to make up for his stature. Mikolajczyk, a jumbo-sized Oakland reject, will put strong pressure on Van Horn. Ellenbogen, a free agent surprise, could just win himself a spot. Gibbons has almost no chance. PERF. QT.: 3.

KICKERS	Ht	Wt	Age	Exp	College
Danelo, Joe (Pk)	5-9	166	23	3	Washington State
Jennings, Dave (P)	6-4	205	25	4	St. Lawrence

(Pk)—Placekicker   (P)—Punter

Danelo can't do it, and if they keep him he'll lose some games. Jennings is among the league's top punters. PERF. QT.: 3.

DEFENSE

FRONT LINEMEN	Ht	Wt	Age	Exp	College
Gregory, Jack (E)	6-5	250	32	11	Delta State
Martin, George (E)	6-4	245	24	3	Oregon
Archer, Troy (T)	6-4	250	22	2	Colorado
Mendenhall, John (T)	6-1	255	28	6	Grambling
Dvorak, Rick (E)	6-4	245	25	4	Wichita State
Pietrzak, Jim (T)	6-5	260	24	3	Eastern Michigan
Gallagher, Dave (E-T)	6-4	256	25	4	Michigan

(E)—End   (T)—Tackle

Gregory refused a knee operation and says he's fine; we'll see. Martin is developing into one of the better young ends in the conference. Archer was the top draft choice in '76 and proved to be a blue-chipper. Mendenhall is ferocious when sound—and happy. Too often he's neither. Dvorak was a project of former Coach Bill Arnsparger; new boss McVay may not pick up the reins, though. Pietrzak, who missed all of '76, may play center. Gallagher can't start here. PERF. QT.: 3.

LINEBACKERS	Ht	Wt	Age	Exp	College
Van Pelt, Brad (O)	6-5	235	26	5	Michigan State
Kelley, Brian (O)	6-3	222	25	5	Cal. Lutheran
Carson, Harry (M)	6-2	235	23	2	South Carolina St.
Lloyd, Dan (M-O)	6-2	225	23	2	Washington
Giblin, Robert (O)	6-2	210	24	2	Houston
Cousino, Brad (O)	6-0	215	24	3	Miami, Ohio
Schmit, Bob (M-O)	6-1	222	27	3	Nebraska

(O)—Outside Linebacker   (M)—Middle Linebacker

Dramatic improvement catapulted Van Pelt to the Pro Bowl plateau. Kelley is consistent, has good range and a knack for hitting hard. Carson, a 1976 rookie, developed quickly; he should star. Lloyd, another head-hunting '76 rookie, worries Kelley now. Giblin is a converted strong safety who can't crack the lineup there. Cousino was a waiver pickup, and his value is on special teams. Schmit tries to come back from serious knee surgery and will likely fail. PERF. QT.: 2.

CORNERBACKS	Ht	Wt	Age	Exp	College
Bryant, Bill	5-11	195	26	2	Grambling
Brooks, Bobby	6-1	195	26	4	Bishop
Ford, Charlie	6-3	185	28	6	Houston

Bryant, an ex-WFLer, started most of last season and played nicely. Brooks, who missed most of '76 with a torn knee, showed real ability before the injury. Ford's another knee case. PERF. QT.: 3.

SAFETIES	Ht	Wt	Age	Exp	College
Powers, Clyde (S)	6-1	195	26	4	Oklahoma
Stienke, Jim (W)	5-11	182	26	5	S.W. Texas State
Volk, Rick (W)	6-3	195	32	10	Michigan
Mallory, Larry (S)	5-11	185	25	2	Tennessee State

(S)—Strong-side   (W)—Weak-side or "Free" Safety

Powers is slowly turning into one of the better strong safeties in the NFC. Stienke is valuable at many positions, but mostly at free safety. Volk used all of his experience when he filled in late last season. Mallory, another WFLer, has a chance. PERF. QT.: 3.

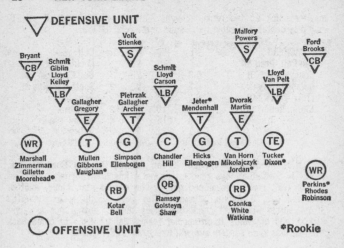

▽ DEFENSIVE UNIT

Volk
Stienke
Ⓢ

Mallory
Powers
Ⓢ

Ford
Brooks
▽
CB

Bryant
▽
CB

Schmit
Giblin
Lloyd
Kelley
Ⓛ
LB

Schmit
Lloyd
Carson
Ⓛ
LB

Lloyd
Van Pelt
Ⓛ
LB

Gallagher
Gregory
Ⓔ

Pietrzak
Gallagher
Archer
Ⓣ

Jeter●
Mendenhall
▽

Dvorak
Martin
Ⓔ

Ⓦ
WR

Ⓣ

Ⓖ

Ⓒ

Ⓖ

Ⓣ

TE

Marshall
Zimmerman
Gillette
Moorehead●

Mullen
Gibbons
Vaughan●

Simpson
Ellenbogen

Chandler
Hill

Hicks
Ellenbogen

Van Horn
Mikolajczyk
Jordan●

Tucker
Dixon●

Ⓦ
WR

RB

QB

RB

Perkins●
Rhodes
Robinson

Kotar
Bell

Ramsey
Golsteyn
Shaw

Csonka
White
Watkins

◯ OFFENSIVE UNIT

●Rookie

1977 DRAFT SELECTIONS

1	Jeter, Gary	DT-DE	6-4	265	So. California
2	Perkins, Johnny	WR	6-2	208	Abilene Christian
3	No Choice				
4	Vaughan, Mike	T	6-5	285	Oklahoma
5	Dean, Randy	QB	6-3	197	Northwestern
6A	Jordan, Bob	T	6-5	260	Memphis State
6B	Moorehead, Emery	RB-WR	6-2	209	Colorado
7	Dixon, Al	TE	6-5	216	Iowa State
8A	Rice, Bill	DT	6-4	250	Brigham Young
8B	Rodgers, Otis	LB	6-3	230	Iowa State
9	Mullins, Ken	LB	6-2	242	Florida A&M
10	Jones, Mike	WR	6-2	182	Minnesota
11	Helms, Bill	TE	6-7	225	San Diego State
12	Simmons, Elmo	RB	5-11	197	Texas-Arlington

Jeter, with 4.8 speed, will step in and win a starting job—maybe Mendenhall's, although the rookie can also play at end. Perkins, too, should be an instant starter. He has 9.6 speed in the 100 and is rangy-tough. Vaughan is a gamble, but if he sheds 20 pounds and plays as he did in his junior year, he's a bargain. Dean, considering the state of flux with QBs, has a chance. Jordan has size and Moorehead could have been a bargain—his college coach swears he'll make it big. He'll be used as WR first, since that area is thin. Dixon has a job—as a reserve—if he shows anything.
PERF. QT.: 2.

WASHINGTON REDSKINS

Prediction: Fourth

What can be said about the Redskins?

They're old. They aren't deep in talent. They have key players coming back from long and sticky injuries. They are in what may be the toughest division in the league.

So what?

It is automatic that they will win more games than they lose. But this year, while the Redskins will be potent, the fans of Washington may have to take in their playoff games from a neutral seat. Dallas and St. Louis both seem too strong, and even the Giants are making menacing gestures.

The Redskins will win games one way or another with an old quarterback, an offensive line that shouldn't perform well but always does, and a defense that should have succumbed to the calendar years ago.

Bill Kilmer is the quarterback. There is no temptation to call him a passer, since his aerials are mostly end-over-end, looking for all the world like dying partridges. Yet they get to the right receiver, somehow. And no one in this world, with the single possible exception of John Wayne, is any tougher than Kilmer.

He'll throw to wide receiver Frank Grant and tight end Jean Fugett, and his backs, and maybe to Charley

Taylor on the other flank. Taylor, 35 shortly after the season begins, missed all of last year with a shoulder injury but insists he's well and is planning a return to glory.

The other veteran receiver of the playoff years, Roy Jefferson, has been waived and is no longer around.

Mike Thomas is the halfback, coming off a superb year in which he gained 1101 yards and caught 28 passes. His partner at fullback will be John Riggins, a 6-2, 230-pound smasher who signed on after playing out his option with the Jets and came into his own in the latter stages of the season. He finished as the team's second-best rusher with 572 yards.

Behind them are former Cowboy All-Pro Calvin Hill, Bob Brunet, former Redskin All-Pro Larry Brown (who may not make it), and hefty Willie Spencer, a 6-4, 235-pounder signed as a free agent after the Vikings won a bidding war for the ex-WFLer and then cut him.

Fugett is the tight end, supported by 34-year-old Jerry Smith until some rookie or retread comes along to force Smith into retirement.

The line is patchwork and makeshift, but it works. At the tackles are Tim Stokes and George Starke. Paul Laaveg, who missed the entire 1976 season, will try to make it back as one starting guard. Terry Hermeling, once a tackle, is the other guard. If Laaveg's plans prove too ambitious, Ron Saul will take over. Len Hauss is the center, close to his previous All-Pro years, and the reserves include such as guard Dan Nugent, tackle Mike Hughes, center-tackle Bob Kuziel and center Ted Fritsch. One or two of the subs will have to go.

Defense, as offense, is operated with sleight of hand. Ron McDole and Dennis Johnson are the ends. McDole will celebrate his 38th birthday as the season opens and he begins his 17th pro year. But when he isn't making big plays, he is playing steadily. Johnson has improved and is one of the team's few young stalwarts. Diron Talbert is one of the tackles, age 33. Bill Brundige is the other, but behind him is massive Dave Butz (6-7, 285) and he finally showed some of his reputed potential last year. He may contest for a job, and it could be Brundige's that he wins.

The listed linebackers are Chris Hanburger (he's 36) and Brad Dusek on the outside, flanking Harold McLinton in the middle. Harold is the weak link, and Greg Hartle, who played out his option with St. Louis, may take over quickly. Reserves are Stu O'Dell, Rusty Tillman (who may be pushed off the roster by Hartle), and Pete Wysocki, which doesn't bode well for depth.

The secondary is old but, like vintage wine, still most appealing. Joe Lavender and Pat Fischer are on the corners. Lavender came over from the Eagles and had a super season. Fischer had a great year simply because, at 36 and too small and plagued by injuries, he lived through 14 games. Gerard Williams will be given every opportunity to send Pat to an old age home.

The safeties are both All-Pros—Ken Houston on the strong-side and Jake Scott the free safety. Neither should yet be defeated by the years, though Houston slipped just a bit. Eddie Brown returns kicks and he and Brig Owens play in the five- and six-back defense and provide some depth.

Not much help is expected from the draft, but that is an old story with George Allen's teams.

This does not look like a true contender. But Allen's teams never do. They just act that way, and 1977 shouldn't be much different, even if the playoffs prove unreachable.

1976 RECORD (10-5)

19	New York Giants	17	24	San Francisco		21
31	Seattle	7	9	New York Giants		12
20	Philadelphia (OT)	17	16	St. Louis		10
7	Chicago	33	24	Philadelphia		0
30	Kansas City	33	37	New York Jets		16
20	Detroit	7	27	Dallas		14
20	St. Louis	10		(Playoff)		
7	Dallas	20	20	Minnesota		35

PASSING

	Atts	Comps	Yds	Lgst	TDs	Ints	Pct
Kilmer	206	108	1252	53	12	10	52.4
Theismann	163	79	1036	44	8	10	48.5

SCORING

	TDs	PATs	FGs	Total
Moseley	0	31	22†	97†
Thomas	9	0	0	54
Fugett	6	0	0	36
Grant	5	0	0	30
Riggins	4	0	0	24
Two tied with	2	0	0	12

RUSHING

	Atts	Yds	TDs	Lgst	Avg
Thomas	254	1101	5	28	4.3
Riggins	162	572	3	15	3.5
Hill	79	301	1	15	3.8
Theismann	17	97	1	22	5.7
L. Brown	20	56	0	11	2.8

RECEIVING

	Recs	Yds	TDs	Lgst	Avg
Grant	50	818	5	53	16.4
Thomas	28	290	4	34	10.4
Jefferson**	27	364	2	27	13.5
Fugett	27	334	6	33	12.4
Riggins	21	172	1	18	8.2
L. Brown	17	98	0	15	5.8

INTERCEPTIONS

	Ints	Yds	TDs	Lgst	Avg
Lavender	8	77	0	28	9.6
Fischer	5	38	0	32	7.6
Houston	4	25	0	12	6.3
Scott	4	12	0	6	3.0

SYMBOLS **—Waived
        †—Conference leader

1977 SCHEDULE

Home: Sept. 25—Atlanta; Oct. 2—St. Louis; Oct. 23—New York Giants; Oct. 30—Philadelphia; Nov. 21—Green Bay; Nov. 27—Dallas; Dec. 17—Los Angeles.

Away: Sept. 18—New York Giants; Oct. 9—Tampa Bay; Oct. 16—Dallas; Nov. 7—Baltimore; Nov. 13—Philadelphia; Dec. 4—Buffalo; Dec. 10—St. Louis.

OFFENSE

QUARTERBACKS	Ht	Wt	Age	Exp	College
Kilmer, Bill	6-0	204	37	16	UCLA
Theismann, Joe	6-0	184	27	4	Notre Dame

It's still Kilmer at the helm if he's healthy. Theismann started some in '76; he lost some games, too. PERF. QT.: 3.

RUNNING BACKS	Ht	Wt	Age	Exp	College
Thomas, Mike	5-11	190	24	3	Nevada-Las Vegas
Riggins, John	6-2	230	28	7	Kansas
Hill, Calvin	6-4	227	30	8	Yale
Brown, Larry	5-11	195	29	9	Kansas State
Brunet, Bob	6-1	205	31	8	Louisiana Tech
Spencer, Willie	6-4	235	24	2	None

Despite the presence of Riggins and Hill, Thomas had his second great, team-leading year. Riggins got into gear late in the season, but then he showed his enormous power. Hill never delivered. He could find himself strictly a spot back. Brown's value is his guts, and his receiving ability. Brunet is Coach Allen's super sub, but he hardly plays except on special teams. Spencer may never live up to his potential. PERF. QT.: 2.

RECEIVERS	Ht	Wt	Age	Exp	College
Grant, Frank (W)	5-11	181	27	5	Southern Colorado
Taylor, Charley (W)	6-3	210	34	14	Arizona State
Fugett, Jean (T)	6-4	226	25	6	Amherst
Fryer, Brian (W)	6-1	185	24	2	Edmonton (Canada)
Jones, Larry (W)	5-10	170	26	4	N.E. Missouri
Smith, Jerry (T)	6-3	208	34	13	Arizona State
Buggs, Danny (W)	6-2	185	24	3	West Virginia
Clune, Don (W)	6-3	195	25	4	Pennsylvania

(W)—Wide Receiver   (T)—Tight End

Grant blossomed into a competent receiver with electric potential. Taylor missed the full '76 season and is cause for concern; he's fine if sound. Fugett is fine; he has the tight end job locked. Fryer didn't play much but is used on specials and does have speed. Jones, the bombshell on kickoff and punt returns, may play regularly now. Smith is on the last lap of a long career and could be derailed. Buggs, a mid-season waiver pickup from the Giants, has speed but no hands. Clune played his option out in Seattle; he's not much. PERF. QT.: 3.

INTERIOR LINEMEN	Ht	Wt	Age	Exp	College
Starke, George (T)	6-5	249	29	5	Columbia
Stokes, Tim (T)	6-5	252	27	4	Oregon

INTERIOR LINEMEN (Contd.)	Ht	Wt	Age	Exp	College
Saul, Ron (G)	6-3	254	29	8	Michigan State
Hermeling, Terry (G)	6-5	255	31	8	Nevada-Reno
Hauss, Len (C)	6-2	235	35	14	Georgia
Laaveg, Paul (G)	6-4	250	28	6	Iowa
Kuziel, Bob (C-T)	6-5	255	27	3	Pittsburgh
Nugent, Dan (G)	6-3	250	27	2	Auburn
Fritsch, Ted (C)	6-2	242	27	6	St. Norbert
Hughes, Mike (T)	6-4	251	22	1	Baylor

(T)—Tackle   (G)—Guard   (C)—Center

Starke has held his starting job for a while, but he still gets beat. Stokes may be a starter only because there's no competition for his spot. Saul played well after coming in late and should present no problem. Hermeling has developed into a sound guard from an average tackle. Hauss is a veteran with Pro Bowl ability, but he may need some relief. Laaveg, coming off a season-long injury, could win a job if he's recovered. Kuziel is the long snapper and has size and youth. Nugent could be a player if he's healthy. Fritsch may be one to go since he's had prior chances and failed. Hughes quit camp as a '76 rookie. He's got potential. PERF. QT.: 3.

KICKERS	Ht	Wt	Age	Exp	College
Moseley, Mark (Pk)	6-0	205	29	6	Stephen F. Austin
Bragg, Mike (P)	5-11	186	30	10	Richmond

(Pk)—Placekicker   (P)—Punter

Moseley led the NFC in scoring and shows no signs of becoming erratic. Bragg is a good and consistent veteran. PERF. QT.: 1.

DEFENSE

FRONT LINEMEN	Ht	Wt	Age	Exp	College
McDole, Ron (E)	6-4	265	38	17	Nebraska
Johnson, Dennis (E)	6-4	260	25	4	Delaware
Brundige, Bill (T-E)	6-5	270	28	8	Colorado
Talbert, Diron (T)	6-5	255	33	11	Texas
Butz, Dave (T)	6-7	285	27	5	Purdue
Hickman, Dallas (E)	6-6	235	25	2	California
Lorch, Karl (E-T)	6-3	258	27	2	Southern California

(E)—End   (T)—Tackle

McDole just keeps playing despite the years; 1977 may be slow-up time. Johnson turned into a sound pass-rusher once given the chance to start. Brundige has been steady but never became the star he could have been. Talbert is a star, huge and quick, but may need rest periods. Butz came along, finally, and now can challenge for a regular job. Hickman showed quickness to go with his lean size, but he's not yet a starter. Lorch should stick as a benchie. PERF. QT.: 3.

LINEBACKERS	Ht	Wt	Age	Exp	College
Hanburger, Chris (O)	6-2	218	36	13	North Carolina
Dusek, Brad (O)	6-2	214	26	4	Texas A&M
McLinton, Harold (M)	6-2	235	30	9	Southern
Hartle, Greg (M)	6-2	225	26	4	Newberry (S.C.)
O'Dell, Stu (O)	6-1	220	25	4	Indiana
Wysocki, Pete (O)	6-2	225	28	3	Western Michigan

(O)—Outside Linebacker   (M)—Middle Linebacker

Hanburger is still Pro Bowl caliber and age hasn't touched him yet. Dusek came on strong two years ago and continued playing well in '76. McLinton is the weak link in the middle; he can be challenged. O'Dell will have to improve to make the final roster. Hartle, from St. Louis, may bench McLinton. Reserve Wysocki is no threat to the first-stringers, but provides depth. PERF. QT.: 3.

CORNERBACKS	Ht	Wt	Age	Exp	College
Lavender, Joe	6-4	190	28	5	San Diego State
Fischer, Pat	5-9	170	37	17	Nebraska
Williams, Gerard	6-1	184	25	2	Langston

Lavender celebrated his escape from Philadelphia with a super year. Fischer can't fool anybody now, and his age and recent injuries will hurt. Williams hasn't had a chance yet. PERF. QT.: 3.

SAFETIES	Ht	Wt	Age	Exp	College
Houston, Ken (S)	6-3	198	32	11	Prairie View
Scott, Jake (W)	6-0	188	32	8	Georgia
Brown, Eddie (S-W)	5-11	190	25	4	Tennessee
Owens, Brig (W-S)	5-11	190	34	12	Cincinnati

(S)—Strong-side   (W)—Weak-side or "Free" Safety

This is an outstanding area. Houston is one of the best strong-side men in the NFL. Scott came up from the Dolphins and showed his old knack for ball-hawking. Brown is mostly the return specialist. He and Owens, who is getting phased out, play on passing downs. PERF. QT.: 2.

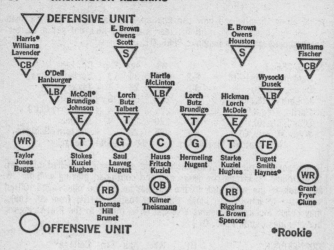

DEFENSIVE UNIT

Harris•
Williams
Lavender
CB

O'Dell
Hanburger
LB

E. Brown
Owens
Scott
S

McColl•
Brundige
Johnson
E

Lorch
Butz
Talbert
T

Hartle
McLinton
LB

Lorch
Butz
Brundige
T

E. Brown
Owens
Houston
S

Hickman
Lorch
McDole
E

Wysocki
Dusek
LB

Williams
Fischer
CB

WR
Taylor
Jones
Buggs

T
Stokes
Kuziel
Hughes

G
Saul
Laaveg
Nugent

C
Hauss
Fritsch
Kuziel

G
Hermeling
Nugent

T
Starke
Kuziel
Hughes

TE
Fugett
Smith
Haynes•

RB
Thomas
Hill
Brunet

QB
Kilmer
Theismann

RB
Riggins
L. Brown
Spencer

WR
Grant
Fryer
Clune

OFFENSIVE UNIT

•Rookie

1977 DRAFT SELECTIONS

1	No Choice				
2	No Choice				
3	No Choice				
4	McColl, Duncan	DE	6-4	237	Stanford
5	No Choice				
6	No Choice				
7	Haynes, Reggie	TE	6-3	225	Nevada-Las Vegas
8	No Choice				
9	Northington, Mike	RB	6-1	210	Purdue
10	Sykes, James	RB	5-11	186	Rice
11	Harris, Don	DB	6-0	185	Rutgers
12	Kirkland, Curt	DE	6-6	235	Missouri

McColl was an All-America who had announced intentions to attend medical school. That's why the draft-poor Redskins were able to get him on the fourth round. But Coach Allen was persuasive, and he was able to convince the son of Hall of Famer Bill McColl to play. That was a coup. Haynes should get a long look because of Washington's depth problems, and Harris, the 11th pick, was rather effective at Rutgers—albeit in a reduced competitive atmosphere. **PERF. QT.: 5.**

PHILADELPHIA EAGLES

Prediction: Fifth

Unless Coach Dick Vermeil does more than is humanly possible in an inhumanly short period of time, he will have locked up fifth place in the NFC East by the middle of August.

The major problem is a lack of depth, for there are starters with much talent. But starters get hurt, and off the current depth chart, the replacements seem to have come from the Happy Hill Nursery School.

The Eagles did get a quarterback—not the foremost of their needs—in Ron Jaworski, who had sulked on the Rams' bench. But in order to get him, they had to give up tight end Charles Young, one of the very best, and that left them with Keith Krepfle and no one else at the tight end spot.

With Jaworski, there is a problem concerning Mike Boryla. He wants to start. Vermeil can't guarantee that. There is an excellent chance that he'll be with another team before the season opens. So behind Jaworski will be has-been Roman Gabriel (37) and never-was Johnny Walton.

There are some runners, however—last year's rookie hot-shot Mike Hogan, for one. He gained 561 yards (and had a 4.6 average) despite missing six full games and parts of others. "If we can keep him healthy," says Vermeil, "he's a good bet to gain 1000 yards." Another important runner is Tom Sullivan, who looms as the other starter. Behind them are Herb Lusk (who could oust Sullivan), Dave Hampton, Bill Olds and Art Malone, trying to come back from major knee surgery.

James McAlister, whose best move is straight-ahead speed, will move from running back to wide receiver.

The line has some things good, some things not so good. Among the good are center Guy Morriss and guard (once a tackle) Jerry Sisemore. Tackle Ed George can become something good. Not so for tackle Stan Walters and guard Wade Key, who should be pushed by Dennis Nelson and Tom Luken, respectively. Luken missed '76 with a knee, and if he's hearty he can wrest away Key's job. Old pro John Niland is trying again for a guard spot; he, too, missed last season because of injury.

The receivers are all right but there is no proved depth. Krepfle is the only tight end, as mentioned. Wide men are Harold Carmichael and Charles Smith, with Vince Papale, last year's 30-year-old rookie, and McAlister behind them.

If the offense hasn't impressed you, neither will the defense, where depth is an even greater problem. Vermeil will consider installing the 3-4 alignment popularized by Oakland, Houston and New England— but that would be a move dictated more by necessity than choice.

Up front are—get this—ends Will Wynn and Carl Hairston, tackles Pete Lazetich, Manny Sistrunk, and retread Mitch Sutton. Manny is the only sure player among them. A 25-year-old rookie from Colorado, Charley Johnson, should win a place if he can walk into camp.

Mired in this muddle is the game's finest middle linebacker, Bill Bergey, who has been flanked by a couple of other good athletes, Frank LeMaster and John Bunting. LeMaster is the better of the two. Depth and, if required, the fourth linebacker spot will come from Tom Ehlers, Terry Tautolo, Drew Mahalic, Dean Halverson (who is coming off the injury list) and free-agent Nate Toran (a 6-2, 230-pound Rutgers All-America end who is projected as a linebacker by the Eagles).

Now we come to the secondary, as will most teams early in each game.

The cornerbacks are John Outlaw and Al Clark. Outlaw had his first good year in eight, but must prove 1976 wasn't a fluke. Clark, another anonymous veteran, didn't do badly but, even if he did, the trade of Joe Lavender to Washington (for Sistrunk) made him a starter. Tommy Campbell was a rookie last year and he could start this season. Also present are three rookie corners (who said Vermeil can't recognize his problems?)—Martin Mitchell, Skip Sharp and Kevin Russell. Mitchell looks like the best of them.

The safeties, like Bergey, are outstanding. Free safety is Bill Bradley, who may have slowed down a bit but who still plays intelligently. Strong safety Randy Logan is on his way to the Pro Bowl. Bradley's job may be challenged for by Artimus Parker.

Horst Muhlmann is the placekicker and an effective one, although Vermeil has signed former Temple hero Don Bitterlich to offer some competition. Bitterlich was cut by Seattle last year, which explains just how much competition he'll offer.

Spike Jones punts. Larry Marshall returns kicks. They will do their things a lot this year.

1976 RECORD (4-10)

7	Dallas	27	10	New York Giants	0
20	New York Giants	7	14	St. Louis	17
17	Washington (OT)	20	3	Cleveland	24
14	Atlanta	13	7	Oakland	26
14	St. Louis	33	0	Washington	24
13	Green Bay	28	7	Dallas	26
12	Minnesota	31	27	Seattle	10

PASSING

	Atts	Comps	Yds	Lgst	TDs	Ints	Pct
Boryla	246	123	1247	48	9	14	50.0
Gabriel	92	46	476	34	2	2	50.0
Walton	28	12	125	33	0	2	42.9

SCORING

	TDs	PATs	FGs	Total
Muhlmann	0	18	11	51
Carmichael	5	0	0	30
Smith	5	0	0	30
Sullivan	3	0	0	18
Boryla	2	0	0	12

RUSHING

	Atts	Yds	TDs	Lgst	Avg
Hogan	123	561	0	32	4.6
Sullivan	99	399	2	26	4.0
Hampton•	83	291	1	59	3.5
McAlister	68	265	0	20	3.9
Lusk	61	254	0	22	4.2
Boryla	29	166	2	22	5.7

RECEIVING

	Recs	Yds	TDs	Lgst	Avg
Carmichael	42	503	5	24	12.0
Young**	30	374	0	29	12.5
Smith	27	412	4	48	15.3
Hogan	15	89	0	18	5.9
Sullivan	14	116	1	20	8.3
Lusk	13	119	0	42	9.2

INTERCEPTIONS

	Ints	Yds	TDs	Lgst	Avg
Bradley	2	63	0	52	31.5
Bergey	2	48	0	37	24.0
Outlaw	2	19	0	19	9.5

SYMBOLS **—Traded
•—Combined Atlanta-Philadelphia record

1977 SCHEDULE

Home: Sept. 18—Tampa Bay; Oct. 16—St. Louis; Oct. 23—Dallas; Nov. 6—New Orleans; Nov. 13—Washington; Dec. 11—New York Giants; Dec. 18—New York Jets.

Away: Sept. 25—Los Angeles; Oct. 2—Detroit; Oct. 9—New York Giants; Oct. 30—Washington; Nov. 20—St. Louis; Nov. 27—New England; Dec. 4—Dallas.

OFFENSE

QUARTERBACKS	Ht	Wt	Age	Exp	College
Jaworski, Ron	6-2	185	26	4	Youngstown
Boryla, Mike	6-3	200	26	4	Stanford
Gabriel, Roman	6-4	225	37	16	North Carolina St.
Walton, John	6-2	210	29	2	Elizabeth City St.

Jaworski came from the Rams, signed and will be given the starting spot. Boryla wanted the same guarantee and he's expected to go elsewhere. Gabriel should be seriously considering a golden retirement by now. Walton is a never-was. PERF. QT.: 3.

RUNNING BACKS	Ht	Wt	Age	Exp	College
Hogan, Mike	6-2	205	23	2	Tenn-Chattanooga
Sullivan, Tom	6-0	190	27	6	Miami, Fla.
Lusk, Herb	6-0	190	24	2	Long Beach State
Hampton, Dave	6-0	210	30	9	Wyoming
Olds, Bill	6-1	224	26	5	Nebraska
Malone, Art	6-0	216	29	8	Arizona State
Green, Art	6-0	202	27	1	Albany State, Ga.

Hogan was the Eagles' '76 highlight, a rookie with big talent from a small school. Sullivan is being counted on; he is capable of doing a good job. Lusk showed promise in his rookie year and could push Sullivan. Hampton came from the Falcons and contributed. Olds is here because the Eagles want a big back; he's not it. Malone probably can't come back from a bad knee. Green starred with Ottawa in the CFL and has big promise. PERF. QT.: 2.

RECEIVERS	Ht	Wt	Age	Exp	College
Carmichael, Harold (W)	6-8	225	27	7	Southern
Smith, Charles (W)	6-1	185	27	4	Grambling
Krepfle, Keith (T)	6-3	225	25	3	Iowa State
Papale, Vince (W)	6-2	195	31	2	St. Joseph's
McAlister, James (W)	6-1	205	25	3	UCLA

(W)—Wide Receiver   (T)—Tight End

This department is thin, but Carmichael is a real danger on any pattern and Smith has lots of speed, though not much size. Krepfle is willing and big, but with little experience (and without a backup). Papale, a pro Cinderella story, could challenge Smith. Former RB McAlister has incredible physical ability but hasn't harnessed it. PERF. QT.: 3.

INTERIOR LINEMEN	Ht	Wt	Age	Exp	College
Walters, Stan (T)	6-6	270	29	6	Syracuse
George, Ed (T)	6-4	270	31	3	Wake Forest

INTERIOR LINEMEN (Contd.)	Ht	Wt	Age	Exp	College
Sisemore, Jerry (G)	6-4	260	26	5	Texas
Luken, Tom (G)	6-3	253	27	5	Purdue
Morriss, Guy (C)	6-4	255	26	5	Texas Christian
Nelson, Dennis (T)	6-5	260	31	8	Illinois State
Key, Wade (G)	6-5	245	30	8	S.W. Texas State
Bleamer, Jeff (G-T)	6-4	253	24	3	Penn State
Franks, Dennis (C)	6-1	236	24	2	Michigan
Niland, John (G)	6-3	250	33	11	Iowa

(T)—Tackle   (G)—Guard   (C)—Center

Walters has the size and experience; it's just that he doesn't play well. George was a gamble but may pay big dividends; he has great strength. Sisemore is easily the team's best lineman, with size, power, agility. Luken comes off the injured reserve list, and the Eagles look for big things from him. Morriss is a quality center. Nelson has size and not much else, but he could bench Walters. Key has been around a while and sometimes starts; he's not recommended. It's now-or-never time in Bleamer's pro career. Franks has to grow and improve before he'll play. Niland shouldn't make it back from a year's injury this time around, but has lots of memories. PERF. QT.: 3.

KICKERS	Ht	Wt	Age	Exp	College
Muhlmann, Horst (Pk)	6-2	219	37	9	None
Jones, Spike (P)	6-2	195	30	8	Georgia
Bitterlich, Don (Pk)	5-7	166	23	2	Temple

(Pk)—Placekicker   (P)—Punter

Muhlmann is normally reliable, though he has troubles at the wrong times. Jones is an adequate punter, but the Eagles will look for better. Bitterlich couldn't make the Seahawks. PERF. QT.: 3.

DEFENSE

FRONT LINEMEN	Ht	Wt	Age	Exp	College
Wynn, Will (E)	6-4	245	28	5	Tennessee State
Hairston, Carl (E)	6-3	245	24	2	Md.-Eastern Shore
Sistrunk, Manny (T)	6-5	275	30	8	Arkansas AM&N
Lazetich, Pete (T)	6-3	245	27	5	Stanford
Sutton, Mitch (T)	6-4	265	26	2	Kansas

(E)—End   (T)—Tackle

Wynn has spent his four years trying to reach a level of competence. Hairston was a rookie last year and he'd better improve fast. Sistrunk is the only quality lineman here, and he can't do it alone. Lazetich, once a linebacker, is barely so-so. Sutton wasn't bad as a rookie in 1974, but then was cut. He tries again. PERF. QT.: 5.

LINEBACKERS	Ht	Wt	Age	Exp	College
LeMaster, Frank (O)	6-2	231	25	4	Kentucky
Bunting, John (O)	6-1	220	27	6	N. Carolina
Bergey, Bill (M)	6-3	245	32	9	Arkansas State
Mahalic, Drew (M)	6-4	225	24	3	Notre Dame
Tautolo, Terry (M)	6-2	235	23	2	UCLA
Ehlers, Tom (O-M)	6-2	218	25	3	Kentucky
Halverson, Dean (O)	6-2	230	31	8	Washington

(O)—Outside Linebacker   (M)—Middle Linebacker

LeMaster has developed into a sound performer with good instincts. Bunting has improved noticeably on the other side and is okay. Bergey is the best middle linebacker in either conference, by a mile. Mahalic has had his moments, even as a starter, and he or Tautolo, who played for Coach Vermeil in college, would probably be the second starting inside backer. Ehlers has managed to spend two years on the squad. Halverson, off the injury list, tries a comeback. PERF. QT.: 2.

CORNERBACKS	Ht	Wt	Age	Exp	College
Outlaw, John	5-10	180	31	9	Jackson State
Clark, Al	6-0	185	29	7	Eastern Michigan
Campbell, Tommy	6-0	188	27	2	Iowa State
Marshall, Larry	5-10	195	27	6	Maryland

Outlaw played far above his established level in 1976. Can he do it again? Clark will only play until someone better arrives. Campbell made strides as a rookie and could push Clark to the bench. Marshall is a good kick return specialist. PERF. QT.: 4.

SAFETIES	Ht	Wt	Age	Exp	College
Logan, Randy (S)	6-1	195	26	5	Michigan
Bradley, Bill (W)	5-11	190	30	9	Texas
Parker, Artimus (W-S)	6-4	200	25	4	Southern California

(S)—Strong-side   (W)—Weak-side or "Free" Safety

Logan is becoming one of the better strong safeties in the league. Bradley may be losing something but he's still capable of starring. Parker wants to play, and he just might. PERF. QT.: 2.

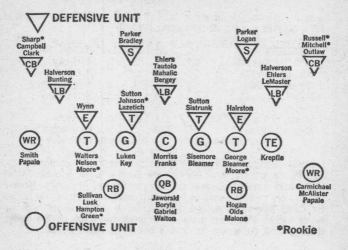

DEFENSIVE UNIT

Sharp*
Campbell
Clark
CB

Halverson
Bunting
LB

Parker
Bradley
S

Ehlers
Tautolo
Mahalic
Bergey
LB

Sutton
Johnson*
Lazetich
E

Wynn
E

Sutton
Sistrunk
T

Hairston
T

Parker
Logan
S

Halverson
Ehlers
LeMaster
LB

Russell*
Mitchell*
Outlaw
CB

WR
Smith
Papale

T
Walters
Nelson
Moore*

G
Luken
Key

C
Morriss
Franks

G
Sisemore
Bleamer

T
George
Bleamer
Moore*

TE
Krepfle

WR
Carmichael
McAlister
Papale

RB
Sullivan
Lusk
Hampton
Green*

QB
Jaworski
Boryla
Gabriel
Walton

RB
Hogan
Olds
Malone

OFFENSIVE UNIT   *Rookie

1977 DRAFT SELECTIONS

1	No Choice				
2	No Choice				
3	No Choice				
4	No Choice				
5	Sharp, Skip	CB	5-11	180	Kansas
6A	Russell, Kevin	CB	6-0	185	Tennessee State
6B	Montgomery, Will	RB	5-10	190	Abilene Christian
6C	Mitchell, Martin	CB	6-0	185	Tulane
7	Johnson, Charley	DT	6-3	255	Colorado
8	Franklin, Cleveland	RB	6-0	217	Baylor
9	Humphreys, T. J.	G	6-4	255	Arkansas State
10	Mastronardo, John	WR	6-2	197	Villanova
11A	Moore, Rocco	T	6-6	257	Western Michigan
11B	Cordova, Mike	QB	6-2	225	Stanford
12	No Choice				

The Philadelphia draft didn't amount to very much, but it hardly could have without a choice until the fifth round. Coach Vermeil went for help at cornerback, help he needs badly, with Sharp, Russell and Mitchell. The best one may be Mitchell, who was highly acclaimed on most scouting reports—though lasting until the sixth round must indicate something less than starting status. Johnson, a 25-year-old three-year Army veteran, was passed by other teams because of his age. He could help this club— maybe even start. He's also experienced in three-man line play. Some experts were surprised Moore lasted until the 11th round. PERF. QT.: 5.

MINNESOTA VIKINGS

Prediction: First

The Minnesota Vikings had a positively typical season in 1976. They won their NFC Central Division in a walk. They lost only two of their 14 regular-season games. They got past Washington and Los Angeles in the playoffs.

And they lost the Super Bowl, this time to Oakland, and in the process cemented their image as the spreaders of joy and winners' shares that has caused AFC teams to love them dearly.

Losing the Super Bowl was not a new experience. The Vikings have played in more of them (four) than any other team. They have also lost more of them than any other team. Right, four.

But it's another season and there is no reason to expect anything but another division championship. Chicago doesn't have a quarterback (yes, we know the Bears traded for Mike Phipps, but the statement still holds). Detroit will simply never get over the hump. Green Bay is too far away. Tampa Bay is the other NFC Central team this year, and anti-vivisectionists everywhere are planning protest demonstrations.

So there are the Vikings, led by fearless quarterback Fran Tarkenton, by superb halfback Chuck Foreman, by Rookie of the Year wide receiver Sammy White, by a monstrous offensive line, by another wide receiver, Ahmad Rashad, who caught even more passes than White did, but who nevertheless didn't catch as many as Foreman did.

And where are they going? Not quite as far this year.

Tarkenton is beginning to wear down, which is only fair since he is 37 years old and has played almost every offensive minute of every game in 16 pro years.

The No. 1 draft pick—wisely—was Rice quarterback Tommy Kramer, who will sit and learn and get ready to create his own legend in Paul Bunyan land.

Some of the luster left tackle Ron Yary, who was one of those automatic Pro Bowl members for years. White and Rashad are dynamite, but they need Tarkenton, who in turn needs a tight end whose name isn't Stu Voigt.

Fullback Brent McClanahan will be replaced. Most folks think it will be by Robert Miller, who sort of shared the position last year. They may be wrong. A kid named Ron Groce, from a school named Macalester, has been driving Coach Bud Grant wild with anticipation. He's 6-2 and 211. And tough.

They would like to replace Voigt, but Steve Craig doesn't look like the answer and Ken Moore, the rookie, can't yet be projected into a starting assignment.

The line will be Yary and Steve Riley at tackles, Ed White (an All-Pro) and Charles Goodrum at guards, Mick Tingelhoff (still) at center. The No. 2 draft pick was a guard, Dennis Swilley, and if he can play Goodrum will go back to tackle to argue with Riley over who should start. Last year's No. 3 pick, guard Wes Hamilton, may be ready to argue a bit, too. Doug

Dumler will back up Tingelhoff, Bart Buetow and Scott Anderson will wave bye-bye and the intriguing body belongs to John Nessel, 6-6 and 270 and twice rejected. But he's young. Grant may scare him into playing better than in the past.

Defense, which always carried the Vikings, did so again. But it remains to be determined how much longer the same old names can hang on, those names being end Jim Marshall (39), end Carl Eller (35) and tackle Alan Page (32).

If they're all right, so are the Vikings. But all three start, along with tackle Doug Sutherland, and if they should all go under together, it will be a disaster. Behind them are end Mark Mullaney and tackle Jim "Duck" White, each a No. 1 pick (1975 and 1976).

The linebackers are excellent. Jeff Siemon is in the middle, flanked by Wally Hilgenberg and Matt Blair. Hilgenberg, however, is 35 and may be ousted by young Fred McNeil. Amos Martin backs up the middle, though he disappointed Grant as Siemon's replacement in the NFC title game, while old Roy Winston (37) and Steve Reese, a free agent signee, will have to get lucky just to stay around.

The secondary was a problem. The corners are Bob Bryant (no problem) and Nate Wright. The safeties are Paul Krause (old and in danger of losing it) and Jeff Wright. Last year, two Wrights made a wrong and help is needed. Nate Allen will get a chance to win Nate Wright's job, while Windlan Hall and Autry Beamon, along with rookies Clint Strozier and Tom Hannon, should figure in spirited rivalries.

So there are problems and questions and weak spots. But the Vikings should be able to win their division. After that, they figure to be spared a fifth Super Bowl defeat.

1976 RECORD (13-3-1)

40	New Orleans	9	17	Green Bay	10
10	Los Angeles (OT)	10	16	San Francisco	20
10	Detroit	9	20	Green Bay	9
17	Pittsburgh	6	29	Miami	7
20	Chicago	19		(Playoff)	
24	New York Giants	7	35	Washington	20
31	Philadelphia	12		(NFC Championship)	
13	Chicago	14	24	Los Angeles	13
31	Detroit	23		(Super Bowl)	
27	Seattle	21	14	Oakland	32

PASSING

	Atts	Comps	Yds	Lgst	TDs	Ints	Pct
Tarkenton	412	255†	2961†	56	17	8	61.9†
Lee	30	15	156	21	0	2	50.0

SCORING

	TDs	PATs	FGs	Total
Cox	0	32	19	89
Foreman	14†	0	0	84
S. White	10	0	0	60
McClanahan	5	0	0	30
Rashad	3	0	0	18

RUSHING

	Atts	Yds	TDs	Lgst	Avg
Foreman	278	1155	13‡	46	4.2
McClanahan	130	382	4	19	2.9
Miller	67	286	0	36	4.3
Johnson•	41	150	2	18	3.7
Tarkenton	27	45	1	20	1.7

RECEIVING

	Recs	Yds	TDs	Lgst	Avg
Foreman	55	567	1	41	10.3
Rashad	53	671	3	47	12.7
S. White	51	906†	10†	56	17.8
McClanahan	40	252	1	23	6.3
Voigt	28	303	1	44	10.8
Miller	23	181	1	19	7.9

INTERCEPTIONS

	Ints	Yds	TDs	Lgst	Avg
N. Wright	7	47	0	21	6.7
Allen	3	44	0	30	14.7
Bryant	2	30	0	25	15.0
Blair	2	25	0	20	12.5
Krause	2	21	0	19	10.5

SYMBOLS †—Conference leader
‡—Tied for conference lead
•—Combined San Francisco-Minnesota record

1977 SCHEDULE

Home: Sept. 18—Dallas; Oct. 2—Green Bay; Oct. 9—Detroit; Oct. 16—Chicago; Nov. 6—St. Louis; Nov. 13—Cincinnati; Dec. 4—San Francisco.

Away: Sept. 24—Tampa Bay; Oct. 24—Los Angeles; Oct. 30—Atlanta; Nov. 20—Chicago; Nov. 27—Green Bay; Dec. 11—Oakland; Dec. 17—Detroit.

OFFENSE

QUARTERBACKS	Ht	Wt	Age	Exp	College
Tarkenton, Fran	6-0	185	37	17	Georgia
Lee, Bob	6-2	195	32	4	Pacific
Berry, Bob	5-11	185	35	13	Oregon

As long as Tarkenton can play, the depth behind him doesn't matter. Lee wants a chance to start and is torn between waiting or leaving. Berry will be leaving. PERF. QT.: 2.

RUNNING BACKS	Ht	Wt	Age	Exp	College
Foreman, Chuck	6-2	207	26	5	Miami, Fla.
McClanahan, Brent	5-10	202	26	5	Arizona State
Miller, Robert	5-11	204	24	3	Kansas
Groce, Ron	6-2	211	23	2	Macalester
Johnson, Sammy	6-1	226	24	4	North Carolina
Kellar, Mark	6-0	225	25	2	Northern Illinois

Foreman is among the best, but says he won't play for the same dough. McClanahan should have done it by now; he'll be pushed hard in camp. Miller will do most of that pushing, having been the "semi-regular" fullback. The reports from the north country on young, interested Groce are wild. In the playoffs, Johnson showed poise and ability. Kellar must do it this year or leave. PERF. QT.: 2.

RECEIVERS	Ht	Wt	Age	Exp	College
White, Sammy (W)	5-11	189	23	2	Grambling
Rashad, Ahmad (W)	6-2	200	27	5	Oregon
Voigt, Stu (T)	6-1	225	29	8	Wisconsin
Willis, Len (W)	5-10	180	24	2	Ohio State
Craig, Steve (T)	6-3	231	26	4	Northwestern
Grim, Bob (W)	6-0	188	32	11	Oregon State

(W)—Wide Receiver   (T)—Tight End

White was spectacular as a rookie and can be projected as a superstar. Rashad finally seems happy, or is he afraid of Coach Grant's iron eyes? Voigt isn't that impressive, and there isn't much behind him. Willis has good speed and could develop; right now, he returns kicks. Craig is the backup for Voigt but a good summer for Steve could change that in a big hurry. They'd like to replace Grim. PERF. QT.: 2.

INTERIOR LINEMEN	Ht	Wt	Age	Exp	College
Yary, Ron (T)	6-6	255	31	10	Southern California
Riley, Steve (T)	6-6	258	24	4	Southern California
White, Ed (G)	6-3	270	30	9	California
Goodrum, Charles (G-T)	6-3	256	27	5	Florida A&M

INTERIOR LINEMEN (Contd.)	Ht	Wt	Age	Exp	College
Tingelhoff, Mick (C)	6-2	240	37	16	Nebraska
Hamilton, Wes (G)	6-3	255	24	2	Tulsa
Dumler, Doug (C)	6-3	242	26	5	Nebraska
Buetow, Bart (T)	6-5	250	26	4	Minnesota
Anderson, Scott (C)	6-5	256	26	3	Missouri
Nessel, John (T)	6-6	270	24	1	Penn State

(T)—Tackle   (G)—Guard   (C)—Center

Yary is still one of the best tackles around despite an off-year in '76. Riley developed, became a starter and could stay that way a while. White is one of the top guards in the conference—at least—and improving. Goodrum may be the line's weak link; he may be better suited to play tackle. Tingelhoff keeps playing, and he does it well. Hamilton, a high draft pick in '76, probably isn't ready to unseat Goodrum. Dumler is a backup and figures to stay that way. Buetow should be gone before camp is disbanded. Anderson hasn't made Grant smile, which is bad for Anderson. Nessel has a chance to stick, especially if Goodrum doesn't move to tackle. PERF. QT.: 2.

KICKERS	Ht	Wt	Age	Exp	College
Cox, Fred (Pk)	5-10	200	38	15	Pittsburgh
Clabo, Neil (P)	6-2	200	24	3	Tennessee

(Pk)—Placekicker   (P)—Punter

Cox does it over and over again, fending off challengers and responding under pressure. Clabo is satisfactory. PERF. QT.: 3.

DEFENSE

FRONT LINEMEN	Ht	Wt	Age	Exp	College
Eller, Carl (E)	6-6	247	35	14	Minnesota
Marshall, Jim (E)	6-4	240	39	18	Ohio State
Page, Alan (T)	6-4	245	32	11	Notre Dame
Sutherland, Doug (T)	6-3	250	29	8	Superior, Wis.
Mullaney, Mark (E)	6-6	242	24	3	Colorado State
White, James (T)	6-3	263	23	2	Oklahoma State

(E)—End   (T)—Tackle

Eller may be slowing noticeably and Marshall, who wants another year, may find it difficult to play up to Viking standards. Page hasn't slowed down much, but he isn't the same invincible star. Sutherland could get pushed off the field with the proper challenge. Mullaney has been Marshall's heir designate, but there's some doubt about the youngster. White was a rookie, and a strong one. PERF. QT.: 3.

LINEBACKERS	Ht	Wt	Age	Exp	College
Blair, Matt (O)	6-5	229	25	4	Iowa State
Hilgenberg, Wally (O)	6-3	229	35	14	Iowa
Siemon, Jeff (M)	6-3	237	27	6	Stanford
McNeill, Fred (O)	6-2	229	25	4	UCLA
Martin, Amos (M)	6-3	228	28	6	Louisville
Winston, Roy (O)	5-11	222	37	16	Louisiana State
Reese, Steve (O)	6-0	223	25	4	Louisville

(O)—Outside Linebacker   (M)—Middle Linebacker

The new order is coming in. Blair is a wonder on the strong-side and will only get better. Hilgenberg will be pushed hard. Siemon is just a notch below Philly's Bill Bergey among middle men. McNeill should have Hilgy's job by the time the season opens. Martin is in the doghouse and may be trade bait. It doesn't seem logical for Winston to get another year. Tampa Bay and Jets flunk-out Reese doesn't have much chance. PERF. QT.: 2.

CORNERBACKS	Ht	Wt	Age	Exp	College
Bryant, Bob	6-1	170	33	9	South Carolina
Wright, Nate	5-11	180	29	9	San Diego State
Allen, Nate	5-11	174	29	7	Texas Southern
Blahak, Joe	5-10	185	27	5	Nebraska

Bryant continues to come up with big plays. He'll stay around. Wright could be improved on and this year could switch roles with Allen, who became the darling of the kick-blocking squad but who can play, too. Blahak isn't the answer, even as a reserve. PERF. QT.: 3.

SAFETIES	Ht	Wt	Age	Exp	College
Wright, Jeff (S)	5-11	190	28	7	Minnesota
Krause, Paul (W)	6-3	200	35	14	Iowa
Hall, Windlan (S)	5-11	175	27	6	Arizona State
Beamon, Autry (W)	6-1	190	23	3	East Texas State

(S)—Strong-side   (W)—Weak-side or "Free" Safety

Wright is competent on pass coverage but doesn't tackle well. Krause wants the NFL interception record, but he may not be a regular long enough to get it. Hall is qualified for a starting job and may get Wright's. Beamon isn't rated all that highly by his coaches. PERF. QT.: 3.

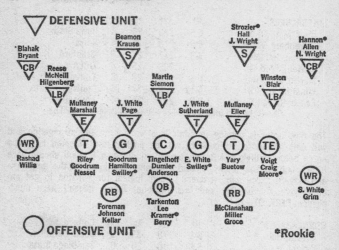

1977 DRAFT SELECTIONS

1	Kramer, Tommy	QB	6-2	190	Rice
2	Swilley, Dennis	G	6-4	245	Texas A&M
3	Hannon, Tom	CB	6-0	196	Michigan State
4	No Choice				
5	Moore, Ken	TE	6-3	225	Northern Illinois
6	No Choice				
7	No Choice				
8	Strozler, Clint	DB	6-4	190	So. California
9	Studwell, Scott	LB	6-3	235	Illinois
10	Beaver, Dan	K	6-2	180	Illinois
11	Hartwig, Keith	WR	6-0	188	Arizona
12	Kelleher, Jim	RB	6-2	214	Colorado

It was a typical Minnesota draft—wise and directly to the team's needs. The selection of Kramer was smart, since he is a player and Tarkenton is 37, Lee is an option problem and Berry has nothing left. Swilley should fill behind the starters and may even push for a job. Hannon will fill a need in the secondary (if he likes to tackle). Moore was picked for another specific need—as either Voigt's backup or replacement. Strozler had good reports and it was a surprise that he was available on the eighth round. PERF. QT.: 2.

CHICAGO BEARS

Prediction: Second

As far as most football professionals are concerned, the most amazing thing about the Chicago Bears last season was how well they did without a quarterback.

They had Bob Avellini, who beat out Gary Huff, who beat out Virgil Carter. But Avellini wasn't good enough. Whether or not he might be in the future is now academic; the Bears traded with Cleveland for Mike Phipps, and if he can't beat out Avellini they will have paid a great deal for a benchwarmer.

The real reason the Bears won seven games and came so close in several others was a halfback named Walter Payton. He led the NFC in rushing with 1390 yards and was involved in a battle for league honors with O.J. Simpson through the final game of the season. He also carried the ball 311 times—far too much.

Roland Harper is the fullback and an adequate one, but he isn't very strong. So in the draft, Coach Jack Pardee grabbed 6-5, 250-pound Robin Earl. He's a fullback—or a tight end.

Behind Payton and Harper are Johnny Musso, Mike Adamle and now Tommy Reamon, another off-season acquisition. If the Bears can control Reamon's natural impulses to run wild, they may have something.

There is a continuing need for wide receivers. The

two returning starters are soph Brian Baschnagel and James (Great) Scott, both of whom did well but neither of whom is All-Pro material. Steve Schubert, Randy Burks and Bo Rather won't do, either, but maybe the return of Ron Shanklin, out much of last season, or seventh-round rookie Gerald Butler will help matters.

The free agent signing of former Viking tight end Doug Kingsriter may help that position, where Greg Latta started but left much to be desired.

Yet the Bears moved the ball. How? With Payton and a very good offensive line.

The line, which may grow into greatness, features Lionel Antoine and Dennis Lick at tackles, Noah Jackson and Jeff Sevy at guards and Dan Neal at center. They are enormous people, averaging 6-4 and slightly over 264 pounds per man. And the reserves, Dan Jiggetts, Revie Sorey, John Ward and Dan Peiffer, are just as big. The No. 1 draft pick, University of California tackle-guard Ted Albrecht, won't hurt the averages, either.

That line is, in fact, bulkier than the defensive front. But the latter is also a volatile group, led by tackles Wally Chambers and Jim Osborne and including ends Mike Hartenstine and Roger Stillwell. Reserves are Royce Berry, Ron Rydalch and Gary Hrivnak, who missed all of last season with a leg injury.

There is a strong but thin corps of linebackers, with Don Rives in the middle, flanked by Waymond Bryant and Ross Brupbacher. The return of veteran Doug Buffone may be short-circuited by his recurring Achilles tendon problems. Tom Hicks is the sub in the middle, and his size, youth and desire may mark him for starting status, perhaps soon. Jerry Muckensturm will try to help on the outside.

The secondary did well, but is also somewhat depleted. On the corners are tiny Virgil Livers and Allan Ellis, who has played surprisingly well and can become even better if he stays healthy. Craig Clemons has become a sound strong-side safety and is young enough to continue improving. Doug Plank is the free safety, and he, too, played well. Terry Schmidt, Bill Knox, Gary Fencik and second-round rookie choice Mike Spivey will provide backup strength. Spivey, in fact, will be tried throughout the secondary and could wind up pushing someone for a starting job or at least displacing one of the reserves on the roster.

The Bears realize they can get more out of Payton by using him somewhat less. Defenses automatically concentrated on him when the obvious running play was coming up, both because they had less concern about Harper and because they knew Avellini's passing was not going to win games.

With Phipps, and perhaps Earl, the situation might change. Phipps lost his job last year, after being injured, to Brian Sipe, and Sipe played so well Phipps became expendable—at his own urging. He wants to start and there are few teams more anxious to find a starter than the Bears.

If he shows the ability that made him a No. 1 draft pick some years ago, he should shine behind that massive line and with the threat of Payton carrying the ball.

The defense, with a few pieces fitted in, could be among the conference's toughest.

The Bears were 7-7 without a quarterback last year. If they have truly found one now, they could be getting ready to challenge the aging Vikings for the Central Division crown in the near future.

1976 RECORD (7-7)

10	Detroit	3	14	Minnesota	13
19	San Francisco	12	27	Oakland	28
0	Atlanta	10	24	Green Bay	13
33	Washington	7	10	Detroit	14
19	Minnesota	20	16	Green Bay	10
12	Los Angeles	20	34	Seattle	7
21	Dallas	31	14	Denver	28

PASSING

	Atts	Comps	Yds	Lgst	TDs	Ints	Pct
Avellini	271	118	1580	63	8	15	43.5
Carter*	5	3	77	55	1	0	60.0

SCORING

	TDs	PATs	FGs	Total
Payton	13	0	0	78
Thomas	0	27	12	63
Scott	6	0	0	36
Musso	4	0	0	26§
Harper	3	0	0	18

RUSHING

	Atts	Yds	TDs	Lgst	Avg
Payton	311†	1390†	13‡	60	4.5
Harper	147	625	2	28	4.3
Musso	57	200	4	11	3.5
Adamle	33	93	0	12	2.8
Avellini	18	58	1	15	3.2

RECEIVING

	Recs	Yds	TDs	Lgst	Avg
Harper	29	291	1	39	10.0
Scott	26	512	6	63	19.7
Latta	18	254	0	58	14.1
Payton	15	149	0	34	9.9
Baschnagel	13	226	0	58	17.4

INTERCEPTIONS

	Ints	Yds	TDs	Lgst	Avg
Brupbacher	7	49	0	25	7.0
Ellis	6	47	1	22	7.8
Plank	4	31	0	15	7.8
Livers	3	34	0	18	11.3
Bryant	2	6	0	3	3.0

SYMBOLS *—Retired
†—Conference leader
‡—Tied for conference lead
§—Includes safety

1977 SCHEDULE

Home: Sept. 18—Detroit; Oct. 2—New Orleans; Oct. 10—Los Angeles; Oct. 23—Atlanta; Nov. 13—Kansas City; Nov. 20—Minnesota; Dec. 11—Green Bay.

Away: Sept. 25—St. Louis; Oct. 16—Minnesota; Oct. 30—Green Bay; Nov. 6 —Houston; Nov. 24—Detroit; Dec. 4—Tampa Bay; Dec. 18—New York Giants.

OFFENSE

QUARTERBACKS	Ht	Wt	Age	Exp	College
Phipps, Mike	6-3	205	29	8	Purdue
Avellini, Bob	6-2	212	24	3	Maryland

The trade for Phipps solves the main problems. The change of uniform should help him. Avellini was not acceptable. PERF. QT.: 3.

RUNNING BACKS	Ht	Wt	Age	Exp	College
Harper, Roland	6-0	205	24	3	Louisiana Tech
Payton, Walter	5-11	204	23	3	Jackson State
Musso, Johnny	5-11	201	27	3	Alabama
Adamle, Mike	5-9	197	26	7	Northwestern
Reamon, Tommy	5-10	192	25	2	Missouri
Schreiber, Larry	6-0	204	30	7	Tennessee Tech

Harper doesn't answer the fullback question totally, but he's satisfactory. No one was better than Payton in the NFC, and that should be the story again. Musso shows some power but lacks consistency. Adamle is a versatile back but not a starter. Reamon can be a help if he gets direction. Schreiber played out his option and is a doubtful returnee. PERF. QT.: 2.

RECEIVERS	Ht	Wt	Age	Exp	College
Baschnagel, Brian (W)	6-0	193	23	2	Ohio State
Scott, James (W)	6-1	193	25	2	Henderson J.C.
Latta, Greg (T)	6-3	235	24	3	Morgan State
Kingsriter, Doug (T)	6-2	225	27	4	Minnesota
Schubert, Steve (W)	5-10	184	26	4	Massachusetts
Rather, Bo (W)	6-1	186	26	5	Michigan State
Burks, Randy (W)	5-10	172	24	2	S.E. Oklahoma St.
Shanklin, Ron (W)	6-1	187	29	8	North Texas State

(W)—Wide Receiver   (T)—Tight End

Baschnagel made a successful conversion from college wingback. Scott has the long-ball speed and moves, but is fragile. Latta is the incumbent tight end and will get a strong challenge from Kingsriter, the former Viking. Schubert has speed, sound moves and could hang on as a reserve. Rather is in over his head; his knees are questionable. Burks is another speed merchant, but it'll be tough for him to break through here. Shanklin, out most of '76, would be a welcome returnee to the ranks. PERF. QT.: 3.

INTERIOR LINEMEN	Ht	Wt	Age	Exp	College
Antoine, Lionel (T)	6-6	263	27	6	Southern Illinois
Lick, Dennis (T)	6-3	275	23	2	Wisconsin

INTERIOR LINEMEN (Contd.)	Ht	Wt	Age	Exp	College
Jackson, Noah (G)	6-2	273	26	3	Tampa
Sevy, Jeff (G-T)	6-5	261	26	3	California
Neal, Dan (C)	6-4	250	28	5	Kentucky
Jiggetts, Dan (T-G)	6-4	276	23	2	Harvard
Sorey, Revie (G)	6-2	269	23	3	Illinois
Ward, John (C-G)	6-4	266	29	7	Oklahoma State
Peiffer, Dan (C)	6-3	254	26	3	S.E. Missouri State

(T)—Tackle   (G)—Guard   (C)—Center

Antoine finally lived up to his reputed potential. Lick, as a rookie, impressed everyone and should be a fixture. Jackson came down from Canada, showed his stuff and won a job. Sevy has size—as do all his linemates—and quickness and versatility. Neal may find some competition for the other job but can win it. Jiggetts, another rookie, was a pleasant surprise; he's versatile, too. Sorey was moved out after starting, and he wants his job back. Ward, the former Viking, has never played up to his notices. He may also get a trial on defense. Peiffer can help, though his knees are questionable. PERF. QT.: 2.

KICKERS	Ht	Wt	Age	Exp	College
Thomas, Bob (Pk)	5-10	174	25	3	Notre Dame
Parsons, Bob (P)	6-5	241	27	6	Penn State

(Pk)—Placekicker   (P)—Punter

Thomas was not much more than borderline acceptable. Parsons is a high, not deep, kicker (and a reserve tight end). PERF. QT.: 3.

DEFENSE

FRONT LINEMEN	Ht	Wt	Age	Exp	College
Hartenstine, Mike (E)	6-3	250	24	3	Penn State
Stillwell, Roger (E)	6-6	250	25	3	Stanford
Chambers, Wally (T-E)	6-6	250	26	5	Eastern Kentucky
Osborne, Jim (T)	6-3	251	27	5	Southern
Berry, Royce (E)	6-3	244	31	9	Houston
Rydalch, Ron (T)	6-4	267	25	3	Utah
Hrivnak, Gary (E-T)	6-5	251	26	4	Purdue
Meyers, Jerry (E-T)	6-4	255	23	2	Northern Illinois

(E)—End   (T)—Tackle

Hartenstine continued to prove his rookie year was no mistake. Stillwell had injury problems as well as a new-found lack of speed. Chambers may be the best tackle in the conference, and he shows it every week. Osborne, helped by Chambers' presence, is valuable in his own right. Berry doesn't have any chance at starting but could be a reserve.

Rydalch is a good pass rusher. He could force his way into the lineup, which would move Chambers to end. Hrivnak tries to come back from Achilles problems. Meyers, a 15th-round pick, did well. PERF. QT.: 2.

LINEBACKERS	Ht	Wt	Age	Exp	College
Brupbacher, Ross (O)	6-3	212	29	5	Texas A&M
Bryant, Waymond (O)	6-3	239	25	4	Tennessee State
Rives, Don (M)	6-2	226	26	4	Texas Tech
Buffone, Doug (O)	6-2	229	33	12	Louisville
Hicks, Tom (M)	6-4	235	24	2	Illinois
Muckensturm, Jerry (O)	6-4	226	23	2	Arkansas State

(O)—Outside Linebacker   (M)—Middle Linebacker

Brupbacher came out of retirement to start and didn't make many mistakes. Bryant was happier on the outside where the job isn't as complicated. He did well. Rives made a comeback and caused the switch that Bryant likes. Buffone underwent second-time leg surgery and must await the results. Chicago coaches think highly of Hicks. He could push Rives. Muckensturm's speed helped on specials. PERF. QT.: 3.

CORNERBACKS	Ht	Wt	Age	Exp	College
Ellis, Allan	5-10	183	26	5	UCLA
Livers, Virgil	5-9	178	25	3	Western Kentucky
Schmidt, Terry	6-0	178	25	4	Ball State

Ellis played well again, made some big interceptions, and can become even better. Livers has almost no size but makes up for it with catch-up speed. Schmidt will have to be lucky to make the squad. PERF. QT.: 3.

SAFETIES	Ht	Wt	Age	Exp	College
Clemons, Craig (S)	5-11	195	28	6	Iowa
Plank, Doug (W)	6-0	203	24	3	Ohio State
Knox, Bill (W-S)	5-9	195	26	4	Purdue
Fencik, Gary (S-W)	6-1	188	23	2	Yale

(S)—Strong-side   (W)—Weak-side or "Free" Safety

Clemons, despite some knocks against him, is one of the better strongsiders. Plank shows savvy and discipline, along with a liking for hitting hard. Knox will make a run at Plank's starting spot. Fencik showed enough as a rookie to merit a further look. PERF. QT.: 2.

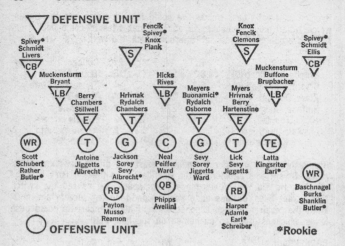

DEFENSIVE UNIT

Spivey•
Schmidt
Livers
CB

Muckensturm
Bryant
LB

Fencik•
Spivey•
Knox
Plank
S

Knox
Fencik
Clemons
S

Spivey•
Schmidt
Ellis
CB

Muckensturm
Buffone
Brupbacher
LB

Berry
Chambers
Stillwell
E

Hrivnak
Rydalch
Chambers
T

Hicks
Rives
LB

Meyers
Buonamici•
Rydalch
Osborne
T

Myers
Hrivnak
Berry
Hartenstine
E

WR
Scott
Schubert
Rather
Butler•

T
Antoine
Jiggetts
Albrecht•

G
Jackson
Sorey
Sevy
Albrecht•

C
Neal
Peiffer
Ward

G
Sevy
Sorey
Jiggetts
Ward

T
Lick
Sevy
Jiggetts

TE
Latta
Kingsriter
Earl•

WR
Baschnagel
Burks
Shanklin
Butler•

QB
Phipps
Avellini

RB
Payton
Musso
Reamon

RB
Harper
Adamle
Earl•
Schreiber

OFFENSIVE UNIT

•Rookie

1977 DRAFT SELECTIONS

1	Albrecht, Ted	T-G	6-4	260	California
2	Spivey, Mike	DB	6-0	203	Colorado
3	Earl, Robin	RB-TE	6-5	250	Washington
4	No Choice				
5	No Choice				
6	Evans, Vince	QB	6-2	204	So. California
7	Butler, Gerald	WR	6-4	206	Nicholls State
8	No Choice				
9	Buonamici, Nick	DT	6-3	242	Ohio State
10	Breckner, Dennis	DE	6-3	241	Miami, Fla.
11	Zelencik, Connie	C	6-4	245	Purdue
12	Irvin, Terry	DB	5-11	185	Jackson State

The Bears made a strange pick in the first round, going for Albrecht when their veteran strength is on the offensive line. But he's a good one and will push for a regular spot. Spivey was one of the top-rated DBs and he, too, requires starting opportunity. Earl is an enigma—he played fullback at 258 pounds—was projected as a TE by some teams, an OT by others. Remember, the Bears need a tight end badly. Butler is a rookie to watch. He can break right through to starting status. Buonamici was an "almost" All-America, and he could stick. **PERF. QT.: 3.**

DETROIT LIONS

Prediction: Third

Once again, the Lions of Detroit came up short. Despite good individual performances and some pleasant defensive statistics, they fell into a hole and crawled out with a 6-8 1976 record. In the face of continued Central Division pressure from Minnesota and the dramatic progress of Chicago, they figure to come up short again in 1977.

The Lions found their offense last season. It involved the return to form of quarterback Greg Landry, an emergent halfback named Dexter Bussey and a rookie fullback named Lawrence Gaines.

Landry had a big year. He hit on 168 of 291 passes for 2191 yards and 17 TDs, while limiting his interceptions to a paltry eight. He also gained 234 yards in 43 carries.

Bussey, in his third pro campaign, used his 210 pounds to gain 858 yards. Gaines, the big rookie, finished with 659. The pair also combined for 51 receptions.

Behind Landry is Joe Reed. Behind Bussey and Gaines are Jim Hooks, Horace King, Andy Bolton and Bobby Thompson.

Landry celebrated his comeback with an equally vital one by wide receiver Larry Walton, who teamed with Ray Jarvis (39 for 822 yards) as the starters. Big tight end Charlie Sanders had another outstanding season (35 for 545).

There is some receiving depth, too, and such as WR J.D. Hill (out for 13 games in '76) and tight end David Hill should push for regular work. Bob Picard, Leonard Thompson and highly regarded rookie Luther Blue will fight for bench spots.

The front line is huge, another Detroit trademark. Tackles are Rockne Freitas (6-6, 275) and Craig Hertwig (6-8, 270). Russ Bolinger (6-5, 255) won a guard job as a rookie and teamed with veteran Bob Kowalkowski (6-3, 245). Kowalkowski and center Jon Morris, who total 26 years of experience, may both be pushed. Lynn Boden and Ken Long want Kowalkowski's job, and this may be the year Mark Markovich (6-5, 255) wins the center assignment.

Defensively, things were good and will be better because Herb Orvis comes back after missing most of the year due to knee surgery. He was an All-Pro the year before.

His return will form a front four of Billy Howard and Ken Sanders on the ends and Jim Mitchell at the other tackle, although John Woodcock, Doug English and veteran Larry Hand will compete for a tackle spot. End Ernest Price had better start showing something.

Strong linebacking is headed up by Jim Laslavic in the middle, flanked by veterans Paul Naumoff and Charlie Weaver. Laslavic is backed up by Penn State teammate Ed O'Neil, while Garth Ten Napel and rookie pick Ron Crosby will be reserves.

The secondary lineup included a 1976 Rookie of the Year, free safety James Hunter. He had seven interceptions for 120 yards and a TD, while cornerback Levi Johnson picked off six passes for a conference-leading 206 yards and another TD. Old pro Lem Barney is on the other corner and Charlie West takes care of the strong safety spot.

They are supported by the gifted Dick Jauron (a regular until he was hurt last season), Maurice Tyler and rookie Walt Williams, a second round pick and Detroit's first selection.

Herman Weaver is a thunderous but erratic punter and Benny Ricardo came in for the last eight games to do the placekicking. He led the team in scoring with 54 points.

Detroit was seldom demolished during the season. Among the eight losses were a 10-3 decision to Chicago, a 10-9 loss to Minnesota, a 17-16 defeat by New Orleans and a 20-17 success by the Rams. Lion victims included New England (30-10) and Chicago (14-10). But it is consistency that has been missing, and still is. The mid-season coaching change that saw Tommy Hudspeth take over from Rick Forzano, who had become embroiled in one-to-one arguments with the players (notably Orvis), as the team got off a 1-3 start, seemed to succeed. The players like Hudspeth, until then the team's personnel director, and after a brief and comical attempt to lure Chuck Knox away from the Rams during the off-season, management gave the job back to the interim coach.

Now the players must keep the coach employed, and that assignment is directly tied to the continued excellence of such as Landry, Bussey, Gaines and the defense, plus finding out how to win on the road, where they were 1-6 last year.

The team is an enigma. On paper, it could be a bona fide contender. But in the standings, it never climbs higher than second. And even that position will be difficult to attain in 1977.

1976 RECORD (6-8)

3	Chicago	10	27	Green Bay	6
24	Atlanta	10	23	Minnesota	31
9	Minnesota	10	16	New Orleans	17
14	Green Bay	24	14	Chicago	10
30	New England	10	27	Buffalo	14
7	Washington	20	10	New York Giants	24
41	Seattle	14	17	Los Angeles	20

PASSING

	Atts	Comps	Yds	Lgst	TDs	Ints	Pct
Landry	291	168	2191	74	17	8	57.7
Reed	62	32	425	57	3	3	51.6

SCORING

	TDs	PATs	FGs	Total
Ricardo°	0	21	11	54
Gaines	5	0	0	30
D. Hill	5	0	0	30
Jarvis	5	0	0	30
C. Sanders	5	0	0	30
Two tied with	3	0	0	18

RUSHING

	Atts	Yds	TDs	Lgst	Avg
Bussey	196	858	3	46	4.4
Gaines	155	659	4	26	4.3
King	93	325	0	22	3.5
Landry	43	234	1	28	5.4

RECEIVING

	Recs	Yds	TDs	Lgst	Avg
Jarvis	39	822	5	74	21.1
C. Sanders	35	545	5	36	15.6
Bussey	28	218	0	27	7.8
Gaines	23	130	1	24	5.7
King	21	163	0	19	7.8
Walton	20	293	3	28	14.7

INTERCEPTIONS

	Ints	Yds	TDs	Lgst	Avg
Hunter	7	120	1	39	17.1
Johnson	6	206†	1	76	34.3
Four tied with 2					

SYMBOLS †—Conference leader
•—Combined Buffalo-Detroit record

1977 SCHEDULE

Home: Sept. 25—New Orleans; Oct. 2—Philadelphia; Oct. 16—Green Bay; Nov. 6—San Diego; Nov. 20—Tampa Bay; Nov. 24—Chicago; Dec. 17—Minnesota.

Away: Sept. 18—Chicago; Oct. 9—Minnesota; Oct. 23—San Francisco; Oct. 30—Dallas; Nov. 13—Atlanta; Dec. 4—Green Bay; Dec. 11—Baltimore.

OFFENSE

QUARTERBACKS	Ht	Wt	Age	Exp	College
Landry, Greg	6-4	205	30	10	Massachusetts
Reed, Joe	6-1	195	29	6	Mississippi State
Danielson, Gary	6-2	195	25	2	Purdue

A magical rejuvenation made Landry fearsome once more; can he retain it? Reed is a journeyman who shows an occasional flash of ability. Danielson? When can he play? PERF. QT.: 3.

RUNNING BACKS	Ht	Wt	Age	Exp	College
Bussey, Dexter	6-1	210	25	4	Texas-Arlington
Gaines, Lawrence	6-1	240	23	2	Wyoming
King, Horace	5-10	210	24	3	Georgia
Thompson, Bobby	5-11	195	30	3	Oklahoma
Hooks, Jim	5-11	225	26	4	Central St. (Okla.)
Bolton, Andy	6-1	205	23	2	Fisk

Bussey blossomed and turned the Lions' offense into a viable unit. Gaines may have been the catalyst. The rookie fullback was great. King has speed and power and can be an important substitute. The aging Thompson and Bolton, salvaged from the Seattle scrapheap as a fill-in, are strictly for depth. Hooks has had knee problems throughout his career. PERF. QT.: 2.

RECEIVERS	Ht	Wt	Age	Exp	College
Jarvis, Ray (W)	6-0	190	28	7	Norfolk State
Walton, Larry (W)	6-0	185	30	9	Arizona State
Sanders, Charlie (T)	6-4	230	31	10	Minnesota
Hill, David (T)	6-2	220	23	2	Texas A&I
Hill, J.D. (W)	6-1	185	28	7	Arizona State
Picard, Bob (W)	6-3	205	28	5	Eastern Washington
Thompson, Leonard (W)	5-10	190	25	3	Oklahoma State
Thomas, Charles (W)	5-10	180	28	2	Tennessee State

(W)—Wide Receiver   (T)—Tight End

Jarvis came from obscurity to lead the team in '76. Walton may have peaked a few years ago, before the injuries came. Sanders is a marvel of fitness, but the years may start to tell. David Hill, as a rookie, showed a propensity for clutch catches. J.D. came expensively—a No. 1 pick—but he missed 13 games with a knee. He could start this year. Picard doesn't have much hope for other than the special teams. Thompson has even less chance. Thomas hasn't played since '75 with the Chiefs. PERF. QT.: 3.

INTERIOR LINEMEN	Ht	Wt	Age	Exp	College
Freitas, Rockne (T)	6-6	275	31	10	Oregon State
Hertwig, Craig (T)	6-8	270	25	3	Georgia
Bolinger, Russ (G)	6-5	255	23	2	Long Beach State
Kowalkowski, Bob (G)	6-3	245	33	12	Virginia
Morris, Jon (C)	6-4	250	35	14	Holy Cross
Yarbrough, Jim (T)	6-5	265	30	9	Florida
Boden, Lynn (G)	6-5	270	24	3	South Dakota State
Long, Ken (G)	6-3	265	24	2	Purdue
Markovich, Mark (C)	6-5	255	25	4	Penn State

(T)—Tackle   (G)—Guard   (C)—Center

Freitas should have been better, but he's still a sound player. Hertwig must improve his technique if he wants to be top flight. Bolinger played well enough to start most of his rookie year. Kowalkowski should be pushed this time, and if he is, he'll lose. Morris could use some pushing at center, but he has outlasted a legion of reserves during his career. Yarbrough has spent recent years angry at everyone; can recover. Boden started as a rookie but sat last year; he could challenge. Long showed much promise. He or Boden could oust Kowalkowski. Markovich is present if Morris falters. PERF. QT.: 3.

KICKERS	Ht	Wt	Age	Exp	College
Ricardo, Benny (Pk)	5-10	175	23	2	San Diego State
Weaver, Herman (P)	6-4	210	28	8	Tennessee

(Pk)—Placekicker   (P)—Punter

Ricardo is just ordinary, so the Lions needed a placekicker badly. Weaver is dramatically erratic. PERF. QT.: 3.

DEFENSE

FRONT LINEMEN	Ht	Wt	Age	Exp	College
Sanders, Ken (E)	6-5	245	27	6	Howard Payne
Howard, Billy (E-T)	6-4	255	27	4	Alcorn A&M
Mitchell, Jim (T)	6-3	250	28	8	Virginia State
Orvis, Herb (T)	6-5	255	30	6	Colorado
Woodcock, John (T)	6-3	240	23	2	Hawaii
Price, Ernest (E)	6-4	245	26	5	Texas A&I
Hand, Larry (T)	6-4	245	37	13	Appalachian State
English, Doug (T)	6-5	255	25	3	Texas
Croft, Don (T)	6-4	255	28	6	Texas-El Paso

(E)—End   (T)—Tackle

Though Sanders is not spectacular, his consistency helps. Howard had best not ease off if he wants to maintain his starting spot. Mitchell is very strong. Orvis should be among the best tackles in the league, but injury doubts are present as he tries a comeback after missing most of '76. Woodcock as a rookie showed much potential. Price, a former No. 1 draft pick, has been very disappointing. Hand, once a Pro Bowl player, is unhappy (because he's 37?). English is still waiting for a chance. Croft, on the other hand, has had plenty of opportunities and hasn't delivered. PERF. QT.: 3.

LINEBACKERS	Ht	Wt	Age	Exp	College
Naumoff, Paul (O)	6-1	215	32	11	Tennessee
Weaver, Charlie (O)	6-2	225	28	7	Southern California
Laslavic, Jim (M)	6-2	240	25	5	Penn State
Ten Napel, Garth (O)	6-1	210	23	2	Texas A&M
O'Neil, Ed (M)	6-3	235	24	4	Penn State

(O)—Outside Linebacker   (M)—Middle Linebacker

Naumoff is quick, smart, intense. But he's at the point where age will become a factor. Weaver continues to surprise scouts who say he isn't strong enough. Laslavic in the middle is good—most of the time. Ten Napel is a player despite his light weight. O'Neil could challenge Laslavic for starting honors. PERF. QT.: 3.

CORNERBACKS	Ht	Wt	Age	Exp	College
Barney, Lem	6-0	190	31	11	Jackson State
Johnson, Levi	6-3	200	26	5	Texas A&I

Barney put together another superb year after a couple of bummers. Johnson is getting better all the time. PERF. QT.: 2.

SAFETIES	Ht	Wt	Age	Exp	College
West, Charlie (S)	6-1	190	31	10	Texas-El Paso
Hunter, James (W)	6-3	195	23	2	Grambling
Tyler, Maurice (S)	6-1	190	27	5	Morgan State
Jauron, Dick (W)	6-0	190	26	4	Yale

(S)—Strong-side   (W)—Weak-side or "Free" Safety

West starts, but he isn't what he used to be. Hunter was a spectacular rookie who has everything he needs to star. Tyler is a fill-in with some speed, some experience. Jauron was a starter before Hunter arrived. He can also double at cornerback. PERF. QT.: 3.

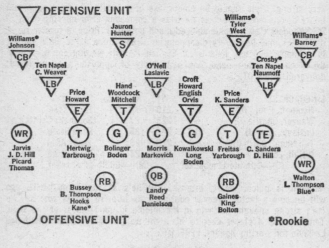

DEFENSIVE UNIT

Williams●
Johnson
CB

Jauron
Hunter
S

Williams●
Tyler
West
S

Williams●
Barney
CB

Ten Napel
C. Weaver
LB

O'Nell
Laslavic
LB

Crosby●
Ten Napel
Naumoff
LB

Price
Howard
E

Hand
Woodcock
Mitchell
T

Croft
Howard
English
Orvis
T

Price
K. Sanders
E

WR
Jarvis
J. D. Hill
Picard
Thomas

T
Hertwig
Yarbrough

G
Bolinger
Boden

C
Morris
Markovich

G
Kowalkowski
Long
Boden

T
Freitas
Yarbrough

TE
C. Sanders
D. Hill

WR
Walton
L. Thompson
Blue●

RB
Bussey
B. Thompson
Hooks
Kane●

QB
Landry
Reed
Danielson

RB
Gaines
King
Bolton

OFFENSIVE UNIT   ●Rookie

1977 DRAFT SELECTIONS

1	No Choice				
2	Williams, Walt	DB	6-3	192	New Mexico State
3	Kane, Rick	RB	6-1	205	San Jose State
4	Blue, Luther	WR	6-0	181	Iowa State
5	Crosby, Ron	LB	6-3	222	Penn State
6	Pinkney, Reggie	DB	6-0	186	East Carolina
7	Black, Tim	LB	6-2	208	Baylor
8	Griffin, Mark	T	6-5	240	North Carolina
9	Mathieson, Steve	QB	6-1	190	Florida State
10	Anderson, Gary	G-T	6-4	251	Stanford
11	Daykin, Tony	LB	6-1	216	Georgia Tech
12	Greenwood, Dave	C-G	6-4	240	Iowa State

Detroit had a puzzling draft, taking "risky" players in most of the upper rounds. It can either be a great draft (for the second straight year) or an embarrassment. Williams has good size and speed but didn't do well man-to-man. He will get trials as a left cornerback, strong safety and kick returner. Kane doesn't have power-strength. Blue has infinite speed, so-so hands. Crosby is another in a long line of Penn State LBs who matriculated to the Lions. PERF. QT.: 3.

GREEN BAY PACKERS

Prediction: Fourth

If Bart Starr gets enough time, he'll finally finish rebuilding the Green Bay Packers. In Green Bay, where he is still considered something more than human, he should get that time.

The question is, what has he done with the team so far?

The answer, sadly, is not much.

There are still too many holes at key positions, and too many borderline players at other positions. But the Starr touch, which is really a part of the Lombardi touch, is starting to take hold.

Starr, as Lombardi, believes in simplicity. But to build a good team he needs players. He is starting to find them, but not in large enough clusters.

Starr, the old quarterback, has committed himself to Lynn Dickey as his starting field leader. Behind Dickey is Randy Johnson; Carlos Brown and Don Milan will fight to see who stays and who goes.

Will Harrell and Barty Smith will be the runners, backed up by Eric Torkelson, slumping John Brockington, young Ken Starch and Cliff Taylor, and a rookie named Terdell Middleton who was so attractive to Starr that he traded cornerback Perry Smith to St. Louis to get him.

The line is getting there, but slowly. Last year's No. 1 pick, Mark Koncar, won a job at tackle and was sensational. The other tackle is veteran Dick Himes. Bruce Van Dyke and Mel Jackson are the guards with Larry McCarren at center. The pickings are lean here —with Bob Hyland, an old vet, and Steve Knutson the only reserves. Rookies Rick Scribner and Greg Koch (who will also get a look at defense tackle) will be expected to win spots on the squad.

When Dickey is well enough to throw, he'll have Ken Payne and Steve Odom as his starting wide men and Rich McGeorge as the tight end. Ollie Smith, from the Raiders, and Gerald Tinker are the backup wide receivers with Bert Askson, once a DE, as the tight end cushion.

At best, the offense is only barely acceptable.

But the defense is further along.

The first-round draft picks (there were two) turned out to be DE Mike Butler of Kansas and DE or LB Ezra Johnson. Butler is a horse, though with a few kneecap problems. Johnson is a 235-pounder who may follow in the tradition of Dave Robinson and Fred Carr, who moved from college line to pro linebacker. The rookies will push starters Alden Roche and Clarence Williams. Mike McCoy and Dave Pureifory are the nominal tackle starters, with only McCoy sure of his status.

Dave Roller, rookie Koch and Bob Barber figure to fight for reserve roles.

Johnson doesn't figure to move out a linebacker immediately, since the duel in the middle will feature Don Hansen trying to hold off Tom Perko and Jim Carter, both of whom return from the injured reserve list, while Carr and Gary Weaver are locked in the outside holes.

Indeed, there is some depth here, too, with such as Johnson, Jim Gueno and Tom Toner all looking for steady work.

In the secondary, M.C. McCoy and Willie Buchanon seem to have the cornerback jobs nailed down, with mediocre veteran Charley Hall listed as the backup for both of them.

That's nice as long as M.C. and Willie stay healthy. Hall has had his chance to start and proved that he couldn't do it.

The safeties show Steve Luke at strong-side and Johnny Gray at weak-side, with young Steve Wagner and rookie Tim Moresco shown as the replacements. Luke doesn't play as well as Gray does, so he figures to have more competition, perhaps from the rookie from Syracuse.

The kicking game is handled excellently, with Chester Marcol coming back from an injury that ruined his '75 season to toe the field goals and placements, and David Beverly booming away the punts.

But there is very little offense, especially if Dickey continues to be hounded by nagging injuries. The Randy Johnson story continues in that he always looks good and always seems to kick away an opportunity. He has served terms in Atlanta, New York and Washington. His salary is up to $80,000-$90,000 by now, and that might work against him if anyone else makes a push.

The other problem, quite simply, is the NFC Central Division competition. Minnesota should win it. Chicago and Detroit were much improved last season and the Bears, with a quarterback, could well make a run at the Vikings.

But the Packers won't finish last this year. Tampa Bay has been moved into the grouping.

1976 RECORD (5-9)

14	San Francisco	26	6	Detroit		27
0	St. Louis	29	32	New Orleans		27
7	Cincinnati	28	13	Chicago		24
24	Detroit	14	10	Minnesota		17
27	Seattle	20	10	Chicago		16
28	Philadelphia	13	9	Minnesota		20
14	Oakland	18	24	Atlanta		20

PASSING

	Atts	Comps	Yds	Lgst	TDs	Ints	Pct
Dickey	243	115	1465	69	7	14	47.3
Johnson	35	21	249	45	0	1	60.0
Brown	74	26	333	47	2	6	35.1

SCORING

	TDs	PATs	FGs	Total
Marcol	0	24	10	54
B. Smith	5	0	0	30
Harrell	4	0	0	24
Payne	4	0	0	24
Three tied with	2	0	0	12

RUSHING

	Atts	Yds	TDs	Lgst	Avg
Harrell	130	435	3	56	3.3
Brockington	117	406	2	29	3.5
B. Smith	97	355	5	16	3.7
Torkelson	88	289	2	15	3.3

RECEIVING

	Recs	Yds	TDs	Lgst	Avg
Payne	33	467	4	57	14.2
McGeorge	24	278	1	28	11.6
Odom	23	456	2	66	19.8
O. Smith	20	364	1	47	18.2
Torkelson	19	140	0	31	7.4
Harrell	17	201	1	69	11.8

INTERCEPTIONS

	Ints	Yds	TDs	Lgst	Avg
Gray	4	101	1	67	25.3
Luke	2	30	0	15	15.0
Buchanon	2	28	0	22	14.0

1977 SCHEDULE

Home: Sept. 25—Houston; Oct. 9—Cincinnati (at Milwaukee); Oct. 30—Chicago; Nov. 13—Los Angeles (at Milwaukee); Nov. 27—Minnesota; Dec. 4—Detroit; Dec. 18—San Francisco (at Milwaukee).

Away: Sept. 18—New Orleans; Oct. 2—Minnesota; Oct. 16—Detroit; Oct. 23—Tampa Bay; Nov. 6—Kansas City; Nov. 21—Washington; Dec. 11—Chicago.

OFFENSE

QUARTERBACKS	Ht	Wt	Age	Exp	College
Dickey, Lynn	6-4	210	27	7	Kansas State
Johnson, Randy	6-3	205	33	10	Texas A&I
Brown, Carlos	6-3	210	25	3	Pacific
Milan, Don	6-3	196	28	3	Cal. Poly-SLO

Dickey is the regular and no one can change that; maybe that's too bad. Johnson may have a year or so left, but he's too unorthodox. Brown has fooled the scouts—they thought he'd make it. Milan is an aging never-quite-there. PERF. QT.: 4.

RUNNING BACKS	Ht	Wt	Age	Exp	College
Harrell, Will	5-9	182	24	3	Pacific
Smith, Barty	6-4	240	25	3	Richmond
Brockington, John	6-1	225	28	6	Ohio State
Torkelson, Eric	6-2	194	25	4	Connecticut
Taylor, Cliff	6-0	195	25	4	Memphis State
Starch, Ken	5-11	219	23	2	Wisconsin
Osborn, Dave	6-0	208	34	13	North Dakota

Harrell shows speed and dogged blocking abilities, but his size hurts him. Smith had better win the job this year or he's off to somewhere else. Brockington is in a down phase, maybe down enough to drown. Torkelson comes up with good efforts and big plays. He blocks well, too. Taylor will try again after a fling with the Bears. He hasn't got enough. Starch showed some speed as a little-known rookie. Osborn must be kidding if he thinks he can still do the job. PERF. QT.: 3.

RECEIVERS	Ht	Wt	Age	Exp	College
Payne, Ken (W)	6-1	185	26	4	Langston
Odom, Steve (W)	5-8	174	24	3	Utah
McGeorge, Rich (T)	6-4	230	28	8	Elon
Smith, Ollie (W)	6-3	200	28	4	Tennessee State
Tinker, Gerald (W)	5-9	170	25	3	Kent State
Askson, Bert (T)	6-2	225	31	5	Texas Southern
Thompson, Aundra (W)	6-0	190	23	1	East Texas State

(W)—Wide Receiver   (T)—Tight End

Payne slipped from 58 catches in '75 to 33, still a lot by Packer standards. Little Odom hasn't really made it except as a return man. McGeorge is steady, with more potential than achievement. Smith has size and speed; Odom shouldn't make any long-range plans with the big man behind him. Tinker missed '76 with injuries; he could surprise. Askson is not more than a reserve. RB Thompson, who spent '76 on the injury list, gets a shot at WR. PERF. QT.: 3.

INTERIOR LINEMEN	Ht	Wt	Age	Exp	College
Koncar, Mark (T)	6-5	268	24	2	Colorado
Himes, Dick (T)	6-4	260	31	10	Ohio State
Van Dyke, Bruce (G)	6-2	255	33	12	Missouri
Jackson, Mel (G)	6-1	267	23	2	Southern California
McCarren, Larry (C)	6-3	248	25	5	Illinois
Knutson, Steve (T)	6-3	254	25	3	Southern California
Hyland, Bob (C)	6-5	255	32	11	Boston College

(T)—Tackle   (G)—Guard   (C)—Center

Koncar, the '76 first-round pick, proved the Packers' selection right and starred. Himes has long since passed a shot at stardom. Van Dyke retains his speed. Jackson came along late in the season and should keep a regular job. McCarren is the best the Packers have at center. He'll have to do. Knutson has youth on his side, lack of poise against him. Hyland is almost past usefulness. The reserves—and some starters —are weak. PERF. QT.: 4.

KICKERS	Ht	Wt	Age	Exp	College
Marcol, Chester (Pk)	6-0	190	27	6	Hillsdale
Beverly, David (P)	6-2	180	27	3	Auburn

(Pk)—Placekicker   (P)—Punter

Marcol is as good as any placekicker when he isn't injured. Beverly solved the team's punting woes last year. PERF. QT.: 2.

DEFENSE

FRONT LINEMEN	Ht	Wt	Age	Exp	College
Williams, Clarence (E)	6-5	255	30	8	Prairie View
Roche, Alden (E)	6-4	255	32	8	Southern
McCoy, Mike (T)	6-5	275	28	8	Notre Dame
Pureifory, Dave (T)	6-1	255	28	6	Eastern Michigan
Roller, Dave (T)	6-2	270	27	4	Kentucky
Barber, Bob (E)	6-3	240	25	2	Grambling

(E)—End   (T)—Tackle

Williams is an able performer with good pass-rushing abilities. Roche seems to have hit the first stage of a slowdown. McCoy, a tower of strength, might be even better if he played a little lighter. Pureifory has reached the time when he must produce or be released. Roller is useful, but he draws too many penalties. Barber shows lots of promise and could push someone. PERF. QT.: 3.

LINEBACKERS	Ht	Wt	Age	Exp	College
Carr, Fred (O)	6-5	240	31	10	Texas-El Paso

LINEBACKERS (Contd.)	Ht	Wt	Age	Exp	College
Hansen, Don (M)	6-2	228	33	11	Illinois
Weaver, Gary (O)	6-1	225	28	5	Fresno State
Perko, Tom (M)	6-3	233	23	2	Pittsburgh
Toner, Tom (O)	6-3	235	27	5	Idaho State
Gueno, Jim (O)	6-2	220	23	2	Tulane
Carter, Jim (M)	6-3	245	28	7	Minnesota

(O)—Outside Linebacker   (M)—Middle Linebacker

Carr hasn't shown signs of age; he still has great abilities. Hansen's experience helps, though he's not the long-range answer. Weaver, a waiver bargain, played well once he got the chance. Perko began as a rookie starter. He's better off learning from the bench. Toner could become a good one. Gueno was another rookie with promise. Carter tries to come back from two years of injuries. He's doubtful to even make the roster. PERF. QT.: 3.

CORNERBACKS	Ht	Wt	Age	Exp	College
Buchanon, Willie	6-0	190	26	6	San Diego State
McCoy, M.C.	5-11	183	24	2	Colorado
Hall, Charley	6-1	190	29	7	Pittsburgh

Buchanon is happy under Coach Starr, which makes him a top performer again. McCoy as a rookie showed great possibilities; he'll replace the departed Perry Smith. Hall will barely hang on. PERF. QT.: 3.

SAFETIES	Ht	Wt	Age	Exp	College
Luke, Steve (S)	6-2	205	23	3	Ohio State
Gray, Johnny (W)	5-11	185	23	3	Cal.-Fullerton
Wagner, Steve (S-W)	6-2	208	23	2	Wisconsin

(S)—Strong-side   (W)—Weak-side or "Free" Safety

Every candidate in camp will battle Luke, a tough hitter. Gray had a second straight sound season after signing as a free agent. Wagner has a slim chance. PERF. QT.: 3.

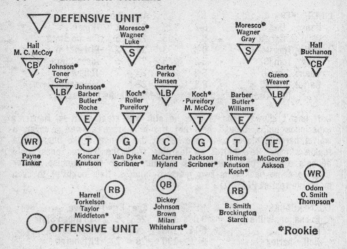

DEFENSIVE UNIT

Moresco●
Wagner
Luke
S

Moresco●
Wagner
Gray
S

Hall
M. C. McCoy
CB

Hall
Buchanon
CB

Johnson●
Toner
Carr
LB

Carter
Perko
Hansen
LB

Gueno
Weaver
LB

Johnson●
Barber
Butler●
Roche
E

Koch●
Roller
Pureifory
T

Koch●
Pureifory
M. McCoy
T

Barber
Butler●
Williams
E

WR
Payne
Tinker

T
Koncar
Knutson

G
Van Dyke
Scribner●

C
McCarren
Hyland

G
Jackson
Scribner●

T
Himes
Knutson
Koch●

TE
McGeorge
Askson

WR
Odom
O. Smith
Thompson●

RB
Harrell
Torkelson
Taylor
Middleton●

QB
Dickey
Johnson
Brown
Milan
Whitehurst●

RB
B. Smith
Brockington
Starch

OFFENSIVE UNIT

●Rookie

1977 DRAFT SELECTIONS

1A	Butler, Mike	DE	6-5	265	Kansas
1B	Johnson, Ezra	LB-DE	6-4	235	Morris Brown
2	Koch, Greg	DT-T	6-4	254	Arkansas
3	Scribner, Rick	G	6-4	250	Idaho State
4	No Choice				
5	Simpson, Nathan	RB	6-1	205	Tennessee State
6	Moresco, Tim	DB	6-0	176	Syracuse
7A	Gofourth, Derrel	C	6-2	253	Oklahoma St.
7B	Tipton, Rell	G	6-3	237	Baylor
8	Whitehurst, Dave	QB	6-2	205	Furman
9	Mullins, Joel	T	6-3	240	Arkansas State
10	Culbreath, Jimmy	RB	5-11	209	Oklahoma
11	Randolph, Terry	DB	6-0	175	American Int.
12	No Choice				

*—Also traded for St. Louis' third-round pick, Terdell Middleton (RB, 6-0, 191, Memphis State).

Butler and Johnson, both first-rounders, must play immediately. But while the Packers have many weaknesses, they are relatively strong at these youngsters' positions. There was some doubt about Butler's "loose knee-caps," but if that fear is unfounded, the Packers stole him. Johnson was a surprise pick as the 28th collegian selected. He was rated as a first-round prospect. Koch, though, was highly rated and will help, probably on offense. Scribner has size. Middleton, from St. Louis, will also help. Safety Moresco, two lower linemen, Gofourth and Tipton, and Randolph may be sleepers. But young Whitehurst is the real dark horse; he has the ability to make this a super draft for the Pack. PERF. QT.: 2.

TAMPA BAY BUCCANEERS

Prediction: Fifth

The Buccaneers are virtually starting all over in 1977. They may as well. They never started anything in 1976. As proof, they have their 0-14 won-lost record.

The Bucs may have to wait until the second "Little Super Bowl," the October 16 meeting with Seattle in the Kingdome, before they can think about breaking their maiden.

When they open the season at Philadelphia, some of the Bucs may still be introducing themselves to each other. Then they play three playoff teams—Minnesota, Dallas and Washington.

John McKay, the Bucs' embarrassed coach, will have an entirely new backfield this season. Two thirds of it played for him at Southern California. The quarterback is the sole non-Trojan. He is Gary Huff, who was supposed to do great things for the Chicago Bears, but never did. He is the second local boy to try to make good in central Florida. Steve Spurrier, former Florida U. Heisman Trophy winner, was hooted out of town. Huff prepped for the pros at Florida State.

Huff will get the fullest shot at the job, despite his lack of productivity in Chicago. Behind him—and pressuring him only if he loses his poise in the face of the defensive rush he is sure to encounter—will be Parnell Dickinson, David Jaynes and rookie Randy Hedberg. Dickinson, a scrambling rookie in '76, hurt a knee that has been slow to heal. If healthy, he is important in the Bucs' future. Jaynes, trying to make it with his fourth team, can be pushed off the roster by eighth-round draft choice Hedberg, a talented youngster from little Minot State in North Dakota.

The two ball carriers will be Anthony Davis, who took the circuitous route from the WFL's Southern California Sun to the Canadian League's Toronto Argonauts to the Bucs, via a trade for his rights with the New York Jets, and Ricky Bell.

Tampa Bay bypassed Tony Dorsett to make Bell the No. 1 pick in the NFL draft. Bell will line up at fullback, where he played for McKay as a college sophomore.

Who will open holes for them? That's a thorny question.

The Buc line shapes up as a mixture of over-the-hill veterans, marginal players and unproved kids. Huge sophomore Steve Young and vet Mike Current are the tackles of record. Howard Fest, another vet, and young Steve Wilson are the guards. Dan Ryczek is the center. There are, of course, no quality reserves behind these non-quality starters, but Dave Reavis, who missed most of the '76 season with a knee injury after winning a tackle job, will try to break into the starting unit.

The receiving is extremely suspect. The best man is Morris Owens, a Miami reject who caught three touchdown passes in Tampa's near-upset of the Dolphins, and J. K. McKay. McKay is the coach's son, which makes his position uncomfortable as well as semi-secure. Bob Moore, the ex-Oakland starter, is the class of the receivers from his tight end position.

About the only place Coach McKay will have offensive depth is in the running back department, with last's year's leading ground gainer, Louis Carter, veteran fullback Ed Williams, sophomore fullback Jimmy DuBose and Harold Hart, a promising former Oakland Raider who missed last season due to a knee injury.

Defensively, the Bucs are virtually committed to the three-man front with four linebackers. The success of that set depends a great deal upon how Lee Roy Selmon, the No. 1 pick in last year's draft, rebounds from his knee injury. Lee Roy was outstanding until he got hurt.

Selmon, an end, is the only definite starter in the line. Dave Pear is semi-established at nose tackle, but he and veterans Pat Toomay and Council Rudolph may find themselves in a battle with rookie Charles Hannah of Alabama. The brother of New England's All-Pro guard, John, young Hannah is strong and quick.

There are plenty of openings in the weak linebacking corps and another rookie, Southern California's Dave Lewis, should be able to fill one. His skills lend themselves to use as a utility man, like Oakland's Ted Hendricks and Miami's Bob Matheson.

Jim Peterson and Cal Peterson, no relation, both were injured last year. If they are healthy, they should start along with rookie Lewis. Lee Roy Selmon's brother, Dewey, was switched from down lineman to inside linebacker to contend with Larry Ball and Richard Wood.

Two rookies, Danny Reece and Mike Washington, started at the cornerback spots last year. Another pro sophomore, Curtis Jordan, may press them for work or take a shot at one of the safeties, where Ken Stone and Mark Cotney are stationed.

1976 RECORD (0-14)

0	Houston	20		19	Kansas City	28
0	San Diego	23		13	Denver	48
9	Buffalo	14		0	New York Jets	34
17	Baltimore	42		7	Cleveland	24
0	Cincinnati	21		16	Oakland	49
10	Seattle	13		0	Pittsburgh	42
20	Miami	23		14	New England	31

PASSING

	Atts	Comps	Yds	Lgst	TDs	Ints	Pct
Spurrier**	311	156	1628	38	7	12	50.2
Dickinson	39	15	210	49	1	5	38.5

SCORING

	TDs	PATs	FGs	Total
Owens	6	0	0	36
Green	0	11	8	35
Johnson**	2	0	0	12
Williams	2	0	0	12
Five tied with	1	0	0	6

RUSHING

	Atts	Yds	TDs	Lgst	Avg
Carter	171	521	1	26	3.0
Williams	87	324	2	19	3.7
Johnson**	47	166	1	27	3.5
McNeill	27	135	0	17	5.0
C. Davis	41	107	1	13	2.6

RECEIVING

	Recs	Yds	TDs	Lgst	Avg
Owens	30	390	6	27	13.0
Johnson**	25	201	1	38	8.0
Moore	24	289	0	31	12.0
Williams	23	166	0	18	7.2
McKay	20	302	1	49	15.1
Carter	20	135	0	19	6.8

INTERCEPTIONS

	Ints	Yds	TDs	Lgst	Avg
Cotney	3	25	0	25	8.3
Stone	2	47	0	26	23.5
Jordan	2	10	0	10	5.0

SYMBOL **—Waived

1977 SCHEDULE

Home: Sept. 24—Minnesota; Oct. 9—Washington; Oct. 23—Green Bay; Nov. 13—New York Giants; Nov. 27—Atlanta; Dec. 4—Chicago; Dec. 18—St. Louis.

Away: Sept. 18—Philadelphia; Oct. 2—Dallas; Oct. 16—Seattle; Oct. 30—San Francisco; Nov. 6—Los Angeles; Nov. 20—Detroit; Dec. 11—New Orleans.

OFFENSE

QUARTERBACKS	Ht	Wt	Age	Exp	College
Huff, Gary	6-1	198	26	5	Florida State
Dickinson, Parnell	6-2	185	24	2	Mississippi Valley
Jaynes, David	6-2	210	24	2	Kansas

The ex-Florida star, Steve Spurrier, couldn't do it for the Bucs so maybe the former Florida State star, Huff, will. He was a Bears' flop. Dickinson could be the eventual answer. Jaynes isn't. PERF. QT.: 5.

RUNNING BACKS	Ht	Wt	Age	Exp	College
Davis, Anthony	5-10	190	24	1	Southern California
Williams, Ed	6-1	245	27	4	Langston
Carter, Louis	5-11	209	24	3	Maryland
DuBose, Jimmy	5-11	217	22	2	Florida
Davis, Charlie	5-11	200	25	3	Colorado
Evans, Charlie	6-1	220	29	5	Southern California
Hart, Harold	6-0	211	24	3	Texas Southern
McNeill, Rod	6-2	220	26	4	Southern California

Anthony Davis can't do anything but upgrade this offense, whether he is running from scrimmage, catching passes or returning punts and kickoffs. They didn't have anyone with his attack skills last year. Williams can be a solid, journeyman fullback. Carter also is a sound runner. DuBose must learn the ropes. Charlie Davis keeps getting hurt. Hart can be a game breaker and kickoff return ace if he can get over his '76 knee injury. Evans and McNeill are former Trojans who may eventually contribute for their old coach. PERF. QT.: 3.

RECEIVERS	Ht	Wt	Age	Exp	College
McKay, J.K. (W)	5-10	175	24	2	Southern California
Owens, Morris (W)	6-0	190	24	3	Arizona State
Moore, Bob (T)	6-3	229	28	7	Stanford
Ragsdale, George (W)	5-11	185	23	1	N.C. Central
Hagins, Isaac (W)	5-9	180	22	1	Southern
Novak, Jack (T)	6-5	240	24	3	Wisconsin
Butler, Gary (T)	6-3	235	26	4	Rice

(W)—Wide Receiver   (T)—Tight End

McKay may be too small, but he's also too slow. Being the coach's son causes a lot of resentment when you don't have ability. Owens upgraded the unit after arriving from Miami. He almost beat the Dolphins in the Florida championship. Moore looked as if he would rather be back in Oakland. Novak, a crude former Bengal, may get more work because of his blocking. Ragsdale and Hagins were hurt in training camp as rookies. Butler is a Bears' reject. PERF. QT.: 5.

INTERIOR LINEMEN	Ht	Wt	Age	Exp	College
Young, Steve (T)	6-8	272	24	2	Colorado
Current, Mike (T)	6-4	270	31	11	Ohio State
Fest, Howard (G-C)	6-6	263	31	10	Texas
Wilson, Steve (G)	6-3	268	23	2	Georgia
Ryczek, Dan (C)	6-3	250	28	5	Virginia
Reavis, Dave (T-G)	6-5	250	27	2	Arkansas
Alward, Tom (G)	6-4	255	24	2	Nebraska
Little, Everett (G-T)	6-4	265	23	2	Houston

(T)—Tackle   (G)—Guard   (C)—Center

This was supposed to be one of the Buccaneer strengths, but the sack total allowed was 50, there was little speed and many flaws. Current and Fest bore small resemblance to their previous reputations in Denver and Cincinnati, respectively. His size alone makes it imperative that the coaches work overtime with Young, who started as a rookie. Wilson falls into that category, also. Ryczek may get better. Reavis was a starter until injury felled him. He could make his presence felt. Alward and Little didn't overwhelm as rookies. PERF. QT.: 5.

KICKER	Ht	Wt	Age	Exp	College
Green, Dave (Pk-P)	6-0	208	27	5	Ohio

(Pk)—Placekicker   (P)—Punter

Green may concentrate strictly on punting in '77. PERF. QT.: 3.

DEFENSE

FRONT LINEMEN	Ht	Wt	Age	Exp	College
Rudolph, Council (E)	6-4	255	27	6	Kentucky State
Selmon, Lee Roy (E)	6-3	263	22	2	Oklahoma
Pear, Dave (T)	6-2	248	24	3	Washington
Toomay, Pat (E)	6-6	244	29	8	Vanderbilt
Robinson, Glenn (E)	6-6	245	25	3	Oklahoma State
Guy, Tim (E)	6-5	243	24	1	Oregon

(E)—End   (T)—Tackle

Defensive coordinator Abe Gibron is committed to a three-man front this year after vacillating through the '76 season. The key is how well Selmon comes back from the injury list. He's a potential All-Pro. Toomay and Rudolph, who started in '76, will fight it out for the other end job. Ex-Colt Pear was a pleasant surprise as a nose tackle. Robinson and Guy are strictly subs. PERF. QT.: 3.

LINEBACKERS	Ht	Wt	Age	Exp	College
Peterson, Calvin (O)	6-3	215	24	4	UCLA

LINEBACKERS (Contd.)	Ht	Wt	Age	Exp	College
Peterson, Jim (O)	6-4	226	27	3	San Diego State
Ball, Larry (M)	6-6	235	27	6	Louisville
Selmon, Dewey (M)	6-1	254	23	2	Oklahoma
Maughan, Steve (O)	6-1	210	23	1	Utah State
Wood, Richard (M)	6-2	215	24	3	Southern California
Gunn, Jimmy (O)	6-2	231	28	7	Southern California
Lemon, Mike (M)	6-2	220	26	3	Kansas

(O)—Outside Linebacker   (M)—Middle Linebacker

Does this team need new linebacking? Are there swallows in Capistrano? The Petersons were healthy for eight games between them last year, so they are potential starters. Selmon, a tackle in his rookie year, gets a long look as an inside linebacker. Maughan, a high draft choice who was hurt last year, gets a fresh start. The rest of the group could be cleared right off the roster by opening day even though three of them—Ball, Wood and Gunn—were starters throughout much of the 1976 campaign. PERF. QT.: 5.

CORNERBACKS	Ht	Wt	Age	Exp	College
Washington, Mike	6-3	190	24	2	Alabama
Reece, Danny	5-11	190	22	2	Southern California
Jordan, Curtis	6-2	182	23	2	Texas Tech
Word, Roscoe	5-11	170	25	4	Jackson State

The Bucs finished seventh in AFC pass defense in '76, a triumph considering the team's season. Washington and Reece come off knee surgery but they are considered bright prospects. Jordan can play safety, also. If Word has to play, the team is in trouble. PERF. QT.: 3.

SAFETIES	Ht	Wt	Age	Exp	College
Cotney, Mark (S)	6-0	207	25	3	Cameron State
Stone, Ken (W)	6-1	180	26	5	Vanderbilt
Davis, Ricky (W)	6-0	178	24	3	Alabama

(S)—Strong-side   (W)—Weak-side or "Free" Safety

Cotney and Stone are not speedsters but they know their way around. Cotney led the team in interceptions with three. Davis may push for work, as may reserve cornerback Jordan. PERF. QT.: 4.

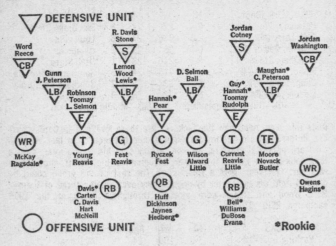

DEFENSIVE UNIT

Word Reece
CB

R. Davis Stone
S

Jordan Cotney
S

Jordan Washington
CB

Gunn
J. Peterson
LB

Lemon Wood Lewis•
LB

D. Selmon Ball
LB

Maughan•
C. Peterson
LB

Robinson
Toomay
L. Selmon
E

Hannah•
Pear
T

Guy•
Hannah•
Toomay
Rudolph
E

WR
McKay
Ragsdale•

T
Young
Reavis

G
Fest
Reavis

C
Ryczek
Fest

G
Wilson
Alward
Little

T
Current
Reavis
Little

TE
Moore
Novack
Butler

WR
Owens
Hagins•

RB
Davis•
Carter
C. Davis
Hart
McNeill

QB
Huff
Dickinson
Jaynes
Hedberg•

RB
Bell•
Williams
DuBose
Evans

OFFENSIVE UNIT

•Rookie

1977 DRAFT SELECTIONS

1	Bell, Ricky	RB	6-2	210	So. California
2	Lewis, Dave	LB	6-4	230	So. California
3	Hannah, Charles	DT-DE	6-6	253	Alabama
4	No Choice				
5	No Choice				
6	No Choice				
7	No Choice				
8	Hedberg, Randy	QB	6-3	195	Minot State
9A	Hemingway, Byron	LB	6-4	205	Boston College
9B	Mucker, Larry	WR	5-11	187	Arizona State
10A	Morgan, Robert	RB	6-2	219	Florida
10B	Ball, Aaron	LB	6-2	229	Cal.-Fullerton
11	Rodgers, Chuck	DB	5-11	168	N. Dakota State
12	Sheffield, Chip	WR	6-2	185	Lenoir Rhyne

This draft wasn't just Southern California chauvinism on Coach McKay's part. Bell will revert to his original USC role as a blocking fullback for Anthony Davis and Lewis should be the class of the Buc linebackers. Hannah also has a chance to start—on the defensive line. Hedberg could upset the team's plans at quarterback by throwing himself in the picture, though he's probably a year or two away. He's a genuine prospect. **PERF. QT.: 2.**

LOS ANGELES RAMS

Prediction: First

This year, critics of the Rams won't be able to point to the lack of an experienced quarterback as the reason why this talent-rich squad has failed to reach the Super Bowl.

This year, the Rams have Joe Namath, and the fans in Los Angeles are already calling travel agents and packing suitcases. The passing master of the last decade, whose option was not picked up by the New York Jets after a dozen years, became a free agent on April 1 and became a Ram on May 12.

He sent Pat Haden down to the No. 2 job and, as one head coach said, "Haden shouldn't mind . . . he can learn a hell of a lot from a guy like Joe."

He probably sent unhappy James Harris to another team. Harris was sure he didn't want to be No. 2 behind Haden. But he was more than positive he didn't want to be No. 3 . . . or No. 4, should Coach Chuck Knox take a liking to rookie Vince Ferragamo of Nebraska, a husky dropback passer.

And one must assume the Rams didn't shell out a bundle of cash for a passer they hope will sit on the bench.

This, then, could be their year. And if it isn't, it may never be.

Lawrence McCutcheon and John Cappelletti are the running backs, supported by Jim Bertelsen, Cullen Bryant, Rod Phillips, Rob Scribner, Brad Davis, Jim Jodat and rookies Wendell Tyler and Art Best. Clearly, they won't all stick, but Jodat was a camp sensation until he got hurt last year, Tyler is a highly touted UCLA product and Best was a college sensation at Notre Dame and Kent State.

The wide receivers are Harold Jackson and Ron Jessie, with Dwight Scales, Tom Geredine, Freeman Johns, another camp hero last year, Willie Miller, and speedy rookie Billy Waddy.

Charles Young, if he signs a contract, will replace tight end Bob Klein, who refused. Young was acquired from Philadelphia (for Ron Jaworski) in a swap of option playouts. Terry Nelson is the reserve.

The offensive line is super, both first and second strings. The starters are John Williams and Doug France at the tackles. Tom Mack and Dennis Harrah are the guards. Rich Saul is the center. The second string includes tackle Jackie Slater, guards Greg Horton and rookies Ed Fulton and Jeff Williams, and center Rick Nuzum.

Mack, an annual All-Pro, slipped a bit last year. Williams was the All-Pro. Harrah and France are on their way to becoming All-Pros.

Defensively, almost no weaknesses exist.

The front four boasts of ends Jack Youngblood and Fred Dryer, tackles Mike Fanning and Larry Brooks. Youngblood and Brooks were All-Pros; Dryer is close; Fanning, who replaces the retired Merlin Olsen, is an All-Pro prospect. Cody Jones and rookie Eary Jones should be the first replacements.

Linebacking? Solid. Jim Youngblood and Isiah Robertson will flank Jack Reynolds in the middle, while

Kevin McLain, Ron McCartney (hurt last year as a rookie), Rick Kay, Mel Rogers and Carl Ekern back them up. And the No. 1 draft pick was Bob Brudzinski of Ohio State—a linebacker.

The secondary, too, is tough. Monte Jackson and Rod Perry are the cornerbacks and they were 1-2 in NFC interceptions. Pat Thomas, a sophomore, is their substitute, as he is for Bill Simpson at free safety. Dave Elmendorf is the strong safety, now backed up by the No. 2 draft pick, Nolan Cromwell of Kansas— a talented but injury-prone youngster.

So there are no serious weaknesses and very few minor problems to boot. Oh, placekicker Tom Dempsey had some trouble with extra points and his contract negotiations and the punter, Rusty Jackson, is totally unacceptable. But draft choice Carson Long and free agent Ian Sunter are lurking, and the kicking problems will be straightened out before training camp disbands.

A more serious problem may be the very abundance of talent. Players like to play, but only a fixed number of them can. The rest resort to sulking and brooding, which does nothing for team morale.

The defense is relatively young, and Reynolds, possibly a weakness, can be moved out by a stern challenge. Maybe McLain, Kay or Brudzinski can free Jim Youngblood for the middle. Kay was the strongside starter early last year and was suddenly demoted to third team, which indicates the depth and quality of the Ram linebackers.

The general feeling is that the only thing the Rams must do to win is win. Just once, just to get over the hump, and they might be invincible for years.

One anticipates the NFC championship game featuring the Rams and the Cowboys. And maybe this time it will have a different ending.

1976 RECORD (11-4-1)

30	Atlanta	14	28	St. Louis		30
10	Minnesota (OT)	10	23	San Francisco		3
24	New York Giants	10	33	New Orleans		14
31	Miami	28	59	Atlanta		0
0	San Francisco	16	20	Detroit		17
20	Chicago	12		**(Playoff)**		
16	New Orleans	10	14	Dallas		12
45	Seattle	6		**(NFC Championship)**		
12	Cincinnati	20	13	Minnesota		24

PASSING

	Atts	Comps	Yds	Lgst	TDs	Ints	Pct
Harris†**	158	91	1460	80	8	6	57.6
Haden	105	60	896	65	8	4	57.1
Jaworski**	52	20	273	42	1	5	38.5

SCORING

	TDs	PATs	FGs	Total
Dempsey	0	36†	17	87
McCutcheon	11	0	0	66
Jessie	6	0	0	36
H. Jackson	5	0	0	30
Haden	4	0	0	24
Two tied with	3	0	0	18

RUSHING

	Atts	Yds	TDs	Lgst	Avg
McCutcheon	291	1168	9	40	4.0
Cappelletti	177	688	1	38	3.9
Phillips	34	206	1	33	6.1
Bertelsen	42	155	2	18	3.7
Haden	25	84	4	16	3.4
Harris**	12	76	2	20	6.3

RECEIVING

	Recs	Yds	TDs	Lgst	Avg
H. Jackson	39	751	5	65	19.3
Jessie	34	779	6	58	22.9†
Cappelletti	30	302	1	32	10.1
McCutcheon	28	305	2	42	10.9
Klein*	20	229	1	26	11.5

INTERCEPTIONS

	Ints	Yds	TDs	Lgst	Avg
M. Jackson	10†	173	3†	46	17.3
Perry	8	79	0	43	9.9
Simpson	4	62	0	30	15.5
Robertson	4	28	0	14	7.0
Two tied with 2					

SYMBOLS   *—Retired
          **—Traded
          †—Conference leader

1977 SCHEDULE

Home: Sept. 25—Philadelphia; Oct. 2—San Francisco; Oct. 16—New Orleans; Oct. 24—Minnesota; Nov. 6—Tampa Bay; Dec. 4—Oakland; Dec. 11—Atlanta.

Away: Sept. 18—Atlanta; Oct. 10—Chicago; Oct. 30—New Orleans; Nov. 13—Green Bay (at Milwaukee); Nov. 20—San Francisco; Nov. 27—Cleveland; Dec. 17—Washington.

OFFENSE

QUARTERBACKS	Ht	Wt	Age	Exp	College
Namath, Joe	6-2	200	34	13	Alabama
Haden, Pat	5-11	182	24	2	Southern California

Namath has arrived and there is little doubt he's wanted as a starter. Haden will learn much from the master. PERF. QT.: 1.

RUNNING BACKS	Ht	Wt	Age	Exp	College
McCutcheon, Lawrence	6-1	205	27	5	Colorado State
Cappelletti, John	6-1	217	25	4	Penn State
Bertelsen, Jim	5-11	205	27	6	Texas
Bryant, Cullen	6-1	235	26	5	Colorado
Phillips, Rod	6-0	220	24	3	Jackson State
Scribner, Rob	6-0	200	26	5	UCLA
Davis, Brad	5-11	215	24	2	Louisiana State
Jodat, Jim	5-11	210	23	1	Carthage

McCutcheon is a powerhouse, one of the NFL's top backs. Cappelletti hasn't begun to tap his vast supply of talent and drive. Bertelsen is the ideal backup, physically and mentally. Bryant has been disappointing, but he's acquiring valuable experience. Phillips has good strength and shows fine speed for a heavyweight. Scribner may be hard-pressed to maintain his reserve's status. Davis is trying again after one failure, but he has good size. Jodat was a training camp flash until felled by an untimely injury. PERF. QT.: 1.

RECEIVERS	Ht	Wt	Age	Exp	College
Jackson, Harold (W)	5-10	175	31	10	Jackson State
Jessie, Ron (W)	6-0	185	29	7	Kansas
Young, Charles (T)	6-4	238	26	5	Southern California
Scales, Dwight (W)	6-2	170	24	2	Grambling
Geredine, Tom (W)	6-2	189	27	4	N.E. Missouri
Nelson, Terry (T)	6-2	230	26	4	Arkansas AM&N
Johns, Freeman (W)	6-1	175	22	1	Southern Methodist
Miller, Willie (W)	5-9	172	30	3	Colorado State

(W)—Wide Receiver   (T)—Tight End

Jackson may have slowed a step, but not many defenders can catch him. Jessie is the perfect complement, though he isn't quite as consistent deep. Young should make it easy to forget the retired Bob Klein. Scales has youth and blurring speed but must refine his moves. Geredine isn't given much of a chance, but he could surprise. Nelson is a satisfactory backup, but not a starting threat. Johns, injured in but his first camp, was a most impressive rookie. Miller has almost no chance; he seems like a "camp body" for July and August. PERF. QT.: 2.

INTERIOR LINEMEN	Ht	Wt	Age	Exp	College
Williams, John (T)	6-3	265	31	10	Minnesota
France, Doug (T)	6-5	272	24	3	Ohio State
Mack, Tom (G)	6-3	250	33	12	Michigan
Harrah, Dennis (G)	6-5	257	24	3	Miami, Fla.
Saul, Rich (C)	6-3	250	29	8	Michigan State
Horton, Greg (G)	6-4	245	26	2	Colorado
Nuzum, Rick (C)	6-4	238	25	1	Kentucky
Slater, Jackie (T)	6-4	270	23	2	Jackson State

(T)—Tackle   (G)—Guard   (C)—Center

Scouts insist that Williams was the team's best lineman in '76. France won a regular job and is young enough to play for a decade. Mack may finally have lost the quickness that made him an All-Pro. Harrah is another youngster with a long and happy future in Smog City. Saul is a poised veteran center who doesn't make many mistakes. Horton is another of the gigantic youngsters who wants to play soon. Nuzum has missed a couple of seasons with injuries, but he is still a prospect. Slater was impressive in limited duty. PERF. QT.: 2.

KICKERS	Ht	Wt	Age	Exp	College
Dempsey, Tom (Pk)	6-1	260	30	9	Palomar J.C.
Jackson, Rusty (P)	6-2	190	26	2	Louisiana State
Sunter, Ian (Pk)	6-0	215	24	2	None

(Pk)—Placekicker   (P)—Punter

Dempsey wasn't reliable, especially on maddening PAT blunders. Jackson frequently hurt the Rams' field position. Sunter can take Dempsey's job if he shows really well. PERF. QT.: 4.

DEFENSE

FRONT LINEMEN	Ht	Wt	Age	Exp	College
Youngblood, Jack (E)	6-4	242	27	7	Florida
Dryer, Fred (E)	6-6	240	31	9	San Diego State
Brooks, Larry (T)	6-3	255	27	6	Va. St.-Petersburg
Fanning, Mike (T)	6-6	260	24	3	Notre Dame
Jones, Cody (T-E)	6-5	240	26	4	San Jose State
Cowlings, Al (E)	6-5	245	30	7	Southern California

(E)—End   (T)—Tackle

Youngblood had a second straight All-Pro year and deserved it. Dryer is still erratic; super on one play, invisible the next. Brooks is the

QUARTERBACK
Jim Hart
St. Louis Cardinals

RUNNING BACK
Walter Payton
Chicago Bears

RUNNING BACK
Chuck Foreman
Minnesota Vikings

WIDE RECEIVER
Sammie White
Minnesota Vikings

WIDE RECEIVER
Drew Pearson
Dallas Cowboys

NFC ALL-STARS/OFFENSE

TIGHT END
Billy Joe DuPree
Dallas Cowboys

CENTER
Tom Banks
St. Louis Cardinals

TACKLE
Dan Dierdorf
St. Louis Cardinals

TACKLE
John Williams
Los Angeles Rams

NFC ALL-STARS/OFFENSE

GUARD
Ed White
Minnesota Vikings

GUARD
Conrad Dobler
St. Louis Cardinals

PLACEKICKER
Jim Bakken
St. Louis Cardinals

PUNTER
John James
Atlanta Falcons

NFC ALL-STARS/DEFENSE

END
Harvey Martin
Dallas Cowboys

END
Jack Youngblood
Los Angeles Rams

TACKLE
Wally Chambers
Chicago Bears

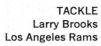

TACKLE
Larry Brooks
Los Angeles Rams

OUTSIDE LINEBACKER
Brad Van Pelt
New York Giants

OUTSIDE LINEBACKER
Isiah Robertson
Los Angeles Rams

NFC ALL-STARS/DEFENSE

MIDDLE LINEBACKER
Bill Bergey
Philadelphia Eagles

CORNERBACK
James Hunter
Detroit Lions

CORNERBACK
Monte Jackson
Los Angeles Rams

NFC ALL-STARS/DEFENSE

**STRONG-SIDE
SAFETY**
Ken Houston
Washington Redskins

FREE SAFETY
Cliff Harris
Dallas Cowboys

OFFENSE

QUARTERBACKS	Ht	Wt	Age	Exp	College
Plunkett, Jim	6-2	219	29	7	Stanford
Bull, Scott	6-5	211	24	2	Arkansas
Lawrence, Larry	6-1	208	28	3	Iowa

Was the cause of Plunkett's off-year physical or mental? Bull started a few games as a rookie, impressed, and could win the job. Lawrence has had a few looks and been found wanting. PERF. QT.: 3.

RUNNING BACKS	Ht	Wt	Age	Exp	College
Williams, Delvin	6-0	197	26	4	Kansas
Jackson, Wilbur	6-1	219	25	4	Alabama
Johnson, Kermit	6-0	202	25	3	UCLA
Hofer, Paul	6-0	195	25	2	Mississippi
Ferrell, Bob	6-0	206	24	2	UCLA

The team's strongest category is led by Williams, who has inside power and speed. Jackson isn't far behind; he has more strength on the third-downers. Johnson still hasn't reached his widely hailed potential, and he may not. Hofer was an unheralded rookie, but he showed flashes of talent. Ferrell will need every break to stick. PERF. QT.: 2.

RECEIVERS	Ht	Wt	Age	Exp	College
Washington, Gene (W)	6-1	187	30	9	Stanford
McGee, Willie (W)	5-11	178	27	5	Alcorn
Mitchell, Tom (T)	6-4	226	33	11	Bucknell
Lash, Jim (W)	6-2	199	25	5	Northwestern
Harrison, Kenny (W)	6-0	170	23	2	Southern Methodist
Rivera, Steve (W)	5-11	184	23	2	California
Obradovich, Jim (T)	6-2	225	24	3	Southern California
Beasley, Terry (W)	5-11	182	27	4	Auburn

(W)—Wide Receiver   (T)—Tight End

Washington remains a dangerous threat; he has speed, moves, discipline, great hands. McGee was a sensation until an injury shelved him; he has pure speed, but it's no sure thing that he can return to full effectiveness. Mitchell is a seasoned veteran; the starting job is clearly his. Lash, a young retread, has moderate talent. Harrison is quick and has some good moves. Rivera isn't fast but exhibited finesse. Obradovich blocks well and can catch but he's so slow. Beasley is trying once more; he shouldn't bother. PERF. QT.: 3.

INTERIOR LINEMEN	Ht	Wt	Age	Exp	College
Banaszek, Cas (T)	6-3	247	31	10	Northwestern
Fahnhorst, Keith (T)	6-6	256	25	4	Minnesota

INTERIOR LINEMEN (Contd.)	Ht	Wt	Age	Exp	College
Lawson, Steve (G)	6-3	265	28	7	Kansas
Peoples, Woody (G)	6-2	252	34	9	Grambling
Cross, Randy (C)	6-3	247	23	2	UCLA
Maurer, Andy (G)	6-3	265	28	8	Oregon
Watson, John (C-G)	6-4	244	28	7	Oklahoma
Barrett, Jean (T)	6-6	248	26	5	Tulsa

(T)—Tackle   (G)—Guard   (C)—Center

Banaszek may need oxygen a little more often, but he can still play. Fahnhorst should blossom now; he has size, agility . . . and smarts. Lawson may still become the accomplished guard he has been billed as. Peoples is heavily counted on to come back from knee surgery that cost him all of 1976. Cross won the center job early in his rookie year, then lost it to Watson. Maurer has the ability to start. Watson has started all along the line. Barrett starts in the event Banaszek finally falters. PERF. QT.: 3.

KICKERS	Ht	Wt	Age	Exp	College
Mike-Mayer, Steve (Pk)	6-0	179	29	3	Maryland
Wittum, Tom (P)	6-1	191	27	5	Northern Illinois

(Pk)—Placekicker   (P)—Punter

Mike-Mayer must improve, but GM Thomas may not give him the opportunity. Wittum is close to the league's best. PERF. QT.: 3.

DEFENSE

FRONT LINEMEN	Ht	Wt	Age	Exp	College
Hardman, Cedrick (E)	6-4	244	28	8	North Texas State
Hart, Tommy (E)	6-4	249	32	10	Morris Brown
Elam, Cleveland (T)	6-4	252	25	3	Tennessee State
Webb, Jimmy (T)	6-4	247	25	3	Mississippi State
Cline, Tony (E)	6-3	244	29	8	Miami, Fla.
Galigher, Ed (T)	6-5	253	26	6	UCLA
Cooke, Bill (E)	6-5	250	26	3	Massachusetts

(E)—End   (T)—Tackle

Hardman is one of the quality ends, and his season in '76 showed it. Hart, who played with surprising ferocity, must show it again to convince skeptics. Elam came on so quickly that he, too, must repeat to quiet the doubters. Webb has all the tools, and he's starting to use them. Cline can be of enormous help if his knee is healed and he's happy. Galigher can be a valuable sub. Cooke, another young one with size, should push someone for more playing time. PERF. QT.: 1.

LINEBACKERS	Ht	Wt	Age	Exp	College
Vanderbundt, Skip (O)	6-3	222	30	9	Oregon State
Washington, Dave (O)	6-5	228	28	8	Alcorn
Bradley, Ed (M)	6-2	239	27	6	Wake Forest
Nunley, Frank (M)	6-2	221	31	11	Michigan
Harper, Willie (O)	6-2	208	27	5	Nebraska
Elia, Bruce (M)	6-1	217	24	3	Ohio State
Mitchell, Dale (O-M)	6-3	223	23	2	Southern California

(O)—Outside Linebacker   (M)—Middle Linebacker

Vanderbundt can still play, but it's near slow-down time. Washington has been overrated, even though 1976 was a good year for him. Bradley, stolen from Seattle, should solve the problem in the middle. Nunley has held that job in the past, and he's a pro, but he can use rest time after three knee operations. Harper, despite his weight, is a ferocious hitter. Elia has brute strength, but lacks speed. Mitchell is a hustler who does well on special teams. PERF. QT.: 3.

CORNERBACKS	Ht	Wt	Age	Exp	College
Taylor, Bruce	6-0	186	29	8	Boston University
Lewis, Eddie	6-0	177	23	2	Kansas
Leonard, Tony	5-11	170	24	2	Virginia Union
Oliver, Frank	6-1	190	25	2	Kentucky State
Austin, Hise	6-4	197	26	3	Prairie View

Taylor, not because of his bad shoulder, gets beat deep too often. Lewis played fairly well as a rookie and will fight for Jimmy Johnson's old job. Leonard may have more speed than Lewis. Oliver is a retread (he was cut by Buffalo) and shouldn't be a factor. Austin, another reclamation case, may surprise. PERF. QT.: 4.

SAFETIES	Ht	Wt	Age	Exp	College
Phillips, Mel (S)	6-1	184	35	13	North Carolina A&T
McGill, Ralph (W)	5-11	178	27	6	Tulsa
Rhodes, Bruce (W-S)	6-0	187	25	2	San Francisco St.

(S)—Strong-side   (W)—Weak-side or "Free" Safety

Phillips plays no matter what his injuries are, but age stops everyone. McGill is no better than average. Rhodes played as a rookie; he can shine. PERF. QT.: 3.

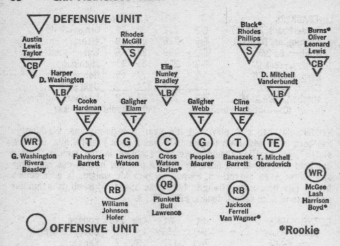

DEFENSIVE UNIT

Austin
Lewis
Taylor
CB

Rhodes
McGill
S

Black*
Rhodes
Phillips
S

Burns*
Oliver
Leonard
Lewis
CB

Harper
D. Washington
LB

Elia
Nunley
Bradley
LB

D. Mitchell
Vanderbundt
LB

Cooke
Hardman
E

Galigher
Elam
T

Galigher
Webb
T

Cline
Hart
E

WR
G. Washington
Rivera
Beasley

T
Fahnhorst
Barrett

G
Lawson
Watson

C
Cross
Watson
Harlan*

G
Peoples
Maurer

T
Banaszek
Barrett

TE
T. Mitchell
Obradovich

WR
McGee
Lash
Harrison
Boyd*

RB
Williams
Johnson
Hofer

QB
Plunkett
Bull
Lawrence

RB
Jackson
Ferrell
Van Wagner*

OFFENSIVE UNIT

*Rookie

1977 DRAFT SELECTIONS

1	No Choice				
2	No Choice				
3	Boyd, Elmo	WR	5-11	190	Eastern Kentucky
4	Black, Stan	S	6-1	205	Mississippi State
5	No Choice				
6A	Burns, Mike	CB	5-11	185	So. California
6B	Harlan, Jim	C	6-3	240	Howard Payne
7	Van Wagner, Jim	RB	6-0	200	Michigan Tech
8	No Choice				
9	Posey, David	K	5-10	166	Florida
10	No Choice				
11	Billick, Brian	TE	6-5	235	Brigham Young
12	Martin, Scott	G	6-4	255	North Dakota

There's not much here to pick from. With nothing until the third round, the brain trust went for a speedy wide receiver, Boyd, whose value will be immediate only if McGee can't come back. Black and Burns (the latter didn't play much in college) were wise selections if only because the secondary is a problem. Van Wagner had a super career at a small school and could be a player. **PERF. QT.: 4.**

ATLANTA FALCONS

Prediction: Third

With a new head coach and a new general manager and a very good draft, the Atlanta Falcons will be expected to do far more football playing than they did last season. But the results they can expect in 1977 still rest on the physical condition of young, potential superstar quarterback Steve Bartkowski.

He was hurt early last season and the job was taken over first by Kim McQuilken and then Scott Hunter. Neither was able to provide the winning spark.

Now Coach Leeman Bennett, who has been given a free hand by General Manager Eddie LeBaron, says Bartkowski is ready to play and has no residual problems from his knee surgery.

That could make the Falcons dangerous, if not winners.

Bartkowski will be able to use a batch of young runners, led by starters Mike Esposito and Sonny Collins and backed up by Haskell Stanback, Bubba Bean, Woody Thompson and Monroe Eley.

The relative disappointment here has been Thompson, a 6-1, 228-pounder with speed who was supposed to be the regular fullback by now.

Wide receivers, who will be better if the ball is thrown by Bartkowski, are John Gilliam, who did not have a good year after signing on as a free agent, little (5-10, 172) Alfred Jenkins, who did have a good year but who is fragile, and a flock of draft choices.

The tight end is big Jim Mitchell (6-1, 236) and he must be brought into the Falcons' offense more frequently. Greg McCrary (watch him) and maybe Bob Adams are reserve TEs, while Wallace Francis and Scott Piper are the veteran wide reserves who are in danger of being swept off the roster by rookies Shelton Diggs, Walter Packer and Billy Ryckman.

The Falcons' major problem was the offensive line, and that has been partially ministered to with the first of two first-round draft choices.

The name is Warren Bryant, the size is 6-5 and 275 and the position is tackle. He's an instant starter, for either Brent Adams or Len Gotshalk. One of them will remain as the other tackle, unless Dave Scott or Phil McKinnely (Bennett likes him) wins the job.

The guards are Larron Jackson and Gregg Kindle, with Royce Smith a strong challenger and Walter Brett in reserve. Jeff Van Note was a Pro Bowl center two years ago, was hurt last year and now finds a No. 2 draft choice, R.C. Theilemann, chasing after his job, as is Paul Ryczek. Thielemann, another member of Atlanta's outstanding rookie crop, can also put pressure on the incumbent guards.

On defense, in addition to the nominal up-front starters—ends Claude Humphrey and Jeff Merrow, tackles Mike Lewis and Mike Tilleman—there are two super draft picks, first-round choice Wilson Faumuina and third-round selection Edgar Fields. They are both tackles, and slowing-up veteran Tilleman is almost sure to be displaced by Faumuina.

The line is further shored up by Jeff Yeates, Jim Bailey and Steve George.

Young linebackers abound. In the middle, to take the place of the retired Tommy Nobis, is Ralph Ortega, in his third season. On the weak-side is Fulton Kuykendall, who showed great improvement as a soph starter last season before being grounded with a back injury. Pushing Greg Brezina, the veteran strong-side starter (and another 1976 injury casualty), is Dewey McClain, a rookie last year. Guy Roberts and Jim Cope handle backup duties.

The problem in the secondary is largely one of depth. The starting (and established) corners are Rolland Lawrence and Frank Reed, and they are backed by Ron Mabra and Rick Byas. Ray Brown is the strong safety and Ray Easterling the weak-side starter, and both played reasonably well last season, though Bob Jones is given a chance to unseat Easterling. Rookie Keith Jenkins of Cincinnati is a draft choice who can make his presence felt here.

Coach Bennett, who came from the Rams, had turned down other jobs in the past while waiting for "the right situation." Clearly, he felt the Falcons were ready to fly. And if Bartkowski is ready, he will have been right.

Patching is necessary, especially among the wide receivers and on the offensive line. Also, a problem exists with placekicker Nick Mike-Mayer, who was far too inconsistent last season and, in fact, could be pushed by No. 3 draft choice Allan Leavitt of Georgia.

The punting is in fine shape with John James, a Pro Bowler and the conference's statistical leader.

But it's all in the hands of Bartkowski. If the 6-4, 213-pound 24-year-old can make it back, he just may become one of the game's top performers . . . and help Bennett win Coach of the Year honors.

1976 RECORD (4-10)

14	Los Angeles	30	23	New Orleans	20
10	Detroit	24	13	Seattle	30
10	Chicago	0	21	San Francisco	16
13	Philadelphia	14	17	Dallas	10
0	New Orleans	30	14	Houston	20
17	Cleveland	20	0	Los Angeles	59
0	San Francisco	15	20	Green Bay	24

PASSING

	Atts	Comps	Yds	Lgst	TDs	Ints	Pct
Hunter	110	51	633	34	5	4	46.4
Bartkowski	120	57	677	50	2	9	47.5
McQuilken	121	48	450	39	2	10	39.7

SCORING

	TDs	PATs	FGs	Total
Mike-Mayer	0	20	10	50
Jenkins	6	0	0	36
Stanback	4	0	0	24
Bean	3	0	0	18
Esposito	2	0	0	12
Gilliam	2	0	0	12

RUSHING

	Atts	Yds	TDs	Lgst	Avg
Bean	124	428	2	30	3.5
Stanback	95	324	3	30	3.4
Collins	91	319	0	47	3.5
Esposito	60	317	2	36	5.3
Thompson	42	152	0	10	3.6

RECEIVING

	Recs	Yds	TDs	Lgst	Avg
Jenkins	41	710	6	34	17.3
Gilliam	21	292	2	49	13.9
Stanback	21	174	1	28	8.3
Mitchell	17	209	0	39	12.3
Esposito	17	88	0	13	5.2

INTERCEPTIONS

	Ints	Yds	TDs	Lgst	Avg
Lawrence	6	43	0	22	7.2
Brown	3	58	0	21	19.3
Reed	3	48	0	42	16.0
Easterling	3	33	0	19	11.0

1977 SCHEDULE

Home: Sept. 18—Los Angeles; Oct. 2—New York Giants; Oct. 30—Minnesota; Nov. 6—San Francisco; Nov. 13—Detroit; Dec. 4—New England; Dec. 18—New Orleans.

Away: Sept. 25—Washington; Oct. 9—San Francisco; Oct. 16—Buffalo; Oct. 23—Chicago; Nov. 20—New Orleans; Nov. 27—Tampa Bay; Dec. 11—Los Angeles.

OFFENSE

QUARTERBACKS	Ht	Wt	Age	Exp	College
Bartkowski, Steve	6-4	213	24	3	California
McQuilken, Kim	6-2	203	26	4	Lehigh
Hunter, Scott	6-2	205	29	7	Alabama

Bartkowski is a potential superstar if his knee has healed properly. McQuilken is better suited to contribute in an off-the-bench capacity. Hunter could stick because of his experience. PERF. QT.: 3.

RUNNING BACKS	Ht	Wt	Age	Exp	College
Collins, Sonny	6-1	196	24	2	Kentucky
Esposito, Mike	6-0	183	24	2	Boston College
Bean, Bubba	5-11	195	23	2	Texas A&M
Stanback, Haskell	6-0	210	25	4	Tennessee
Thompson, Woody	6-1	228	25	3	Miami, Fla.
Eley, Monroe	6-2	210	28	2	Arizona State

Collins didn't play like a rookie and should even improve. Esposito showed the form that made him a college All-America. Bean, too, mastered his pro assignments without undue difficulty. Stanback plays hard all the time. Thompson has great size and good speed; he may be the blocker this backfield needs. Eley, injured in '76, had been a CFL standout. PERF. QT.: 3.

RECEIVERS	Ht	Wt	Age	Exp	College
Gilliam, John (W)	6-1	187	32	11	S. Carolina State
Jenkins, Alfred (W)	5-10	172	25	3	Morris Brown
Mitchell, Jim (T)	6-1	236	29	9	Prairie View
Francis, Wallace (W)	5-11	190	25	5	Arkansas AM&N
Piper, Scott (W)	6-1	184	23	2	Arizona
McCrary, Greg (T)	6-3	230	25	2	Clark
Adams, Bob (T)	6-2	225	31	9	Pacific

(W)—Wide Receiver   (T)—Tight End

Gilliam wasn't the savior he was expected to be, but he's dangerous. Jenkins emerged as the star; he has great speed, gluey hands. Mitchell is most effective when Bartkowski is quarterbacking. Francis is quick but he won't press the starters. Piper showed some moves as a rookie but his job, as well as Francis', is in jeopardy. McCrary, hurt last season, has a lot of ability. Adams is your average ordinary pro performer. PERF. QT.: 3.

INTERIOR LINEMEN	Ht	Wt	Age	Exp	College
Adams, Brent (T)	6-5	256	25	3	Tenn.—Chattanooga
Gotshalk, Len (T)	6-4	259	27	7	Humboldt State

INTERIOR LINEMEN (Contd.)	Ht	Wt	Age	Exp	College
Jackson, Larron (G)	6-3	260	28	7	Missouri
Kindle, Gregg (G)	6-4	265	26	4	Tennessee State
Van Note, Jeff (C)	6-2	247	31	9	Kentucky
McKinnely, 'Phil (T)	6-4	248	23	2	UCLA
Smith, Royce (G)	6-3	250	28	6	Georgia
Scott, Dave (T)	6-4	285	23	2	Kansas
Ryczek, Paul (C)	6-2	230	25	4	Virginia
Brett, Walter (G)	6-5	241	23	2	Montana

(T)—Tackle   (G)—Guard   (C)—Center

Adams plays fairly well and has satisfactory size, but somehow he isn't the answer. Gotshalk definitely isn't the answer to anything except a rising QB sack count. Jackson was a plus and should have plenty left for another few years. Kindle will have difficulty holding off a challenge from Smith or any other aspirant. Van Note is a Pro Bowl quality center who must feel very lonely in this company. McKinnely can make a run at a starting job, though he's not a great talent. Smith has been tried before, but in this crowd he could wind up a starter. Scott has a weight problem; he'll lose some poundage or his spot on the roster. Ryczek has long-snapping ability. Brett will go early. PERF. QT.: 4.

KICKERS	Ht	Wt	Age	Exp	College
Mike-Mayer, Nick (Pk)	5-9	187	27	5	Temple
James, John (P)	6-3	200	28	6	Florida

(Pk)—Placekicker   (P)—Punter

Mike-Mayer will be in trouble if anyone else shows up. James is a proved star punter. PERF. QT.: 3.

DEFENSE

FRONT LINEMEN	Ht	Wt	Age	Exp	College
Humphrey, Claude (E)	6-5	265	33	9	Tennessee State
Merrow, Jeff (E)	6-4	230	24	3	West Virginia
Lewis, Mike (T)	6-4	261	28	7	Arkansas AM&N
Tilleman, Mike (T)	6-7	278	33	11	Montana
Yeates, Jeff (T)	6-3	248	26	5	Boston College
Bailey, Jim (E-T)	6-5	260	29	8	Kansas
George, Steve (T)	6-6	265	26	2	Houston

(E)—End   (T)—Tackle

Humphrey came back, and was good, but not at his pre-injury level. Merrow, despite his quickness, proves that the John Zook trade was idiotic. Lewis is still improving and with motivation could be a good one. Tilleman is too heavy now that his age has caught up with him.

Yeates has had other chances; at best, he's a reserve. Bailey isn't much either, though he's versatile. This is George's last chance to live up to the good scouting reports. PERF. QT.: 4.

LINEBACKERS	Ht	Wt	Age	Exp	College
Brezina, Greg (O)	6-1	221	31	10	Houston
Kuykendall, Fulton (O)	6-5	225	26	3	UCLA
Ortega, Ralph (M)	6-2	220	24	3	Florida
McClain, Dewey (O)	6-3	236	23	2	East Central Okla.
Roberts, Guy (O)	6-1	220	27	6	Maryland
Cope, Jim (M)	6-2	230	24	2	Ohio State

(O)—Outside Linebacker   (M)—Middle Linebacker

Brezina, an old pro, still plays with fire and determination. His presence will help the young starters. Kuykendall should make it big if he learns to defend the run better. Ortega must fill Tommy Nobis' shoes; the youngster can be a good one. McClain, a '76 rookie, could push Brezina if the veteran doesn't fully recover from a '76 injury. Roberts and Cope are average, certainly not starting material. PERF. QT.: 3.

CORNERBACKS	Ht	Wt	Age	Exp	College
Lawrence, Rolland	5-10	179	26	5	Tabor
Reed, Frank	5-11	193	23	2	Washington
Mabra, Ron	5-10	164	26	3	Howard
Byas, Rick	5-9	180	26	4	Wayne State

Lawrence won his job a few seasons ago and keeps improving. Reed won his job as a rookie but will have to fight to keep it. Mabra has hung on for two years and seems to do best on special teams. Byas, once a safety reserve, may have to seek work elsewhere. PERF. QT.: 3.

SAFETIES	Ht	Wt	Age	Exp	College
Brown, Ray (S)	6-2	202	28	7	West Texas State
Easterling, Ray (W)	6-0	192	27	6	Richmond
Jones, Bob (W)	6-2	193	26	5	Virginia Union

(S)—Strong-side   (W)—Weak-side or "Free" Safety

Brown was a lot better a few year ago, though he still has talent. Easterling is not so established that he won't be challenged. Jones is the threat to unseat him. PERF. QT.: 3.

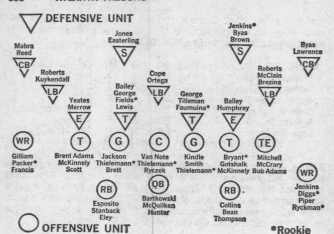

DEFENSIVE UNIT

Jenkins*
Byas
Brown

Jones
Easterling
S

Mabra
Reed
CB

S

Byas
Lawrence
CB

Roberts
Kuykendall
LB

Roberts
McClain
Brezina
LB

Yeates
Merrow
E

Bailey
George
Fields*
Lewis
T

Cope
Ortega
LB

George
Tilleman
Faumuina*
T

Bailey
Humphrey
E

WR
Gilliam
Packer*
Francis

T
Brent Adams
McKinnely
Scott

G
Jackson
Thielemann*
Brett

C
Van Note
Thielemann*
Ryczek

G
Kindle
Smith
Thielemann*

T
Bryant*
Gotshalk
McKinnely

TE
Mitchell
McCrary
Bob Adams

WR
Jenkins
Diggs*
Piper
Ryckman*

RB
Esposito
Stanback
Eley

QB
Bartkowski
McQuilken
Hunter

RB
Collins
Bean
Thompson

OFFENSIVE UNIT

*Rookie

1977 DRAFT SELECTIONS

1A	Bryant, Warren	T	6-5	275	Kentucky
1B	Faumuina, Wilson	DT	6-5	275	San Jose State
2	Theilemann, R. C.	C-G	6-4	247	Arkansas
3	Fields, Edgar	DT	6-3	253	Texas A&M
4	Leavitt, Allan	K	6-1	180	Georgia
5	Diggs, Shelton	WR	6-2	200	So. California
6	Jenkins, Keith	S	6-3	190	Cincinnati
7	No Choice				
8	Packer, Walter	WR	6-0	180	Mississippi State
9A	Maxwell, John	T	6-6	265	Boston College
9B	Speer, Robert	DE	6-5	230	Arkansas State
10	Ryckman, Billy	WR	5-10	167	Louisiana Tech
11	Farmer, Dave	RB	6-2	210	So. California
12	Parrish, Don	DE	6-3	248	Pittsburgh

The Falcons got at least two instant starters, Bryant for the offense and
Faumuina for the defense, and both should be solid. Theilemann won't
unseat Van Note, but he could make waves at a guard spot. Fields is still
another starting prospect, though his chances are slimmer. Diggs was expected to be picked on a higher round. Packer can be a steal. Jenkins,
Speer, Ryckman and Parrish have ability and could surprise. And placekicker
Leavitt could unseat Mike-Mayer. **PERF. QT.: 1**

NEW ORLEANS SAINTS

Prediction: Fourth

Don't look now, but the New Orleans Saints may have finally had a good draft. And thereby, they may have made a strong move toward improvement.

It's about time. This franchise has been a bad joke since its expansion inception.

Now there is Hank Stram as the head coach and mover-and-shaker, and he will start his second season totally familiar with the Saints' weaknesses and strengths.

He needed defensive linemen, for example, so he went heavily in that direction in the first two rounds of the draft and lookie-here, he came up with end Joe Campbell of Maryland and huge tackle Mike Fultz of Nebraska.

What Henry did was create an over-abundance among his down linemen, and he will no doubt want to use the surplus to trade for fillings elsewhere.

But quarterback is still his major source of concern. Archie Manning hasn't been healthy for two years, and the 6-3, 200-pounder must play this time around or seriously consider a premature retirement. He says he's fine. Stram says he's fine. We'll soon see. Behind him, as last year, are Bobby Scott and Bobby Douglass. Stram is still looking for another one, perhaps a starter, and former Steeler Joe Gilliam, rehabilitated from his drug problems, may get a chance.

The running backs were taken care of last season, when Stram drafted Chuck Muncie and Tony Galbreath. As rookies, they were outstanding, and as starters working together they figure to get even better. Behind them are qualified backs such as Mike Strachan and Alvin Maxson, plus a 6-4, 243-pound fullback named Kim Jones, who saw only light duty as a rookie, and Leon McQuay.

Don Herrmann and Larry Burton are the wide receivers, with Tinker Owens, the long-ball threat, and Joel Parker (out all of last season and once a starter) in reserve. Henry Childs is a strong tight end, and so is Paul Seal, who'll fight to regain his old first-string job. James Thaxton is a reserve TE-WR who can prove to be a late bloomer.

The offensive line is and was and has always been a problem. This time the tackles will be Marv Montgomery and Don Morrison, the guards will be Terry Stieve or Kurt Schumacher and Emanuel Zanders and the center will be John Hill. It's not good enough, nor should Stram expect to find pearls from among the subs, who include tackles Tom Wickert and Jeff Hart, and center Lee Gross. A free agent center from Boston College, 6-3, 255-pound Joe Prendergast, may make some waves.

The defense is what will do it for the Saints this year, if anything at all is to be done.

In addition to Campbell and Fultz up front, there are returnees Steve Baumgartner and Bob Pollard at ends, Derland Moore and Elex Price at tackles, and veteran reserves Andy Dorris, Elois Grooms and Maulty Moore. Campbell should win a job, probably

Baumgartner's, and Fultz stands a good chance to beat out Price.

Good linebackers will aid the front. The best is strong-side man Jim Merlo. In the middle there is Joe Federspiel, the target of several other teams with trade on their minds. Greg Westbrooks is the weak-side starter, but he'll be pushed by young Ken Bordelon and veteran Pat Hughes. Warren Capone, Rick Kingrea and rookie Bob Watts of Boston College, will fill out the reserve corps.

There is trouble, however, in the secondary. On the corners will be Ernie Jackson and Maurice Spencer, both vulnerable to a challenge and both expecting one from Benny Johnson, the only sub at either spot.

Help is needed here, although nothing exciting was selected in the draft.

And there are only two established safeties, unless Stram wants to put Watts back there; he achieved All-America recognition last season as a college linebacker but may be suited to play pro safety. The starters are Chuck Crist on the strong-side, a big hitter with coverage deficiencies, and Tom Myers on the weak-side, a proved professional who needs only to stay healthy to improve.

Stram's situation is this: He has pieces of offense and pieces of defense, but nary a full unit on either side of the line. While his running backs and receivers are classy, he has quarterback and line woes. Defensively, his front four and his linebackers should be strong, but the secondary will give up what the big guys try to stop.

But it has been a long time since New Orleans looked competitive, if only on paper, and if Manning, some offensive linemen and some defensive backs come through, the club could start the long climb upward.

1976 RECORD (4-10)

9	Minnesota	40	20	Atlanta	23
6	Dallas	24	27	Green Bay	32
27	Kansas City	17	17	Detroit	16
26	Houston	31	51	Seattle	27
30	Atlanta	0	14	Los Angeles	33
3	San Francisco	33	6	New England	27
10	Los Angeles	16	7	San Francisco	27

PASSING

	Atts	Comps	Yds	Lgst	TDs	Ints	Pct
Scott	190	103	1065	60	4	6	54.2
Douglass	213	103	1288	74	4	8	48.4

SCORING

	TDs	PATs	FGs	Total
Szaro	0	25	18	79
Galbreath	8	0	0	48
Childs	4	0	0	24
Five tied with	2	0	0	12

RUSHING

	Atts	Yds	TDs	Lgst	Avg
Muncie	149	659	2	51	4.4
Galbreath	136	570	7	74	4.2
Strachan	66	258	2	31	3.9
Maxson	34	120	1	16	3.5
Douglass	21	92	2	19	4.4

RECEIVING

	Recs	Yds	TDs	Lgst	Avg
Galbreath	54	420	1	35	7.8
Herrmann	34	535	0	57	15.7
Muncie	31	272	0	33	8.8
Childs	26	349	3	46	13.4
Burton	18	297	2	69	16.5

INTERCEPTIONS

	Ints	Yds	TDs	Lgst	Avg
Merlo	4	142	2	83†	35.5
Athas**	2	22	0	22	11.0
Jackson	2	5	0	5	2.5

SYMBOLS **—Waived
†—Conference leader

1977 SCHEDULE

Home: Sept. 18—Green Bay; Oct. 9—San Diego; Oct. 30—Los Angeles; Nov. 13—San Francisco; Nov. 20—Atlanta; Dec. 4—New York Jets; Dec. 11—Tampa Bay.

Away: Sept. 25—Detroit; Oct. 2—Chicago; Oct. 16—Los Angeles; Oct. 23—St. Louis; Nov. 6—Philadelphia; Nov. 27—San Francisco; Dec. 18—Atlanta.

OFFENSE

QUARTERBACKS	Ht	Wt	Age	Exp	College
Manning, Archie	6-3	200	28	7	Mississippi
Scott, Bobby	6-1	197	28	6	Tennessee
Douglass, Bobby	6-4	228	29	9	Kansas
Gilliam, Joe	6-2	187	26	5	Tennessee State

This has to be about Manning's last chance to show he's over injury problems. Scott did well as a starter and can win the job by default if Manning can't make it. Douglass is big, strong, and not very good. Gilliam is getting yet another chance. PERF. QT.: 4.

RUNNING BACKS	Ht	Wt	Age	Exp	College
Muncie, Chuck	6-3	220	24	2	California
Galbreath, Tony	6-0	220	23	2	Missouri
Maxson, Alvin	5-11	201	25	4	Southern Methodist
Strachan, Mike	6-0	200	24	3	Iowa State
Jones, Kim	6-4	243	25	2	Colorado State
McQuay, Leon	5-9	195	27	4	Tampa

Muncie showed enough of his Superman potential to excite coaches. Galbreath, the other rookie hero, looked even better and stronger. Maxson is a qualified pro but sometimes loses his poise. Strachan should be starting somewhere—like on another team in '77? Jones has impressive size but if he can move it he'll be a help. McQuay won't last with any coach. PERF. QT.: 2.

RECEIVERS	Ht	Wt	Age	Exp	College
Herrmann, Don (W)	6-2	193	30	9	Waynesburg
Burton, Larry (W)	6-1	193	25	3	Purdue
Childs, Henry (T)	6-2	220	26	4	Kansas State
Owens, Tinker (W)	5-11	170	22	2	Oklahoma
Parker, Joel (W)	6-5	215	25	3	Florida
Seal, Paul (T)	6-4	223	25	4	Michigan
Thaxton, James (T-W)	6-2	230	28	4	Tennessee State

(W)—Wide Receiver   (T)—Tight End

Herrmann has great moves, fine temperament. Burton has blazing speed but sometimes has a problem with his hands. Childs can become a superstar if he learns the routes. Owens, a big-play specialist, showed that trait even as a rookie. Parker missed last season with injury; now he'll push for a first-string job. Seal, who had the starting job early in '76, will prod Childs. Thaxton is interesting, versatile, and getting his last chance. PERF. QT.: 3.

INTERIOR LINEMEN	Ht	Wt	Age	Exp	College
Montgomery, Marv (T)	6-6	255	29	7	Southern California
Morrison, Don (T)	6-5	250	27	7	Texas-Arlington
Stieve, Terry (G)	6-2	242	23	2	Wisconsin
Zanders, Emanuel (G)	6-1	248	26	4	Jackson State
Hill, John (C)	6-2	246	27	6	Lehigh
Wickert, Tom (T)	6-4	252	25	4	Washington State
Schumacher, Kurt (G)	6-3	246	24	3	Ohio State
Gross, Lee (C)	6-3	235	24	3	Auburn
Hart, Jeff (T)	6-5	252	23	3	Oregon State

(T)—Tackle   (G)—Guard   (C)—Center

Montgomery started in the last half of '76 and showed enough to warrant a further look. Morrison is about as good as the team has—satisfactory but not outstanding. Stieve, a youngster, has moderate promise. Zanders always tries hard; he may be the line's best operative. Hill is an established veteran, neither a star nor an embarrassment. Wickert was a starter until injured; he's nice to have around. Schumacher was a No. 1 draft, but he doesn't play to that level. Gross has more potential than he's displayed. Hart isn't much. The team needs help here. PERF. QT.: 4

KICKERS	Ht	Wt	Age	Exp	College
Szaro, Rich (Pk)	5-11	204	29	3	Harvard
Blanchard, Tom (P)	6-0	180	29	7	Oregon

(Pk)—Placekicker   (P)—Punter

Szaro settled the Saints' placekicking problems. Blanchard had planned to retire but changed his mind. PERF. QT.: 2.

DEFENSE

FRONT LINEMEN	Ht	Wt	Age	Exp	College
Pollard, Bob (E)	6-3	251	28	7	Weber State
Baumgartner, Steve (E-T)	6-7	255	26	5	Purdue
Moore, Derland (T)	6-4	253	25	5	Oklahoma
Price, Elex (T)	6-3	253	27	5	Alcorn
Dorris, Andy (E)	6-4	240	26	5	New Mexico State
Grooms, Elois (E)	6-4	250	24	3	Tennessee Tech
Moore, Maulty (T)	6-5	265	31	6	Bethune Cookman

(E)—End   (T)—Tackle

Pollard shows strength and good speed, but there's something missing. Baumgartner was a starter because of others' deficiences. Moore is the best of the linemen; he's capable of starting for most NFL clubs. Price is another who can be displaced by a strong challenger. Dorris has been around long enough to do the job; he hasn't. Grooms also hasn't executed his assignments to the coach's satisfaction. Moore is vagabonding nowadays. PERF. QT.: 3.

LINEBACKERS	Ht	Wt	Age	Exp	College
Merlo, Jim (O)	6-1	220	25	4	Stanford
Westbrooks, Greg (O)	6-2	217	24	3	Colorado
Federspiel, Joe (M)	6-1	230	27	6	Kentucky
Bordelon, Ken (O)	6-4	236	23	2	Louisiana State
Hughes, Pat (O)	6-2	225	30	8	Boston University
Kingrea, Rick (M)	6-1	222	28	7	Tulane
Capone, Warren (O)	6-1	218	26	3	Louisiana State

(O)—Outside Linebacker   (M)—Middle Linebacker

Merlo is becoming one of the league's best. Westbrooks should be pushed, but who is here to push him? Federspiel played better a few years ago, but he still has a lot of ability. Bordelon has a good chance to move up, as has Hughes, a long-time starter with the Giants. Kingrea somehow manages to stick on the final roster each year. Capone came from Dallas and the WFL; his main strength is his quickness and special teams ability. PERF. QT.: 3.

CORNERBACKS	Ht	Wt	Age	Exp	College
Jackson, Ernie	5-10	176	27	6	Duke
Spencer, Maurice	6-0	176	25	4	N. Carolina Cen.
Johnson, Benny	5-11	178	29	6	Johnson C. Smith

Jackson is developing, but not quickly enough, and his lack of size hurts. Spencer has similar problems but is lightning-quick. Johnson will press hard for a starting spot. PERF. QT.: 3.

SAFETIES	Ht	Wt	Age	Exp	College
Crist, Chuck (S)	6-2	205	27	6	Penn State
Myers, Tom (W)	5-11	180	26	6	Syracuse
Cassady, Craig (W)	5-10	175	24	1	Ohio State

(S)—Strong-side   (W)—Weak-side or "Free" Safety

Crist has been a regular since being cut by the Giants; he's mediocre. Myers is a solid pro, though not of Pro Bowl stature. Cassady didn't survive his '76 rookie training camp. PERF. QT.: 3.

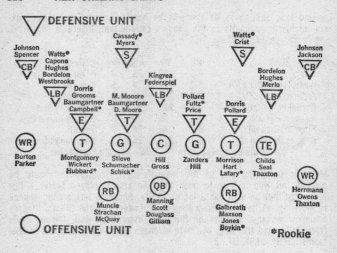

DEFENSIVE UNIT

Johnson
Spencer
CB

Watts●
Capone
Hughes
Bordelon
Westbrooks

Cassady●
Myers
S

Dorris
Grooms
Baumgartner
Campbell●
LB

Kingrea
Federspiel
LB

M. Mooore
Baumgartner
D. Moore

Pollard
Fultz●
Price
T

Watts●
Crist
S

Dorris
Pollard
E

Bordelon
Hughes
Merlo
LB

Johnson
Jackson
CB

E   **T**

OFFENSIVE UNIT

WR
Burton
Parker

T
Montgomery
Wickert
Hubbard●

G
Stieve
Schumacher
Schick●

C
Hill
Gross

G
Zanders
Hill

T
Morrison
Hart
Lafary●

TE
Childs
Seal
Thaxton

RB
Muncie
Strachan
McQuay

QB
Manning
Scott
Douglass
Gilliam

RB
Galbreath
Maxson
Jones
Boykin●

WR
Herrmann
Owens
Thaxton

●Rookie

1977 DRAFT SELECTIONS

1	Campbell, Joe	DE	6-6	255	Maryland
2	Fultz, Mike	DT	6-5	275	Nebraska
3	Watts, Robert	S-LB	6-2	217	Boston College
4	No Choice				
5A	Lafary, Dave	T	6-8	288	Purdue
5B	Hubbard, Dave	T	6-7	270	Brigham Young
6A	Parsley, Cliff	P	6-1	210	Oklahoma State
6B	Schick, Tom	G	6-4	247	Maryland
7	Boykin, Greg	RB	6-0	230	Northwestern
8	Stewart, Jim	DB	6-0	190	Tulsa
9	Knowles, Dave	T	6-6	247	Indiana
10	Septien, Rafael	K	5-9	171	S. W. Louisiana
11	Blain, John	T	6-5	255	San Jose State
12	Dalton, Oakley	DE	6-3	245	Jackson State

The Saints needed defense and that's what Coach Stram got in the draft.
Campbell should start immediately, and it wouldn't surprise if Fultz did the
same. Watts, a linebacker at B.C., may move to strong safety; he'll make
it big somewhere, some time, if not immediately. Lafary and Hubbard offer
great size but must prove they can play on the pro level. Parsley could
replace Blanchard if the vet insists on his retirement. Schick, the "second
best" Maryland guard, may prove to be a find. Boykin is worth a long look
as a reserve. PERF. QT.: 2.

AMERICAN FOOTBALL CONFERENCE

The 14 teams that make up the American Football Conference are described in comprehensive detail on the following 112 pages. After reading the facts and figures we have assembled, you will be eminently prepared to follow your favorite team and its rivals through the action-filled season.

Each club receives the following treatment: a text analysis of the club's strong points and weak spots; the important statistics of the 1976 season; the team's 1977 schedule; a detailed roster of veteran club personnel—including each player's height, weight, age as of Aug. 31, 1977, years of professional experience and college; our own Performance Quotient ratings for each unit on offense and defense (quarterbacks, running backs, receivers, interior linemen, kickers, defensive linemen, linebackers, cornerbacks, and safeties); a depth chart showing first-team, second-team and third-team players at each position; and the team's 1977 rookie selections, also with a Performance Quotient rating of the club's freshman class. Our experts' evaluation of all of this material led to their prediction of the team's final standing in its division. We have considered the club's tangible strengths, as reflected in our Performance Quotients, as well as the intangibles that affect a team's performance in making our predictions.

A bit of explanation is required for you to fully understand the Performance Quotient rating system. Each area of the team under examination gets an appraisal and a ranking. For a given team, running backs may get a ranking of 2, for example; linebackers may be worth a 1; rookies could earn a 3. The rating scale is based on evaluations from 1 to 5. A unit that is best or tied for best in the conference is valued at 1; 2 equals excellent; 3 stands for good; 4 is fair; and 5 is poor. If you add up all the ratings of each team's 10 categories, you can readily compare that club's overall quality to the skills of any other team.

The teams appear in the order in which we forecast they will finish the season. The winning team in each division—we predict they will be the New England Patriots in the East, the Cincinnati Bengals in the Central and the Oakland Raiders in the West—of course qualifies for the postseason playoff round, which is filled out with the team that has the best second-place record—and we predict that will be the Baltimore Colts. Who, then, will survive the playoffs and win a trip to the Super Bowl to oppose the National Conference champion?

This season's AFC representative will again be the Oakland Raiders, the same team that successfully carried the American Conference's colors into Super Bowl XI, we forecast. To find out the National Conference team we predict the Raiders will face, see the complete NFC section that begins on page 1.

NEW ENGLAND PATRIOTS

Prediction: First

A year ago, when the New England Patriots traded quarterback Jim Plunkett to the San Francisco 49ers for a fortune in draft choices, the NFL railbirds suggested that the Pats had made the mistake of their lives.

Plunkett, they said, would go on to become one of the elite quarterbacks in the NFL. Who knows what the draft choices would turn out to be?

A year later, Coach Chuck Fairbanks' decision to deal with the 'Niners looks like one of the grandest moves in the history of the league.

Last year it gave Fairbanks a total of three first-round draft choices and the Pats' selectors turned them into the Defensive Rookie of the Year, cornerback Mike Haynes, and the All-Rookie free safety, Tim Fox, plus a future star in center Pete Brock.

This year it gave them extra first- and second-round selections. The first choice was used to draft another high-quality cornerback, Texas' Raymond Clayborn, and then the team used its own pick on the opening round to name Tennessee's exciting wide receiver-kick returner, Stanley Morgan. In the second go-around the Patriots reupholstered their already versatile backfield with Oklahoma halfback Horace Ivory (with the choice they had from San Francisco) and then chose Colorado tight end Don Hasselback, whom they can use as a backup for Russ Francis or convert to an offensive tackle.

But the best thing the deal did for the Pats was to force Fairbanks to commit his quarterbacking to young Steve Grogan.

Last season, Grogan was no worse than the third-most valuable player in the AFC, behind only Oakland's Ken Stabler and Baltimore's Bert Jones.

Grogan passed for 18 touchdowns, ran for 12 and picked up a fumble for another. His passing accounted for 1903 yards, his running for 397.

This year Grogan should be even better, and it couldn't come at a better time. The Patriots, without question, have the easiest schedule in the NFL.

The Patriots play only three games in 1977 against teams that had winning records last year. Their opponents had an aggregate won-lost record of 74-122 in 1976.

Grogan supervised a running game that produced an average of 210.6 yards a game. Sam Cunningham led the ground gainers with 824 yards in the 11 games he started before being injured; he was followed by another fullback, Don Calhoun, with 721, most of them accumulated in the three starting assignments he got when he replaced Cunningham. Halfback Andy Johnson added 699.

Everyone was provided with impressive running room by the Pats' awesome young line.

Both guard John Hannah and tackle Leon Gray made the Pro Bowl, and center Bill Lenkaitis had, by far, the best year of his career. The other guard, Sam Adams, is solid, but the fight for the starting assignment at right tackle may be a derby among Bob

McKay, Shelby Jordan, who returns after a one-year stretch in jail on a drug rap, and aging Tom Neville.

When Grogan isn't looking for Francis, his most obvious target, he can go to Darryl Stingley, who averaged 21.8 yards on his 17 catches, two other veteran wide receivers, Randy Vataha and Marlin Briscoe, or running backs Johnson and Cunningham, the team's two leading catchers.

Haynes and Fox were the best news the Patriot pass defense received in years. Mike led the team in interceptions with eight and in punt returns with a 13.5-yard average. Fox intercepted three passes. But their value was in coverage and tackling as well as when they handled the ball.

Prentice McCray blossomed as a strong safety and veteran Bob Howard turned in a solid year. Clayborn is his eventual heir.

The linebacking is solid. Evidence of that is that the best man in the unit, inside backer Steve Nelson, missed the playoffs, but no great weakness was discovered in his absence. The other inside guy, Sam Hunt, is a head-hunter. Steve Zabel had a strong year on the outside and veterans George Webster, Steve King and Pete Barnes vie for the other spot, but it may go to Rod Shoate, whose debut has been delayed by injuries the last two years.

The three-man front is manned by a wave of defenders. Noseguard Ray Hamilton and ends Julius Adams and Mel Lunsford are the nominal starters, but Richard Bishop, Tony McGee and Craig Hanneman, who was hurt last year, will play a lot.

Placekicker John Smith is solid and Mike Patrick's punting average jumped over the 40-yard mark.

The playoff experience the Patriots got last season will be put to good use in 1977.

1976 RECORD (11-4)

13	Baltimore	27	20	Buffalo	10
30	Miami	14	21	Baltimore	14
30	Pittsburgh	27	38	New York Jets	24
48	Oakland	17	38	Denver	14
10	Detroit	30	27	New Orleans	6
41	New York Jets	7	31	Tampa Bay	14
26	Buffalo	22		(Playoff)	
3	Miami	10	21	Oakland	24

PASSING

	Atts	Comps	Yds	Lgst	TDs	Ints	Pct
Grogan	302	145	1903	58	18	20	48.0
Owen	5	1	7	7	0	0	20.0

SCORING

	TDs	PATs	FGs	Total
Smith	0	42	15	87
Grogan	13	0	0	78
Johnson	10	0	0	60
Stingley	4	0	0	24
Three tied with	3	0	0	18

RUSHING

	Atts	Yds	TDs	Lgst	Avg
Cunningham	172	824	3	24	4.8
Calhoun	129	721	1	54	5.6†
Johnson	169	699	6	69	4.1
Grogan	60	397	12	41	6.6
Phillips	24	164	1	46	6.8
Forte	25	100	1	26	4.0

RECEIVING

	Recs	Yds	TDs	Lgst	Avg
Johnson	29	343	4	53	11.8
Cunningham	27	299	0	41	11.1
Francis	26	367	3	38	14.1
Stingley	17	370	4	58	21.8
Calhoun	12	56	0	12	4.7
Vataha	11	192	1	44	17.5

INTERCEPTIONS

	Ints	Yds	TDs	Lgst	Avg
Haynes	8	90	0	28	11.3
McCray	5	182†	2‡	63	36.4
Fox	3	67	0	29	22.3
Howard	3	28	0	15	9.3
Two tied with 2					

SYMBOLS †—Conference leader
‡—Tied for conference lead

1977 SCHEDULE

Home: Sept. 18—Kansas City; Oct. 9—Seattle; Oct. 23—Baltimore; Oct. 30—New York Jets; Nov. 6—Buffalo; Nov. 27—Philadelphia; Dec. 11—Miami.

Away: Sept. 26—Cleveland; Oct. 2—New York Jets; Oct. 16—San Diego; Nov. 13—Miami; Nov. 20—Buffalo; Dec. 4—Atlanta; Dec. 18—Baltimore.

OFFENSE

QUARTERBACKS	Ht	Wt	Age	Exp	College
Grogan, Steve	6-4	200	24	3	Kansas State
Owen, Tom	6-1	194	24	4	Wichita State

Grogan emerged as one of the NFL's new stars, accounting for 31 touchdowns. Owen once started for the 49ers. PERF. QT.: 1.

RUNNING BACKS	Ht	Wt	Age	Exp	College
Cunningham, Sam	6-3	224	27	5	Southern California
Johnson, Andy	6-0	204	24	4	Georgia
Calhoun, Don	6-0	198	25	4	Kansas State
Forte, Ike	6-0	196	23	2	Arkansas
Phillips, Jess	6-1	208	30	10	Michigan State

The Patriots got an aggregate total of 2244 yards from Cunningham, Johnson and Calhoun. Cunningham is in the top echelon of NFL fullbacks, and the quick, rugged Calhoun has developed as he didn't in Buffalo. Johnson is a versatile back, but the team could use a speedster. Forte has quickness but lots to learn. Phillips is handy. PERF. QT.: 2.

RECEIVERS	Ht	Wt	Age	Exp	College
Stingley, Darryl (W)	6-0	195	25	4	Purdue
Vataha, Randy (W)	5-10	170	28	7	Stanford
Francis, Russ (T)	6-6	240	24	3	Oregon
Briscoe, Marlin (W)	5-11	180	31	10	Nebraska-Omaha
Burks, Steve (W)	6-5	211	24	3	Arkansas State
Chandler, Al (T)	6-3	229	27	4	Oklahoma

(W)—Wide Receiver   (T)—Tight End

Grogan throws to his backs a lot, but Francis is emerging as the killer receiver. Stingley also is fulfilling his potential. Vataha and Briscoe could fight it out for the other starting wide spot, but look for Burks to be more useful, particularly if he can avoid the injuries that hexed his first two seasons. Chandler is a competent fill-in who's never fulfilled his college rep. PERF. QT.: 3.

INTERIOR LINEMEN	Ht	Wt	Age	Exp	College
Gray, Leon (T)	6-3	256	25	5	Jackson State
McKay, Bob (T)	6-5	265	29	8	Texas
Hannah, John (G)	6-2	265	26	5	Alabama
Adams, Sam (G)	6-3	252	28	6	Prairie View
Lenkaitis, Bill (C)	6-4	250	31	10	Penn State
Jordan, Shelby (T)	6-7	260	25	2	Washington, Mo.
Brock, Pete (C)	6-5	253	23	2	Colorado
Neville, Tom (T)	6-4	253	34	12	Mississippi State

INTERIOR LINEMEN (Contd.)	Ht	Wt	Age	Exp	College
Sturt, Fred (G)	6-4	255	26	2	Bowling Green

(T)—Tackle   (G)—Guard   (C)—Center

This is the heart of New England's success. Some experts say Gray ranks with Oakland's Art Shell as the best tackle in the league. He was reclaimed from Miami. McKay will be challenged by Jordan, out of prison after serving a year on a drug charge. Hannah is All-Pro class now, and Adams is not far behind. Lenkaitis, who has had a mediocre career, was super in '76. Brock, a first-round draftee last year, may give Lenkaitis a big push this time. Neville is fighting age. Sturt is average. One liability is the loss of line coach Red Miller, now head man with the Denver Broncos. PERF. QT.: 1.

KICKERS	Ht	Wt	Age	Exp	College
Smith, John (Pk)	6-0	185	27	3	Southampton, Eng.
Patrick, Mike (P)	6-0	213	24	2	Mississippi State

(Pk)—Placekicker   (P)—Punter

Smith was 15-for-25 in field goals. Patrick's punting average was 40.1. This department is sound. PERF. QT.: 3.

DEFENSE

FRONT LINEMEN	Ht	Wt	Age	Exp	College
Adams, Julius (E)	6-4	260	29	7	Texas Southern
Lunsford, Mel (E)	6-3	250	27	5	Central State, Ohio
Hamilton, Ray (T)	6-1	245	26	5	Oklahoma
Bishop, Richard (T)	6-1	260	27	2	Louisville
McGee, Tony (E)	6-4	245	28	7	Bishop
Moore, Arthur (T)	6-5	253	26	4	Tulsa
Hanneman, Craig (E)	6-4	245	28	5	Oregon State
Cusick, Pete (T)	6-1	255	24	2	Ohio State

(E)—End   (T)—Tackle

What Coach Fairbanks doesn't have in talent, he tries to compensate for in numbers. Adams came back strongly from his '75 injury, but he wasn't the destroyer of previous times. Lunsford's career, in limbo for years, revived last season. Hamilton is effective as long as he gets some rest. Bishop, the ex-Bengal, gave him some last year. McGee led the team in quarterback sacks. If Moore is recovered from illness, he could give Hamilton even more rest in '77. Hanneman is average. Cusick is too frequently hurt. PERF. QT.: 3.

LINEBACKERS	Ht	Wt	Age	Exp	College
Zabel, Steve (O)	6-4	235	29	8	Oklahoma

LINEBACKERS (Contd.)	Ht	Wt	Age	Exp	College
Barnes, Pete (O)	6-1	240	32	10	Southern
Nelson, Steve (M)	6-2	230	26	4	North Dakota State
Hunt, Sam (M)	6-1	240	26	4	Stephen F. Austin
King, Steve (O)	6-4	230	26	5	Tulsa
Shoate, Rod (O)	6-1	211	24	2	Oklahoma
Thomas, Donnie (M)	6-2	245	24	2	Indiana
Webster, George (O)	6-4	230	31	11	Michigan State

(O)—Outside Linebacker   (M)—Middle Linebacker

The "safety in numbers" route is followed here, too. Fairbanks' former Oklahoma star, Zabel, had his finest season as a pro. Aging Barnes (and aging Webster) were okay for spot duty, but neither is a full-time answer. The strength in this department lies with Nelson and Hunt. Nelson is one of the NFL's best. King played hurt; he has talent. The biggest lift would come if Shoate can avoid the injuries that have plagued his pro career; he can capture a starting place. Thomas has heft and promise. Webster could even be forced out. PERF. QT.: 2.

CORNERBACKS	Ht	Wt	Age	Exp	College
Haynes, Mike	6-2	189	24	2	Arizona State
Howard, Bob	6-2	177	32	11	San Diego State
Sanders, John	6-1	178	26	4	South Dakota
Germany, Willie	6-0	192	28	5	Morgan State

Haynes, everybody's Rookie of the Year, not only played with the NFL's best as a cornerback but was the most productive punt returner in Pat history. Howard had the best year of his career. Sanders returns from injury. Germany is average here and at safety. PERF. QT.: 2.

SAFETIES	Ht	Wt	Age	Exp	College
McCray, Prentice (S)	6-1	187	26	4	Arizona State
Fox, Tim (W)	5-11	186	23	2	Ohio State
Beaudoin, Doug (W)	6-1	200	23	2	Minnesota
Conn, Dick (S)	6-0	180	26	4	Georgia

(S)—Strong-side   (W)—Weak-side or "Free" Safety

Fox was the other half of the Pats' gold strike in the first round of the '76 draft. McCray, now in his fourth pro season, has become solid. Beaudoin was ill for much of his rookie campaign. Conn, the former Steeler, adds valuable experience. PERF. QT.: 3.

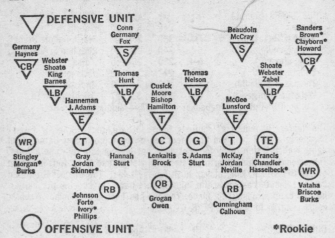

DEFENSIVE UNIT

OFFENSIVE UNIT

*Rookie

1977 DRAFT SELECTIONS

1A	Clayborn, Raymond	CB	6-1	183	Texas
1B	Morgan, Stanley	WR	5-11	171	Tennessee
2A	Ivory, Horace	RB	5-10	193	Oklahoma
2B	Hasselbeck, Don	TE	6-7	241	Colorado
3	Brown, Sid	CB	6-0	183	Oklahoma
4	Skinner, Gerald	T	6-5	262	Arkansas
5	No Choice				
6	No Choice				
7	Smith, Ken	WR	6-2	187	Ark.-Pine Bluff
8	Benson, Brad	G-T	6-3	260	Penn State
9	Vogele, Jerry	LB	6-3	235	Michigan
10A	Rasmussen, John	T	6-4	280	Wisconsin
10B	Alexander, Giles	DE	6-6	250	Tulsa
11	Costict, Ray	LB	6-0	215	Mississippi St.
12	Preston, Dave	RB	5-11	200	Bowling Green

The Jim Plunkett deal may be listed as one of the all-time one-sided trades. Clayborn, the eventual successor to CB Howard, and Ivory, who will give the backfield some needed versatility, are this year's yield. Morgan is a super return man and a scary long-ball catcher. Hasselbeck probably will be converted to offensive tackle. He's a risk. Skinner may be a better bet. Brown has a chance. PERF. QT.: 2.

BALTIMORE COLTS

Prediction: Second

If you are a fan of the Eastern Division of the American Conference, circle October 23 and December 18 on your calendar. These are the dates on which the defending-champion Baltimore Colts and New England Patriots go head-to-head this season. Both have easy schedules, although the Colts' slate is not quite as cushy as the Patriots; and both are hungry to go far in the playoffs.

It could be that the race will go all the way to the final Sunday of the season; that's the December 18 rematch of the teams in Baltimore. They are that closely matched.

When Pittsburgh blew the Colts out of last season's playoffs, 40-14, the Baltimore organization immediately set for itself the task of strengthening an already strong team. There are at least two areas, probably three, in which the Colts are now stronger.

The most obvious is at cornerback, where there was a definite lack of quality until former Cardinal Norm Thompson was signed after he played out his option in St. Louis.

The second improvement is at outside linebacker, where Tom MacLeod, one of the NFL's finest, returns from a year on the injury list.

Improvement at middle linebacker is also probable. A trade is a distinct possibility unless young Sanders Shiver challenges incumbent Jim Cheyunski. Cheyunski's many knee injuries finally are taking a big toll.

The Colts don't need improvement from Bert Jones; just a copy of his 1976 heroics will do fine. Jones is the best young quarterback in the sport.

Last year he completed 207 of 343 passes for a league-leading 3104 yards and 24 touchdowns. He was intercepted only nine times. He was voted the AFC's Most Valuable Player upon the conclusion of his fourth year in pro ball.

The Colts' passing game is the team's most dangerous offensive weapon. Glenn Doughty is the consistent, possession receiver. He caught 40 balls last year. Tight end Raymond Chester is a big play guy. He averaged 19.5 yards on his 24 grabs. The home run catcher is Roger Carr, who scored 11 touchdowns with his 43 receptions, leading the league in yardage (1112) and average (25.9 per catch). First-round draft Randy Burke and young speedsters Marshall Johnson, Freddie Scott and Ricky Thompson vie for backup roles.

If Jones hadn't been quite so outstanding last year, running back Lydell Mitchell would have made a serious run at the Most Valuable Player Award. He ran for 1200 yards, second in the AFC to O.J. Simpson, and led the Colts with 60 catches, good for 555 yards.

His partner, Roosevelt Leaks, is not in such sturdy shape. Leak is valued for his blocking, but young Ron Lee averaged 5.4 yards on 41 carries as a halfback, so he is being switched to fullback. If he can block well enough (and at 6-4 and 222, he has the equipment), the job probably is his.

To power its offense, Baltimore gets amazingly consistent play from its offensive line.

George Kunz, obviously, is one of the NFL's best tackles, but the rest of the line is somewhat non-descript. Ken Mendenhall made himself into a sturdy center. At 32, Elmer Collett shows no sign of slowing, although young Ken Huff is hungrily awaiting a chance to break into the starting lineup. Bob Pratt, the other guard, produces beyond expectations. David Taylor, the other tackle, is another surprise.

The strength of the defense is the line. John Dutton and Fred Cook at ends and Mike Barnes and Joe Ehrmann at tackles led a contingent that slam-banged for 56 sacks, best in the AFC last year.

Coach Ted Marchibroda isn't taking any chances on that unit slipping through injury or anything else. Last year the No. 1 draftee was another defensive tackle, Ken Novak, and this year the second-round choice was an end, Virginia's Mike Ozdowski.

MacLeod is counted on to return to his strong-side linebacking post, although in his absence last season Derrel Luce did a competent job. Stan White mans the weak-side and calls defensive signals. The middle backer's spot will be fought over by young Shiver and elderly Cheyunski unless a trade is made.

Nelson Munsey is expected to come off the injury list to pair with Thompson at corner. Lloyd Mumphord provides admirable relief and special-teams play. Bruce Laird had a top-notch season at strong safety. The weak link is free safety Jackie Wallace, and every DB in camp will get a shot at his position.

Toni Linhart had a Pro Bowl placekicking year with 20 field goals in 27 tries. Punter David Lee kicked for a 39.7-yard average, with 21 of his 59 boots nestling inside the 20-yard line.

1976 RECORD (11-4)

27	New England	13	37	San Diego		21
28	Cincinnati	27	14	New England		21
27	Dallas	30	17	Miami		16
42	Tampa Bay	17	33	New York Jets		16
28	Miami	14	17	St. Louis		24
31	Buffalo	13	58	Buffalo		20
20	New York Jets	0		(Playoff)		
38	Houston	14	14	Pittsburgh		40

PASSING

	Atts	Comps	Yds	Lgst	TDs	Ints	Pct
Jones	343	207	3104†	79	24	9	60.3
Troup	18	8	117	32	0	1	44.4

SCORING

	TDs	PATs	FGs	Total
Linhart	0	49†	20	109†
Carr	11	0	0	66
McCauley	11	0	0	66
Mitchell	8	0	0	48
Leaks	7	0	0	42
Doughty	5	0	0	30

RUSHING

	Atts	Yds	TDs	Lgst	Avg
Mitchell	289	1200	5	43	4.2
Leaks	118	445	7	42	3.8
McCauley	69	227	9	16	3.3
R. Lee	41	220	1	69	5.4
Jones	38	214	2	17	5.6

RECEIVING

	Recs	Yds	TDs	Lgst	Avg
Mitchell	60	555	3	40	9.3
Carr	43	1112†	11	79	25.9†
Doughty	40	628	5	41	15.7
McCauley	34	347	2	44	10.2
Chester	24	467	3	40	19.5

INTERCEPTIONS

	Ints	Yds	TDs	Lgst	Avg
Wallace	5	105	0	41	21.0
White	3	26	0	15	8.7
Oldham	2	40	0	33	20.0
Luce	2	7	0	7	3.5

SYMBOL †—Conference leader

1977 SCHEDULE

Home: Oct. 2—Buffalo; Oct. 9—Miami; Oct. 30—Pittsburgh; Nov. 7—Washington; Nov. 20—New York Jets; Dec. 11—Detroit; Dec. 18—New England.

Away: Sept. 18—Seattle; Sept. 25—New York Jets; Oct. 16—Kansas City; Oct. 23—New England; Nov. 13—Buffalo; Nov. 27—Denver; Dec. 5—Miami.

OFFENSE

QUARTERBACKS	Ht	Wt	Age	Exp	College
Jones, Bert	6-3	212	25	5	Louisiana State
Troup, Bill	6-5	215	26	4	South Carolina
Kirkland, Mike	6-1	195	23	2	Arkansas

Jones Is pro football's newest superstar. Passing or running, he is dynamite. Troup bears him small resemblance. Some think Kirkland has some pro potential. PERF. QT.: 1.

RUNNING BACKS	Ht	Wt	Age	Exp	College
Mitchell, Lydell	6-0	195	28	6	Penn State
Leaks, Roosevelt	5-11	225	24	3	Texas
McCauley, Don	6-1	215	28	7	North Carolina
Lee, Ron	6-4	222	23	2	West Virginia
Stevens, Howard	5-5	165	27	5	Louisville

Mitchell would have received more recognition had Jones not enjoyed his sensational season. Lydell was first-rate. The Colts seek a better running mate for him than Leaks. McCauley is a super sub, but big Lee has the moves of a halfback. If he can improve his blocking, he can have Leaks' job. Stevens returns kicks. PERF. QT.: 2.

RECEIVERS	Ht	Wt	Age	Exp	College
Carr, Roger (W)	6-3	196	25	4	Louisiana Tech
Doughty, Glenn (W)	6-2	202	26	6	Michigan
Chester, Raymond (T)	6-4	236	29	8	Morgan State
Johnson, Marshall (W)	6-1	190	24	2	Houston
Scott, Freddie (W)	6-2	175	25	4	Amherst
Kennedy, Jimmie (T)	6-3	230	25	3	Colorado State
Thompson, Ricky (W)	6-0	170	23	2	Baylor

(W)—Wide Receiver   (T)—Tight End

If the starters don't get hurt, the Colts have top-notch play at all three spots. Carr increased his TD catches from two in '76 to 11 last year while accumulating 1112 yards. Doughty caught 39 passes in '75 and 40 last year. Chester's statistics dwindled, but Coach Marchibroda felt the vet made more big plays. He can block, too. The subs caught only five passes among them. It would help if Johnson comes off the injured list at 100 per cent effectiveness. PERF. QT.: 2.

INTERIOR LINEMEN	Ht	Wt	Age	Exp	College
Kunz, George (T)	6-6	261	30	9	Notre Dame
Taylor, David (T)	6-5	264	27	5	Catawba
Collett, Elmer (G)	6-5	246	32	11	San Francisco State
Pratt, Robert (G)	6-4	248	26	4	North Carolina

INTERIOR LINEMEN (Contd.)	Ht	Wt	Age	Exp	College
Mendenhall, Ken (C)	6-3	250	29	6	Oklahoma
Huff, Ken (G)	6-4	257	24	3	North Carolina
Van Duyne, Bob (T-G-C)	6-3	249	25	4	Idaho
Blue, Forrest (C)	6-6	260	31	10	Auburn

(T)—Tackle   (G)—Guard   (C)—Center

Kunz is the solid All-Pro who helped show this line how to join the NFL's elite. Taylor gets better every year. Collett seems to improve with age. Pratt does well enough to keep his highly touted fellow North Carolina alumnus, Huff, out of the lineup—though that task may prove difficult this year. Mendenhall made himself into a top center. Van Duyne is a multi-position handyman. Blue is not the man he used to be with the 49ers. There is room for ambitious young kids to sit on the bench and learn the ropes. PERF. QT.: 2.

KICKERS	Ht	Wt	Age	Exp	College
Linhart, Toni (Pk)	5-11	179	35	5	Austria Tech
Lee, David (P)	6-5	224	33	12	Louisiana Tech

(Pk)—Placekicker   (P)—Punter

Linhart had a Pro Bowl year with 20 FGs in 27 tries. Lee averaged a solid 39.7 yards and puts many punts out of bounds. PERF. QT.: 1.

DEFENSE

FRONT LINEMEN	Ht	Wt	Age	Exp	College
Cook, Fred (E)	6-4	246	25	4	Southern Mississippi
Dutton, John (E)	6-7	266	26	4	Nebraska
Ehrmann, Joe (T)	6-4	254	28	5	Syracuse
Barnes, Mike (T)	6-6	256	26	5	Miami, Fla.
Novak, Ken (T)	6-7	275	23	2	Purdue
Fernandes, Ron (E)	6-4	239	25	3	Eastern Michigan

(E)—End   (T)—Tackle

The Sack Pack dropped passers 56 times last year, and the frightening thing is that none of them has been around for more than four seasons. Cook is almost as effective as Dutton, the line's heaviest hitter. Ehrmann is the spiritual leader, and Barnes may be the most underrated tackle in the league. Novak, last year's first-rounder, didn't play much. Fernandes helps out. PERF. QT.: 1.

LINEBACKERS	Ht	Wt	Age	Exp	College
MacLeod, Tom (O)	6-3	228	26	4	Minnesota
White, Stan (O)	6-1	223	27	6	Ohio State
Cheyunski, Jim (M)	6-1	220	31	10	Syracuse

LINEBACKERS (Contd.)	Ht	Wt	Age	Exp	College
Luce, Derrel (O)	6-3	227	24	3	Baylor
Shiver, Sanders (M-O)	6-2	222	22	2	Carson-Newman
Simonini, Ed (M)	6-0	220	23	2	Texas A&M
Dickel, Dan (O)	6-4	230	25	4	Iowa

(O)—Outside Linebacker   (M)—Middle Linebacker

MacLeod is expected to beat out Luce, who competently replaced Mac while he was hurt. Shiver will challenge for Cheyunski's job, and if the youngster doesn't win that spot, he'll slide over and make the solid White earn his job again. Baltimore brass thinks Shiver is going to be a top player. Chey is a marked man, mostly because of his knee trouble. Simonini is limited by his size. Dickel is not a serious challenger for a starting role. PERF. QT.: 3.

CORNERBACKS	Ht	Wt	Age	Exp	College
Thompson, Norm	6-1	180	32	7	Utah
Munsey, Nelson	6-1	198	29	6	Wyoming
Mumphord, Lloyd	5-10	178	30	9	Texas Southern
Nettles, Doug	6-0	178	26	3	Vanderbilt

The big news is the addition of Thompson, whose experience upgrades the entire secondary by quite a bit. Munsey is coming back from surgery, but he's counted on to start. Mumphord is best utilized in relief situations. Nettles can find himself jobless. PERF. QT.: 2.

SAFETIES	Ht	Wt	Age	Exp	College
Laird, Bruce (S)	6-1	198	27	6	American Inter.
Wallace, Jackie (W)	6-3	198	26	4	Arizona
Hall, Randy (W)	6-3	194	25	3	Idaho
Baylor, Tim (W)	6-6	191	23	2	Morgan State
Oldham, Ray (S)	5-11	192	26	5	Middle Tenn. State
Salter, Bryant (W)	6-5	196	27	7	Pittsburgh

(S)—Strong-side   (W)—Weak-side or "Free" Safety

Laird had his finest season as a Colt. Wallace is another story entirely. Everybody will be taking aim at his job, and somebody figures to win it. If Hall or Baylor can't push him, Oldham (who is also a cornerback), will move over from his reserve spot on the strong-side or the team will try to find the answer via the trade route. Salter doesn't figure to return. PERF. QT.: 3.

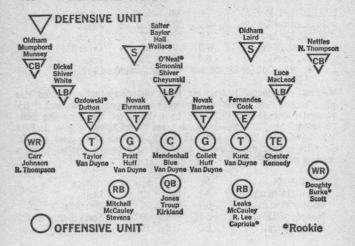

DEFENSIVE UNIT

Oldham
Mumphord
Munsey

Salter
Baylor
Hall
Wallace

Oldham
Laird

Nettles
N. Thompson

CB

Dickel
Shiver
White

O'Neal●
Simonini
Shiver
Cheyunski

Luce
MacLeod

CB

LB

Ozdowski●
Dutton

Novak
Ehrmann

Novak
Barnes

Fernandes
Cook

LB

LB

E

T

G

C

G

T

E

WR
Carr
Johnson
R. Thompson

T
Taylor
Van Duyne

G
Pratt
Huff
Van Duyne

C
Mendenhall
Blue
Van Duyne

G
Collett
Huff
Van Duyne

T
Kunz
Van Duyne

TE
Chester
Kennedy

RB
Mitchell
McCauley
Stevens

QB
Jones
Troup
Kirkland

RB
Leaks
McCauley
R. Lee
Capriola●

WR
Doughty
Burke●
Scott

OFFENSIVE UNIT

●Rookie

1977 DRAFT SELECTIONS

1	Burke, Randy	WR	6-1	186	Kentucky
2	Ozdowski, Mike	DE	6-5	244	Virginia
3	No Choice				
4	No Choice				
5	No Choice				
6	O'Neal, Calvin	LB	6-1	235	Michigan
7	Carter, Blanchard	T	6-4	262	Nevada-Las Vegas
8	Helms, Ken	T-C	6-4	251	Georgia
9	Capriola, Glen	RB	5-11	220	Boston College
10	Baker, Ron	G	6-3	238	Oklahoma State
11	Ruff, Brian	LB	6-1	222	Citadel
12	Deutsch, Bill	FB	6-3	227	North Dakota

Burke, a quick, slick receiver provides some needed backup depth. Ozdowski is able to break in slowly, behind the Sack Pack. O'Neal's problem in college was poor diagnostic ability. Capriola could be the surprise of this rather thin group. PERF. QT.: 4.

MIAMI DOLPHINS

Prediction: Third

It is said that fortunes even out over the long run. The Miami Dolphins won't argue with that—not with what's happened to them of late.

Everything came up roses for them in the days when they were going to Super Bowls. But then there was the reversal. First Larry Csonka, Paul Warfield and Jim Kiick signed with the World Football League and didn't return when that enterprise turned belly-up. Then injuries began to strike the famed "No-Name" defense.

Tackle Manny Fernandez hasn't played in two years and probably won't this season. Onetime All-Pro end Bill Stanfill has had two sub-par campaigns due to chronic neck injuries, and his career, too, might come to a premature end. Linebacker Mike Kolen missed most of two seasons with knee injuries. Young linebackers by the score hurt their knees—almost as if such injuries were a communicable disease. Safety Dick Anderson hasn't played much since suffering an injury in 1975. Cornerback Tim Foley is in something of the same boat. Safeties Charlie Babb and Barry Hill got hurt last year.

Then Nick Buoniconti finally lost it.

It didn't stop last winter.

Offensive tackle Darryl Carlton got involved in a nightclub hassle, stormed out of the place and got involved in a fiery automobile crash that left him with severe burns. Just after the draft, starting defensive tackles Randy Crowder and Donald Reese were arrested for allegedly dealing in cocaine.

Coach Don Shula would like to know just where the adversity ends.

The Dolphins can't be all bad, however, as long as Bob Griese still plays quarterback for them. He had an off year in '76, but he should be a factor in their comeback over the next few seasons.

The famed offensive line is still sturdy—from guard to guard. Jim Langer is still the most prominent center in the NFL. Bob Kuechenberg and Larry Little continue to be a noble pair of guards, although Little may have to move over and play Carlton's tackle unless Darryl makes a complete recovery. If that switch happens, seasoned sub Ed Newman will step into Little's guard position. The other tackle, Wayne Moore, also has experienced health problems.

Finding healthy running backs is another task for Shula. The Dolphins keep saying Benny Malone will be a 1000-yard runner someday, but he keeps getting hurt. Norm Bulaich should really be just a spot guy now, and Don Nottingham is useful only in certain situations.

That's why Shula plans to employ his star receiver, Nat Moore, as a third-down running back upon occasion. Moore was a great college runner at Florida. And Leroy Harris of Arkansas State, one of the top sleepers in the collegiate draft, is now a Dolphin. The stocky youngster, chosen by the Dolphins as their second selection on the fifth round, could move right up through the ranks to a starting spot.

The receiving corps is more than adequate. In addition to Moore, Fred Solomon and Duriel Harris are young and have considerable promise. And the tight end troika of Jim Mandich, Andre Tillman and Loaird McCreary gets the job done in fine style.

The best news the defense got is that Bill Arnsparger is back to run it after a three-year sabbatical as head coach of the New York Giants.

Was it a premonition or a tip that led the Dolphins to draft two defensive linemen in the first two rounds of the draft, shortly before Crowder and Reese were busted? The linemen are A.J. Duhe of Louisiana State and Bob Baumhower of Alabama.

The most reliable man up front is veteran end Vern den Herder. If Stanfill can't go, John Andrews will step in at end. Bob Heinz, a stay-home tackle, is another possible starter.

Steve Towle is the starting middle linebacker again. Larry Gordon, who started as a rookie, will be one outside linebacker. The other will be veteran Bob Matheson or Kim Bokamper, a '76 first-round draftee whose rookie year was postponed by knee surgery. He'd earned raves from Shula before being sidelined.

Jeris White, who experienced a nightmare season for the league's worst pass defense, is one cornerback. Curtis Johnson is the other. Ken Ellis may press White if Shula finds enough healthy safeties.

Out of the safeties' knee surgery group—Babb, Anderson and Hill—the coach hopes that two will be ready to report for duty, but he won't know who they are until the hitting starts in training camp.

Garo Yepremian hit on 16 of 23 field goals. Larry Seiple is a short punter but an accurate one whose hang-time is more than satisfactory.

1976 RECORD (6-8)

30	Buffalo	21	10	New England	3
14	New England	30	27	New York Jets	7
16	New York Jets	0	3	Pittsburgh	14
28	Los Angeles	31	16	Baltimore	17
14	Baltimore	28	13	Cleveland	17
17	Kansas City (OT)	20	45	Buffalo	27
23	Tampa Bay	20	7	Minnesota	29

PASSING

	Atts	Comps	Yds	Lgst	TDs	Ints	Pct
Griese	272	162	2097	47	11	12	59.6
Strock	47	21	359	53	3	2	44.7
Morrall*	26	10	148	67	1	1	38.5

SCORING

	TDs	PATs	FGs	Total
Yepremian	0	29	16	77
Bulaich	4	0	0	24
Malone	4	0	0	24
Mandich	4	0	0	24
N. Moore	4	0	0	24
Solomon	4	0	0	24

RUSHING

	Atts	Yds	TDs	Lgst	Avg
Malone	186	797	4	31	4.3
Bulaich	122	540	4	35	4.4
Winfrey	52	205	1	13	3.9
Nottingham	63	185	3	13	2.9
Davis	31	160	1	57	5.2

RECEIVING

	Recs	Yds	TDs	Lgst	Avg
N. Moore	33	625	4	67	18.9
Bulaich	28	151	0	25	5.4
Solomon	27	453	2	53	16.8
Harris	22	372	1	44	16.9
Mandich	22	260	4	31	11.8
Twilley	14	214	1	39	15.3

INTERCEPTIONS

	Ints	Yds	TDs	Lgst	Avg
Ellis	2	40	0	40	20.0
Matheson	2	34	0	34	17.0
Babb	2	20	0	20	10.0
White	2	4	0	4	2.0

SYMBOL *—Retired

1977 SCHEDULE

Home: Oct. 2—Houston; Oct. 16—New York Jets; Oct. 23—Seattle; Oct. 30—San Diego; Nov. 13—New England; Dec. 5—Baltimore; Dec. 17—Buffalo.

Away: Sept. 18—Buffalo; Sept. 25—San Francisco; Oct. 9—Baltimore; Nov. 6—New York Jets; Nov. 20—Cincinnati; Nov. 24—St. Louis; Dec. 11—New England.

OFFENSE

QUARTERBACKS	Ht	Wt	Age	Exp	College
Griese, Bob	6-1	190	32	11	Purdue
Strock, Don	6-5	203	26	4	Virginia Tech

Griese sagged a bit in '76, but there will be no Dolphin comeback without him. Strock shows occasional signs of a future. PERF. QT.: 2.

RUNNING BACKS	Ht	Wt	Age	Exp	College
Malone, Benny	5-10	193	25	4	Arizona State
Bulaich, Norm	6-1	218	30	8	Texas Christian
Nottingham, Don	5-10	210	28	7	Kent State
Davis, Gary	5-10	202	22	2	Cal. Poly-Obispo
Winfrey, Stan	5-11	223	24	3	Arkansas State

This is Coach Shula's No. 1 offensive trouble spot. Malone is skilled, but he's always hurt, it seems. The time is passed for Bulaich to contribute greatly. Nottingham is a decent third back. Late last season speedy Davis got a couple of shots and showed some promise. It's time for Winfrey to make his move. PERF. QT.: 4.

RECEIVERS	Ht	Wt	Age	Exp	College
Moore, Nat (W)	5-9	180	25	4	Florida
Solomon, Fred (W)	5-11	181	24	3	Tampa
Tillman, Andre (T)	6-5	230	24	3	Texas Tech
Mandich, Jim (T)	6-2	215	29	8	Michigan
McCreary, Loaird (T)	6-5	227	24	2	Tennessee State
Harris, Duriel (W)	5-11	175	22	2	New Mexico State
Smith, Barry (W)	6-1	190	26	5	Florida State
Twilley, Howard (W)	5-10	185	33	12	Tulsa
(W)—Wide Receiver			(T)—Tight End		

There's not a lot of size here, but much talent. In fact Shula may convert Moore to running back, his position at the U. of Florida. Solomon seems ready to become a star. Tight end was shared by Mandich, the clutch-receiving veteran, and Tillman last year. This season McCreary could nose in there somewhere, or one of them could be used in a trade. Harris showed flashes of brilliance as a rookie. Smith, a former first-round draftee, is getting his last shot. Twilley may retire, but, then, he's said that before. PERF. QT.: 2.

INTERIOR LINEMEN	Ht	Wt	Age	Exp	College
Moore, Wayne (T)	6-7	265	32	8	Lamar Tech
Carlton, Darryl (T)	6-6	260	24	3	Tampa
Kuechenberg, Bob (G)	6-1	252	29	8	Notre Dame
Little, Larry (G-T)	6-1	265	31	11	Bethune-Cookman

INTERIOR LINEMEN (Contd.)	Ht	Wt	Age	Exp	College
Langer, Jim (C)	6-2	253	29	8	South Dakota State
Newman, Ed (G)	6-2	245	26	5	Duke
Drougas, Tom (T)	6-4	255	27	6	Oregon
Mitchell, Melvin (G)	6-3	260	24	2	Tennessee State
Young, Randy (T-C)	6-5	250	23	2	Iowa State

(T)—Tackle   (G)—Guard   (C)—Center

Miami used to boast of the best line in the universe. It's still a dandy from guard to guard. Then the trouble starts. Moore has been cursed with injuries lately. Carlton played poorly last season, then got hurt in the postseason and may never be able to come back. But there isn't any better guard tandem than Kooch and Little, who could find himself at tackle if Carlton isn't up to it. Langer is still the All-Pro center. Newman could step right in if Little moves over. Drougas has had every chance. Mitchell is learning and could develop into something special. Young is a reclamation project. PERF. QT.: 2.

KICKERS	Ht	Wt	Age	Exp	College
Yepremian, Garo (Pk)	5-8	175	33	11	None
Seiple, Larry (P)	6-0	214	32	11	Kentucky

(Pk)—Placekicker   (P)—Punter

Garo went 16 for 23 last year. He's about as effective as ever. Seiple is a steady punter and spot receiver. PERF. QT.: 2.

DEFENSE

FRONT LINEMEN	Ht	Wt	Age	Exp	College
Stanfill, Bill (E)	6-5	252	30	9	Georgia
den Herder, Vern (E)	6-6	252	28	7	Central Iowa
Crowder, Randy (T)	6-2	236	25	4	Penn State
Reese, Don (T)	6-7	260	25	4	Jackson State
Andrews, John (E)	6-6	251	25	3	Morgan State
Heinz, Bob (T)	6-6	265	30	8	Pacific
Fernandez, Manny (T)	6-2	250	31	9	Utah

(E)—End   (T)—Tackle

The Dolphins had the third fewest QB sacks in the NFL in '76 and finished last in pass defense. Stanfill's neck injury destroyed his effectiveness and jeopardizes his pro future. Only den Herder is of certified ability. Crowder and Reese almost certainly won't be back; they didn't play that well, anyway. Andrews will play if Stanfill can't. The youngster is only average, as is vet Heinz. Injuries have cost Fernandez two years; he tries again. PERF. QT.: 4.

LINEBACKERS	Ht	Wt	Age	Exp	College
Gordon, Larry (O)	6-4	230	24	2	Arizona State
Bokamper, Kim (O)	6-5	240	23	1	San Jose State
Towle, Steve (M)	6-2	233	23	3	Kansas
Matheson, Bob (O)	6-4	235	32	11	Duke
Kolen, Mike (O-M)	6-2	222	29	7	Auburn
Rhone, Earnie (O)	6-2	212	24	2	Henderson State
Selfridge, Andy (O)	6-3	220	28	5	Virginia

(O)—Outside Linebacker   (M)—Middle Linebacker

Gordon started as a rookie and should get better. Bokamper was a gem in his rookie ('76) training camp, then hurt a knee. He's recovered. Towle is no Nick Buoniconti, but he'll do. Aging Matheson will again help when Miami uses the 3–4, which will happen plenty. The bonus would be a full recovery by Kolen, whose knees have failed him for the last two years. Rhone and Selfridge are two more potential helpers who return from knee injuries. PERF. QT.: 3.

CORNERBACKS	Ht	Wt	Age	Exp	College
White, Jeris	5-11	180	24	4	Hawaii
Johnson, Curtis	6-1	196	29	8	Toledo
Foley, Tim	6-0	194	29	7	Purdue
Bachman, Ted	6-0	190	25	2	New Mexico State

White was singed more than anyone in last season's pass defense horror. Johnson is still sound. Foley probably will be switched to free safety, where he could help a lot if his knee is healed. Bachman isn't much. PERF. QT.: 4.

SAFETIES	Ht	Wt	Age	Exp	College
Babb, Charlie (S)	6-0	190	27	6	Memphis State
Hill, Barry (W)	6-3	185	24	3	Iowa State
Anderson, Dick (S)	6-2	196	31	9	Colorado
Ellis, Ken (W)	5-11	190	29	8	Southern

(S)—Strong-side   (W)—Weak-side or "Free" Safety

Babb is the only safe player back here. Hill was considered a potential star at free safety. He may do it yet. Anderson hasn't played much in the last three years. Ellis was an emergency pickup in '76. He'll either show something or be gone in '77. PERF. QT.: 4.

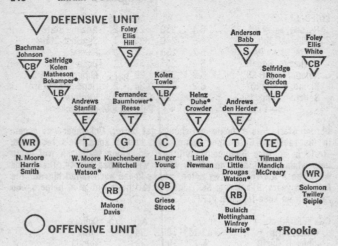

1977 DRAFT SELECTIONS

1	Duhe, A. J.	DT	6-4	248	Louisiana State
2	Baumhower, Bob	DT	6-5	237	Alabama
3	Watson, Mike	T	6-6	265	Miami, Ohio
4	No Choice				
5A	Michel, Mike	Pk	5-11	180	Stanford
5B	Harris, Leroy	RB	5-11	215	Arkansas State
6	No Choice				
7	Herron, Bruce	LB	6-2	220	New Mexico
8	Perkins, Horace	DB	5-10	170	Colorado
9	Turner, Robert	RB	5-11	192	Oklahoma State
10	Carter, Mark	T	6-6	235	Eastern Michigan
11	Alexander, John	DE	6-3	240	Rutgers
12	Anderson, Terry	WR	5-9	182	Bethune-Cookman

Whether it was irony or advance information, the Dolphins made fortunate selections with their first two picks, since both of their starting defensive tackles, Reese and Crowder, face cocaine-peddling charges now. Duhe and Baumhower will get crash courses in pro technique. Watson should help to relieve the uncertainty about Carlton. But what do they want with Michel when they already have Yepremian? Harris could be a real find. **PERF. QT.: 3.**

American Conference • Eastern Division

BUFFALO BILLS

Prediction: Fourth

There is a school of thought around the National Football League that says there is little wrong with the Buffalo Bills that the returns to good health of quarterback Joe Ferguson and fullback Jim Braxton won't cure.

That school of thought ignores some elementary facts:

1. The Bills lost their last 10 games of the 1976 season.

2. In their final two games, the Bills' opponents scored 103 points against them.

3. Their head coach, Jim Ringo, hasn't won a game after more than half a season on the job. He went 0-9 last year in relief of Lou Saban.

If the Bills are going to move out of the pits of the NFL into mediocrity, then Ferguson and Braxton have to get healthy, certainly, but there's more to the Bills' problems than that.

Braxton, one of the top fullbacks in the league, suffered a knee injury on the first play from scrimmage in the first game last year and never played again. Ferguson suffered broken bones in his back in game seven and never played again. The season before, he threw a conference-leading 25 touchdown passes.

Braxton and Ferguson have to be healthy because the only way Buffalo is going to win is to outscore people. The Bills' offensive unit, centered around O.J. Simpson, is still among the jewels of the NFL.

There seems little question that Buffalo should have traded the Juice for some defensive help last year. Such a deal probably could have been made with the Los Angeles Rams, bringing running back Lawrence McCutcheon and three defensive starters to Buffalo. But it wasn't made, and O.J. remains with the Bills, an orchid in the onion patch.

The Juice gained 1503 yards last year to lead the league—without benefit of a training camp. He broke his own single-game record with 273 yards against the Detroit Lions, then the No. 1 ranked defensive team in the National Conference. He rang up his fifth and sixth 200-yard games, an all-time record.

The only name that stands between him and the NFL's career record for ground gaining is that of Cleveland's Jim Brown.

Simpson's offensive line, one of the best in the league, may be even better in '77. Joe Devlin beat out veteran offensive tackle Donnie Green in the last month of the season and the Bills think Devlin can be an All-Pro. The rest of the line includes one certified All-Pro, guard Joe DeLamielleure, another top guard in Reggie McKenzie, plus veteran tackle Dave Foley and center Mike Montler.

The chief offensive problem is that the Bills' passing attack has only one receiver of quality. Bob Chandler was even triple-teamed at times last season because no qualified partner could be found for him. The chief hope this year is that third-round rookie selection John (The Comet) Kimbrough, a :09.4 sprinter from St. Cloud State, can take some heat off Chandler. If that turns out not to be the case, the Bills may play an awful lot of double tight end again, with Paul Seymour, a superior blocker but not much of a catching threat, joined by Reuben Gant.

On defense is where you'll find the team's critical—maybe fatal—problems.

The Bills made a defensive lineman, Oklahoma State's Phil Dokes, their No. 1 draftee. He is a player of considerable skill, but the word is that he must be motivated. That puts him in a class with the player who probably will start at right defensive end, ex-Bengal Sherman White. Tackle Mike Kadish and end Ben Williams should be the other starters.

Last year's best rookie was a linebacker, Dan Jilek. That makes him the only solid man in that position, since John Skorupan, the other outside linebacker, had his worst season and Merv Krakau is not the answer in the middle. The new linebacker coach is former Detroit defensive coordinator Jimmy Carr; his priority assignment is to resurrect the career of Tom Ruud, the No. 1 draftee of two years ago who has been a flop so far.

The Bills had better luck with their first-rounder of 1976, cornerback Mario Clark. He made the All-Rookie team. The other corner, Dwight Harrison, has some hairy games, but he is a super athlete.

The safeties, weak-sider Tony Greene and strong-sider Doug Jones, are veterans. Something may have to give at a corner or safety for Keith Moody, a talented youngster who played well as a spot man in the secondary and did a top job of returning punts.

Marv Bateman's punting average, 42.3, led the NFL, but rookie Neil O'Donoghue will challenge place-kicker George Jakowenko.

1976 RECORD (2-12)

21	Miami	30	14	New York Jets	19
3	Houston	13	10	New England	20
14	Tampa Bay	9	10	Dallas	17
50	Kansas City	17	13	San Diego	34
14	New York Jets	17	14	Detroit	27
13	Baltimore	31	27	Miami	45
22	New England	26	20	Baltimore	58

PASSING

	Atts	Comps	Yds	Lgst	TDs	Ints	Pct
Ferguson	151	74	1086	58	9	1	49.0
Marangi	232	82	998	39	7	16	35.3

SCORING

	TDs	PATs	FGs	Total
Chandler	10	0	0	60
Jakowenko	0	21	12	57
Simpson	9	0	0	54
Gant	3	0	0	18
Holland	3	0	0	18

RUSHING

	Atts	Yds	TDs	Lgst	Avg
Simpson	290†	1503†	8	75	5.2
Kinney•	117	482	1	22	4.1
Marangi	39	230	2	21	5.9
Hooks	25	116	0	24	4.6

RECEIVING

	Recs	Yds	TDs	Lgst	Avg
Chandler	61	824	10	58	13.5
Simpson	22	259	1	43	11.8
Seymour	16	169	0	22	10.6
Holland	15	299	2	58	19.9
Kinney	14	78	0	15	5.6
Gant	12	263	3	39	21.9

INTERCEPTIONS

	Ints	Yds	TDs	Lgst	Avg
Greene	5	135	1	101†	27.0
Moody	3	63	0	44	21.0
D. Jones	3	5	0	5	1.7
Jilek	2	33	0	28	16.5
Clark	2	21	0	21	10.5

SYMBOLS †—Conference leader
       •—Combined Kansas City-Buffalo record

1977 SCHEDULE

Home: Sept. 18—Miami; Oct. 9—New York Jets; Oct. 16—Atlanta; Oct. 23—Cleveland; Nov. 13—Baltimore; Nov. 20—New England; Dec. 4—Washington.

Away: Sept. 25—Denver; Oct. 2—Baltimore; Oct. 30—Seattle; Nov. 6—New England; Nov. 28—Oakland; Dec. 11—New York Jets; Dec. 17—Miami.

OFFENSE

QUARTERBACKS	Ht	Wt	Age	Exp	College
Ferguson, Joe	6-1	184	27	5	Arkansas
Marangi, Gary	6-2	203	25	4	Boston College

The Bills must have Ferguson back from the injury list, since Marangi was unbelievably bad in relief. PERF. QT.: 3.

RUNNING BACKS	Ht	Wt	Age	Exp	College
Simpson, O.J.	6-1	212	30	9	Southern California
Braxton, Jim	6-1	242	28	6	West Virginia
Hooks, Roland	6-0	197	24	2	N. Carolina State
Kinney, Jeff	6-2	215	27	6	Nebraska
Powell, Darnell	6-0	197	23	2	Chattanooga

What can you say about the Juice? It's just too bad he isn't with a big winner. Braxton was hurt on the first down of the season and didn't play again. He deserves a big raise off what his successors didn't do. Hooks showed some signs of helping out as a spot player. Kinney and Powell aren't much. PERF. QT.: 1.

RECEIVERS	Ht	Wt	Age	Exp	College
Chandler, Bob (W)	6-1	180	28	7	Southern California
Holland, John (W)	6-1	190	25	4	Tennessee State
Seymour, Paul (T)	6-5	245	27	5	Michigan
Gant, Reuben (T)	6-4	225	25	4	Oklahoma State
Bell, Eddie (W)	5-10	160	29	6	Idaho State
Coleman, Fred (T)	6-4	240	24	2	Northwest Louisiana
Edwards, Emmett (W)	6-1	187	25	3	Kansas

(W)—Wide Receiver   (T)—Tight End

It's Chandler against the world. He may have been the NFL's most un-derrated offensive player last year. No one playing the opposite position belonged in the league, and that included Holland. Seymour is a great blocker, but as a pass catcher he's a third tackle. Gant is handy to have when the Bills go into a double tight end alignment. Bell may get work in an emergency. Coleman is a prospect; Edwards isn't. Help is desperately needed at the wide spots. PERF. QT.: 4.

INTERIOR LINEMEN	Ht	Wt	Age	Exp	College
Foley, Dave (T)	6-5	247	29	8	Ohio State
Devlin, Joe (T)	6-4	258	23	2	Iowa
DeLamielleure, Joe (G)	6-3	248	26	5	Michigan State
McKenzie, Reggie (G)	6-4	242	27	6	Michigan
Montler, Mike (C)	6-4	245	33	9	Colorado

INTERIOR LINEMEN (Contd.)	Ht	Wt	Age	Exp	College
Green, Donnie (T)	6-7	252	29	7	Purdue
Adams, Bill (G)	6-2	246	27	5	Holy Cross
Parker, Willie (C-G)	6-3	245	28	5	North Texas State
Jones, Ken (T-G)	6-5	252	24	2	Arkansas State
Patton, Bob (C)	6-1	240	22	2	Delaware

(T)—Tackle   (G)—Guard   (C)—Center

Foley is no ballet dancer, but he can drive block. Devlin moved in ahead of Green late last season. Coach Ringo thinks the youngster can be in DeLamielleure's class—and Joe D. is a Pro Bowl regular. McKenzie remains one of the class guards in the league. Montler shows no signs of slowing down, despite his age. Green, Adams and Parker are savvy, skilled subs who might be starting elsewhere. Any of them may be used in a trade to bring defensive help. Jones switches over to this side of the line after an unsuccessful try on defense. Patton is the least of this group—and remember to consider TE Seymour as part of this brotherhood. PERF. QT.: 1.

KICKERS	Ht	Wt	Age	Exp	College
Jakowenko, George (Pk)	5-9	180	29	3	Syracuse
Bateman, Marv (P)	6-4	214	27	6	Utah

(Pk)—Placekicker   (P)—Punter

Jakowenko is a "hold-your-breath" field-goaler. Bateman's average led the NFL but he's no clutch guy. PERF. QT.: 3.

DEFENSE

FRONT LINEMEN	Ht	Wt	Age	Exp	College
Williams, Ben (E)	6-2	258	22	2	Mississippi
White, Sherman (E)	6-5	250	28	6	California
Kadish, Mike (T)	6-5	270	27	5	Notre Dame
Dunstan, Bill (T)	6-4	250	28	5	Utah State
Smith, Marty (T)	6-3	250	23	2	Louisville
Lloyd, Jeff (T)	6-6	255	23	2	West Texas State

(E)—End   (T)—Tackle

Williams did some good things as a rookie and he's quick, but he gets overpowered. White still hasn't been coaxed to play up to his ability. Kadish makes the effort, but he's limited. Dunstan was a spear carrier in Philly last year, but he may start with Buffalo. Things are that bad. Smith and Lloyd are expendable . . . and that's the case even though Smith started last year. PERF. QT.: 5.

LINEBACKERS	Ht	Wt	Age	Exp	College
Jilek, Dan (O)	6-2	212	23	2	Michigan
Skorupan, John (O)	6-2	221	26	5	Penn State
Krakau, Merv (M)	6-2	233	26	5	Iowa State
Rudd, Tom (O)	6-2	223	23	3	Nebraska
Nelson, Bob (O-M)	6-4	232	24	3	Nebraska
Cornell, Bo (O)	6-1	222	28	7	Washington
Johnson, Mark (O)	6-2	236	24	3	Missouri

(O)—Outside Linebacker   (M)—Middle Linebacker

A new assistant coach, Gummy Carr, will try to revive the linebacking. Jilek was the best Buffalo had in his rookie year. Skorupan must snap out of his slump. Krakau gives everything he has, but it's not enough. Ruud, a one-time No. 1 draftee, is a Carr development project. Nelson also falls into the reclamation category. Cornell and Johnson are valued as special-teams players, but that's all. What the Bills need is a beneficial trade. PERF. QT.: 4.

CORNERBACKS	Ht	Wt	Age	Exp	College
Clark, Mario	6-2	190	23	2	Oregon
Harrison, Dwight	6-2	186	28	7	Texas A&I
Moody, Keith	5-11	171	24	2	Syracuse
Brooks, Clifford	6-1	190	28	5	Tennessee State
James, Robert	6-1	184	30	7	Fisk

Clark made the All-Rookie team in '76, but he has much to learn. Harrison is erratic but a fine athlete. Moody has big possibilities and may move someone in this secondary to the bench. Brooks has no such prospects. Former All-Pro James tries again to come back from his knee injury. He's missed 1½ seasons. PERF. QT.: 2.

SAFETIES	Ht	Wt	Age	Exp	College
Jones, Doug (S)	6-2	205	27	4	California State
Greene, Tony (W)	5-10	170	28	7	Maryland
Green, Van (S)	6-1	197	26	5	Shaw
Freeman, Steve (W)	5-11	185	24	3	Mississippi State

(S)—Strong-side   (W)—Weak-side or "Free" Safety

Jones has some good games and some very bad ones. Greene hasn't played up to his All-Pro '75 season since hurting his knee. Green and Freeman can play in spots, but Moody may be switched back here. He is a top prospect. PERF. QT.: 3.

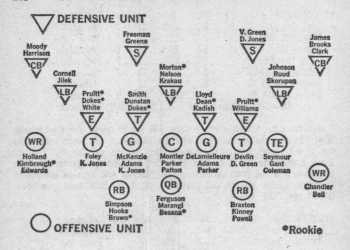

▽ **DEFENSIVE UNIT**

Moody
Harrison
CB ▽

Cornell
Jilek
LB ▽

Freeman
Greene
S ▽

V. Green
D. Jones
S ▽

James
Brooks
Clark
CB ▽

Johnson
Ruud
Skorupan

Pruitt●
Dokes●
White
E ▽

Smith
Dunstan
Dokes●
T ▽

Morton●
Nelson
Krakau
LB ▽

Lloyd
Dean●
Kadish
T ▽

Pruitt●
Williams
E ▽

WR
Holland
Kimbrough●
Edwards

T
Foley
K. Jones

G
McKenzie
Adams
K. Jones

C
Montler
Parker
Patton

G
DeLamielleure
Adams
Parker

T
Devlin
D. Green

TE
Seymour
Gant
Coleman

WR
Chandler
Bell

RB
Simpson
Hooks
Brown●

QB
Ferguson
Marangi
Besana●

RB
Braxton
Kinney
Powell

◯ **OFFENSIVE UNIT**

●**Rookie**

1977 DRAFT SELECTIONS

1	No Choice				
2	Dokes, Phil	DT-DE	6-4	269	Oklahoma State
3A	Brown, Curtis	RB	5-10	203	Missouri
3B	Kimbrough, John	WR	5-10	165	St. Cloud State
4	Dean, Jim	DT	6-4	252	Texas A&M
5A	Besana, Fred	QB	6-4	200	California
5B	O'Donoghue, Neil	P	6-6	205	Auburn
6	Pruitt, Ron	DE	6-3	251	Nebraska
7	Nelms, Mike	DB	6-0	183	Baylor
8	Morton, Greg	LB	6-1	230	Michigan
9	No Choice				
10	No Choice				
11	Jackson, Nate	RB	6-1	226	Tennessee State
12	Romes, Charles	DB	6-1	190	N. C. Central

Dokes was a motivation problem in college, but he's a sure starter with this talent-hungry defense. Kimbrough also has a shot at starting if he can acquire some technique to go with his speed and quickness. He and Brown should help as the kick returners. O'Donoghue is a good bet to take Jakowenko's job. Dean, Besana and Pruitt all have chances to stick, although if they play a lot it may be an indication of problems with higher-touted players. Morton is an MLB prospect; he's got talent, but he used it in college as a defensive tackle. **PERF. QT.: 3.**

NEW YORK JETS

Prediction: Fifth

The sentimentalists say it's a tragedy that Joe Namath will not be a New York Jet in 1977. The realists say it's a good thing Namath is gone. The *real* tragedy, according to them, is that Tony Dorsett won't be a Jet in 1977. The New Yorkers could almost see him in green and white before Seattle made the silly trade that allowed the Dallas Cowboys to draft the Heisman Trophy winner.

Despite failing to get Dorsett, the Jets did appear to have a good draft. But the new coach, Walt Michaels, is building one step at a time. All but one of the premium picks were used for offensive players.

The defense will have to wait a year.

The No. 1 pick was the finest offensive lineman in the draft, possibly in the last five drafts, Southern California tackle Marvin Powell. If he doesn't start for the Jets there should be an investigation.

The No. 2 pick was Wesley Walker, the California comet who was the highest rated of the college receivers until he tore up a knee last November. The knee is supposed to be healed. If it is, he may beat out David Knight to give the Jets some breathtaking receivers.

It would not be a shock to see the fourth-round

pick, Purdue fullback Scott Dierking, starting. The Jets just aren't that deep in ball-carriers.

The X factor in any improvement by the Jet offense is quarterback Richard Todd, who played a lot as a rookie but may not have benefited from the exposure. The former head coach, Lou Holtz, couldn't seem to make up his mind what he wanted to do with Todd. Holtz used some veer formation, some shotgun, a little of this and a little of that before fleeing south to rejoin the collegians at Arkansas.

Michaels will make or break Todd from the pro set.

Todd's rookie statistics were not thrilling. He had a 40.1 per cent completion average, 870 yards and three touchdowns, and 12 interceptions. But he kept looking over his shoulder and seeing Namath.

If he can stabilize, he'll have some fantastic catchers. Jerome Barkum spent most of last season on the injury list, but when well he'll terrorize any cornerback. Richard Caster may be the most dangerous pass receiver among NFL tight ends, even though his '76 stats don't testify to it. Knight averaged 20.2 yards on his 20 catches, but Walker is a flyer with good hands who could chase him back to the bench if Wes is healthy and ready to go.

Powell will go directly to right offensive tackle. The left tackle is improving Robert Woods. Left guard Randy Rasmussen still has plenty left at 32. If Darrell Austin doesn't get nicked again, he can beat out Gary Puetz at right guard. Joe Fields is the center—which doesn't excite—and there's little behind him.

Ed Marinaro had consecutive 100-yard games before getting hurt last year. He's a sound runner if the foot he hurt gets better, but it continued to trouble him well into the off-season. Free agent Clark Gaines picked up 724 yards and made the All-Rookie team in Marinaro's absence. Former Steeler Steve Davis is another experienced back, but he is the soul of inconsistency. Little Louie Giammona and Bob Gresham are also available, with the latter probably the greatest preseason runner in NFL history.

Defensively, last season's Jets have to get better on their own.

The best bet for improvement is at linebacker, where three top rookies were developed in 1976. The cream of that crop is Greg Buttle, whom Michaels characterizes as a "future All-Pro." Buttle is listed as an outside backer, but he'll take over in the middle if Larry Keller, a special teams ace, proves he can start. The third kid, Bob Martin, did excellent work on the weakside. If Buttle stays on the outside, veteran John Ebersole will man the middle.

The Jets had one of the lowest sack totals in history, 16. The only hope for improvement lies in a bunch of *"ifs"*: If Billy Newsome comes back from injury; if Carl Barzilauskas regains his rookie form; if kids like Lawrence Pillers and Larry Faulk continue to improve; if Richard Neal has something left; if third-round rookie Tank Marshall proves to be of immediate help.

With a pass rush, the secondary could be decent. The safeties are respected, with Burgess Owens at free safety and Phil Wise on the strong-side. Ed Taylor, a hitter, and Shafer Suggs, who showed moxie when he started as a rookie, are the cornerbacks.

The kicking isn't bad. Pat Leahy tried 16 field goals and made 11. Punter Duane Carrell, the ex-Cowboy, averaged 39.7 yards, but Coach Michaels hopes to find more efficiency at that spot. It could come from Mike Burke, who'll get first crack at the job.

1976 RECORD (3-11)

17	Cleveland	38	19	Buffalo		14
3	Denver	46	7	Miami		27
0	Miami	16	34	Tampa Bay		0
6	San Francisco	17	24	New England		38
17	Buffalo	14	16	Baltimore		33
7	New England	41	16	Washington		37
0	Baltimore	20	3	Cincinnati		42

PASSING

	Atts	Comps	Yds	Lgst	TDs	Ints	Pct
Namath**	230	114	1090	35	4	16	49.6
Todd	162	65	870	44	3	12	40.1

SCORING

	TDs	PATs	FGs	Total
Leahy	0	16	11	49
Gaines	5	0	0	30
Davis	3	0	0	18
Knight	2	0	0	12
Marinaro	2	0	0	12

RUSHING

	Atts	Yds	TDs	Lgst	Avg
Gaines	157	724	3	33	4.6
Davis	94	418	3	26	4.4
Marinaro	77	312	2	17	4.1
Giammona	39	150	1	35	3.8
Todd	28	107	1	22	3.8
Gresham	30	92	0	24	3.1

RECEIVING

	Recs	Yds	TDs	Lgst	Avg
Gaines	41	400	2	27	9.8
Caster	31	391	1	41	12.6
Marinaro	21	168	0	35	8.0
Knight	20	403	2	44	20.2
Giammona	15	145	0	28	9.7

INTERCEPTIONS

	Ints	Yds	TDs	Lgst	Avg
Sowells	2	46	0	27	23.0
Taylor	2	22	0	11	11.0
Buttle	2	20	0	14	10.0
Martin	2	15	0	12	7.5

SYMBOL **—Waived

1977 SCHEDULE

Home: Sept. 25—Baltimore; Oct. 2—New England; Oct. 23—Oakland; Nov. 6—Miami; Nov. 13—Seattle; Nov. 27—Pittsburgh; Dec. 11—Buffalo.

Away: Sept. 18—Houston; Oct. 9—Buffalo; Oct. 16—Miami; Oct. 30—New England; Nov. 20—Baltimore; Dec. 4—New Orleans; Dec. 18—Philadelphia.

OFFENSE

QUARTERBACKS	Ht	Wt	Age	Exp	College
Todd, Richard	6-2	210	23	2	Alabama
Joachim, Steve	6-3	215	25	2	Temple

In his debut, Todd didn't look up to making Jet fans forget Joe Namath. Joachim can't play at the pro level. PERF. QT.: 5.

RUNNING BACKS	Ht	Wt	Age	Exp	College
Gaines, Clark	6-1	195	23	2	Wake Forest
Marinaro, Ed	6-2	207	27	6	Cornell
Davis, Steve	6-1	210	27	6	Delaware State
Giammona, Louie	5-9	180	24	2	Utah State
Gresham, Bob	5-11	195	29	7	West Virginia

Gaines came out of nowhere to win a spot on the All-Rookie team. If Marinaro gets over foot problems, he could contribute. Davis seems unable to make up his mind whether to play or to retire. Giammona can only help as a spot player and kick returner. Gresham has shown that he can't do it, despite preseason splurges. PERF. QT.: 4.

RECEIVERS	Ht	Wt	Age	Exp	College
Barkum, Jerome (W)	6-4	212	27	6	Jackson State
Knight, David (W)	6-2	175	26	5	William & Mary
Caster, Richard (T)	6-5	230	28	8	Jackson State
Osborne, Richard (T)	6-4	230	23	2	Texas A&M
Satterwhite, Howard (W)	5-11	185	24	2	Sam Houston
Piccone, Lou (W)	5-8	184	28	4	West Liberty State
Haslerig, Clint (W)	6-0	189	25	4	Michigan

(W)—Wide Receiver   (T)—Tight End

Barkum is quality; he should recover from the injury that ruined 1976. Knight is in-and-out; he's not up to the standards of the other starters. The Jet front office avoided disaster by signing Caster after he played out his option. The drop in quality behind the starters is precipitous. Osborne isn't bad in a double tight end formation. Satterwhite and Piccone don't matter, though Lou is good on special teams. Haslerig has floated from team to team. PERF. QT.: 3.

INTERIOR LINEMEN	Ht	Wt	Age	Exp	College
Woods, Robert (T)	6-4	259	27	5	Tennessee State
Krevis, Al (T)	6-6	263	25	3	Boston College
Rasmussen, Randy (G)	6-2	255	32	11	Kearney State
Puetz, Gary (G)	6-4	267	25	5	Valparaiso
Fields, Joe (C)	6-2	240	23	3	Widener
Austin, Darrell (G-C)	6-4	252	25	3	South Carolina

INTERIOR LINEMEN (Contd.)	Ht	Wt	Age	Exp	College
Roman, John (T-G)	6-4	247	25	2	Idaho State
Hill, Winston (T)	6-4	272	35	15	Texas Southern
King, Steve (T)	6-5	245	24	1	Michigan

(T)—Tackle   (G)—Guard   (C)—Center

There should be some shaking up here once training camp gets underway. Woods has the best future among the starters. He's finally settling down to improve his play. Krevis never justified his high draft selection (Cincinnati picked him on the second round). Rasmussen is first-rate, but he's 32. Puetz is only so-so. Fields, Austin and Roman are the type usually found on waiver lists. Hill will probably pack it in before the season starts; he's had a distinguished career. King was a prospect last season; there's question whether he can come back from the injury that sidelined him. PERF. QT.: 4.

KICKERS	Ht	Wt	Age	Exp	College
Leahy, Pat (Pk)	6-0	200	26	4	St. Louis
Carrell, Duane (P)	5-10	185	27	4	Florida State
Burke, Mike (P)	5-10	188	27	2	Miami, Fla.

(Pk)—Placekicker   (P)—Punter

Leahy does a quietly competent job. He connected on 11 of 16 field goals. Carrell was with the team last year; both he and Burke have been around, and neither has proved to be exceptional. PERF. QT.: 3.

DEFENSE

FRONT LINEMEN	Ht	Wt	Age	Exp	College
Neal, Richard (E)	6-3	263	29	9	Southern
Pillers, Lawrence (E)	6-3	250	24	2	Alcorn
Faulk, Larry (T)	6-3	256	24	2	Kent State
Barzilauskas, Carl (T)	6-6	265	26	4	Indiana
Newsome, Billy (E)	6-5	250	29	9	Grambling
Lomas, Mark (E)	6-4	250	29	7	Northern Arizona
Wasick, Dave (E)	6-3	220	23	1	San Jose State

(E)—End   (T)—Tackle

If there were new bodies available, there could be a total turnover among the starters. Patience is running out with Neal. Pillers and Faulk get partial pardons because they're young. Barzo might be salvaged, though he's never played as well as in his first year. Newsome got hurt last year, Lomas in 1974. Neither of them is to be counted on this time around. Wasick was a prospect for Kansas City in 1976, then got hurt. At 220, he's awfully light for the line. PERF. QT.: 5.

LINEBACKERS	Ht	Wt	Age	Exp	College
Buttle, Greg (O-M)	6-2	235	23	2	Penn State
Martin, Bob (O)	6-1	217	23	2	Nebraska
Ebersole, John (M)	6-3	235	28	8	Penn State
Keller, Larry (O)	6-2	220	23	2	Houston
Poole, Steve (M-O)	6-1	232	25	2	Tennessee
Hennigan, Mike (O)	6-2	230	25	5	Tennessee Tech
Russ, Carl (M)	6-2	227	24	3	Michigan
Coleman, Don (O)	6-2	222	25	3	Michigan

(O)—Outside Linebacker　　(M)—Middle Linebacker

Coach (and former LB) Michaels can hang his hat on these youngsters. He says Buttle is a sure All-Pro, and the kid played very well as a rookie. Martin is small, but he's smart and he'll hit. Ebersole is the man in the middle only by default. Keller came up with some big plays to help win two games—no small thing on a 3–11 team. If he wins a spot, Buttle goes to the middle and Ebersole to the bench. Poole deserves a patient look. Hennigan never made it in Detroit. Russ and Coleman are longshots. PERF. QT.: 3.

CORNERBACKS	Ht	Wt	Age	Exp	College
Suggs, Shafer	6-1	200	24	2	Ball State
Taylor, Ed	6-0	181	24	3	Memphis State
Sowells, Rich	6-0	180	28	7	Alcorn
Dunlap, Len	6-2	198	28	6	North Texas State

Suggs gave the Jets something to pin future hopes on until he got hurt. Taylor will hit anything that moves. Jet fans are getting tired of watching Sowells make mistakes. Dunlap, once a Colts' No. 1, gets a last look. He could help. PERF. QT.: 3.

SAFETIES	Ht	Wt	Age	Exp	College
Wise, Phil (S-W)	6-0	193	28	7	Nebraska-Omaha
Owens, Burgess (W)	6-2	200	26	5	Miami, Fla.
Marvaso, Tommy (S-W)	6-1	191	23	2	Cincinnati

(S)—Strong-side　　(W)—Weak-side or "Free" Safety

Wise does a competent job. Owens is about to become a polished player. These starters' ability makes this the Jets' best defensive area. Marvaso, a Redskin reject, hasn't shown much. PERF. QT.: 2.

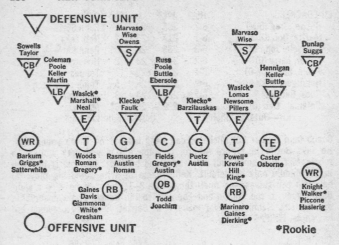

DEFENSIVE UNIT

Sowells
Taylor

CB
Coleman
Poole
Keller
Martin

LB
Wasick●
Marshall●
Neal

Marvaso
Wise
Owens
S

E
Klecko●
Faulk

T

Russ
Poole
Buttle
Ebersole
LB

T
Klecko●
Barzilauskas

G

Marvaso
Wise
S

Wasick●
Lomas
Newsome
Pillers
LB

E
Powell●
Krevis
Hill
King●

Hennigan
Keller
Buttle

Dunlap
Suggs
CB

OFFENSIVE UNIT

WR
Barkum
Griggs●
Satterwhite

T
Woods
Roman
Gregory●

G
Rasmussen
Austin
Roman

C
Fields
Gregory●
Austin

G
Puetz
Austin

T
Powell●
Krevis
Hill
King●

TE
Caster
Osborne

Gaines
Davis
Giammona
White●
Gresham
RB

QB
Todd
Joachim

RB
Marinaro
Gaines
Dierking●

WR
Knight
Walker●
Piccone
Haslerig

●**Rookie**

1977 DRAFT SELECTIONS

1	Powell, Marvin	T	6-4	264	So. California
2	Walker, Wesley	WR	6-0	172	California
3	Marshall, Tank	DE	6-3	256	Texas A&M
4	Dierking, Scott	RB	5-10	220	Purdue
5A	Griggs, Perry	WR	5-9	175	Troy State
5B	Gregory, Gary	C-T	6-3	242	Baylor
6	Klecko, Joe	DT	6-3	262	Temple
7A	White, Charles	RB	6-0	190	Bethune-Cookman
7B	Grupp, Bob	DB	6-0	190	Duke
7C	Long, Kevin	RB	6-1	205	South Carolina
8A	Alexander, Don	DT	6-4	242	Louisiana State
8B	Thompson, Ed	LB	6-1	220	Ohio State
9	Robinson, Matt	QB	6-2	188	Georgia
10	Hennessy, John	DE	6-4	235	Michigan
11	Butterfield, Dave	DB	5-10	182	Nebraska
12A	Gargis, Phil	RB-DB	6-0	185	Auburn
12B	Conrad, Dave	T	6-4	245	Maryland

Powell should be a top NFL tackle for the next decade. The Jets have to build a line so that Todd can be protected. Then maybe he can connect with his first-rate receivers, who will include Walker, providing his knee mended. Marshall should beef up the pass rush. Dierking and White should get to play a lot. Griggs, Gregory and Klecko can all make this squad, not so much because of their potential as because of the team's lack of quality. PERF. QT.: 2.

CINCINNATI BENGALS

Prediction: First

For the true definition of building a football team, inspect what the Cincinnati Bengals have done over the last few years.

Last season they had six selections in the first three rounds of the college draft. Five of the players chosen became regulars. Two high picks from 1975 refreshed the defensive unit. In all, 13 first-year players made the 1976 Cincinnati roster.

This year the Bengals had three first-round picks.

Cincinnati is headed for the Super Bowl. How quickly the team gets there depends upon the development of those kids. But this is a team to watch in the next couple of years.

The Bengal mover and shaker is still Ken Anderson, the remarkably accurate passer who skillfully quarterbacks the club. Anderson threw for 2367 yards and 19 touchdowns last year when the Bengals were developing a running game to give them championship balance.

One of the rookie starters was Archie Griffin, Ohio State's two-time Heisman Trophy winner. He averaged 4.5 yards a carry as a pro, gaining 625 yards. Another was Billy Brooks, who did so well as Isaac Curtis' wide receiver partner that former starter Chip Myers was traded to San Diego after the season. Then there was

Reggie Williams, a little-known linebacker out of Dartmouth, who got to play when Ron Pritchard got hurt; when he got well, Pritchard couldn't win his job back. Chris Bahr, the former Penn State All-America soccer player, won the placekicking job and, to round out the remarkable high-round rookie contingent, Glenn Bujnoch became one of the messenger guards.

This year's draft also brought a multitude of prospects.

The Bengals used their three first-round picks for a pair of incredibly quick defensive linemen, end Eddie Edwards and tackle Wilson Whitley, plus a promising tight end, Mike Cobb.

Edwards should be ready when Coy Bacon, who had a fantastic season at age 34, is through. Whitley may contend right now with quick Bill Kollar for the job of 37-year-old Bob Brown.

Cobb, and a later pick, UCLA's Rick Walker, will vie for the honor of backing up veteran Bob Trumpy, the only other tight end on the roster.

But the Bengals aren't merely a team of youth. They have sound veterans at most positions.

Boobie Clark is Griffin's fullback partner and now he'll be pushed by another rookie prize, Ohio State's Pete Johnson. Stan Fritts, Lenvil Elliott and Tony Davis supply reserve strength at this position, and rookie Mike Voight will join them this year.

The receiving boasts Trumpy and Curtis, still one of the most-feared speed receivers in football. He caught 41 passes and scored six touchdowns last year. John McDaniel is a fleet reserve.

The offensive line is seasoned, with Rufus Mayes and Vernon Holland at tackles, Bob Johnson at center, Dave Lapham at the anchor guard and John Shinners and sophomore Bujnoch the messengers.

Anderson's backup, John Reaves, is one of the most experienced relief signal-callers in the league.

Defensively, the Bengals line up with Bacon, eight-year pro Ron Carpenter, Brown and another bright young star, end Gary Burley, who started as a rookie last year.

Something may have to give—with Edwards, Whitley and Kollar standing by—but Bacon, who was obtained from San Diego in exchange for Charlie Joiner before the 1976 season, had 26 quarterback sacks last year, and he doesn't seem ready for retirement. His personal sack total exceeded the entire team's mark of a year earlier.

The linebacking will have undergone an almost total turnover in the last couple of seasons if Williams continues to keep veteran Pritchard out of the lineup. Jim LeClair has become a top middle backer and Bo Harris won a starting job last year after Al Beauchamp was dealt to St. Louis.

Any NFL club would like to have the Bengals' cornerbacks, Lemar Parrish and Ken Riley. Parrish was selected to the Pro Bowl for the third straight year, and Riley had one of the better seasons among NFL corners, gathering nine interceptions to lead the conference.

Strong-side safety Tommy Casanova also played in the Pro Bowl after his best pro season. Marvin Cobb, who passed up a pro baseball contract to play with the Bengals, won the free safety assignment.

The Bengals even get mileage out of their punter, Pat McInally, the former Harvard star. He's a spare receiver.

This is a young team that may be most dangerous at playoff time, a team that is building toward a Super Bowl peak in the near future.

1976 RECORD (10-4)

17	Denver	7	21	Cleveland	6
27	Baltimore	28	20	Los Angeles	12
28	Green Bay	7	31	Houston	27
45	Cleveland	24	27	Kansas City	24
21	Tampa Bay	0	3	Pittsburgh	7
6	Pittsburgh	23	20	Oakland	35
27	Houston	7	42	New York Jets	3

PASSING

	Atts	Comps	Yds	Lgst	TDs	Ints	Pct
Anderson	338	179	2367	85	19	14	53.0
Reaves	22	8	76	19	2	1	36.4

SCORING

	TDs	PATs	FGs	Total
Bahr	0	39	14	81
Clark	8	0	0	48
Trumpy	7	0	0	42
Curtis	6	0	0	36
Four tied with	3	0	0	18

RUSHING

	Atts	Yds	TDs	Lgst	Avg
Clark	151	671	7	24	4.4
Griffin	138	625	3	77†	4.5
Elliott	69	276	0	24	4.0
Fritts	47	200	3	13	4.3
Davis	36	178	1	16	4.9
Anderson	31	134	1	25	4.3

RECEIVING

	Recs	Yds	TDs	Lgst	Avg
Curtis	41	766	6	85	18.7
Clark	23	158	1	19	6.9
Elliott	22	188	3	29	8.5
Trumpy	21	323	7	48	15.4
Myers**	17	267	1	63	15.7

INTERCEPTIONS

	Ints	Yds	TDs	Lgst	Avg
Riley	9†	141	1	53	15.7
Casanova	5	109	2‡	33	21.8
Cobb	3	55	0	28	18.3
Parrish	2	0	0	0	0.0
Harris	2	—3	0	0	—1.5

SYMBOLS **—Traded
†—Conference leader
‡—Tied for conference lead

1977 SCHEDULE

Home: Sept. 18—Cleveland; Sept. 25—Seattle; Oct. 23—Denver; Oct. 30—Houston; Nov. 20—Miami; Nov. 27—New York Giants; Dec. 10—Pittsburgh.

Away: Oct. 2—San Diego; Oct. 9—Green Bay (at Milwaukee); Oct. 17—Pittsburgh; Nov. 6—Cleveland; Nov. 13—Minnesota; Dec. 4—Kansas City; Dec. 18—Houston.

OFFENSE

QUARTERBACKS	Ht	Wt	Age	Exp	College
Anderson, Ken	6-2	210	28	7	Augustana
Reaves, John	6-4	202	27	6	Florida

Anderson is a Super Bowl-quality quarterback who has never been to the Super Bowl. Reaves is a top-flight backup. PERF. QT.: 2.

RUNNING BACKS	Ht	Wt	Age	Exp	College
Griffin, Archie	5-9	191	23	2	Ohio State
Clark, Boobie	6-2	245	26	5	Bethune-Cookman
Fritts, Stan	6-2	215	24	3	North Carolina State
Elliott, Lenvil	5-11	207	25	5	Northeast Missouri
Davis, Tony	5-10	210	24	2	Nebraska
Shelby, Willie	5-10	190	24	2	Alabama

The Bengals run better than they used to, mostly because of the addition of Griffin, the comeback made by Clark and the beefed-up offensive line. There were no 1000-yard rushers, just a lot of guys who could step in and perform. Fritts, Elliott and Davis are underrated. Shelby returns kicks. Archie could be more valuable now that his teammates are used to his style. PERF. QT.: 3.

RECEIVERS	Ht	Wt	Age	Exp	College
Curtis, Isaac (W)	6-1	195	26	5	San Diego State
Brooks, Billy (W)	6-4	215	24	2	Oklahoma
Trumpy, Bob (T)	6-6	231	32	10	Utah
McDaniel, John (W)	6-1	194	25	4	Lincoln
McInally, Pat (W)	6-5	200	24	2	Harvard
(W)—Wide Receiver		(T)—Tight End			

Despite lower passing production, the Bengals still have the burners. Curtis continues to scare the opposition to death. With Brooks broken in on the other side, both of these speedsters should thrive. Trumpy is the only vet tight end, but a good one. McDaniel has had outstanding games. McInally hasn't had much chance. PERF. QT.: 2.

INTERIOR LINEMEN	Ht	Wt	Age	Exp	College
Holland, Vernon (T)	6-5	272	29	7	Tennessee State
Mayes, Rufus (T)	6-5	268	29	9	Ohio State
Shinners, John (G)	6-2	259	30	9	Xavier
Lapham, Dave (G)	6-4	258	25	4	Syracuse
Johnson, Bob (C)	6-5	255	31	10	Tennessee
Bujnoch, Glenn (G)	6-5	260	23	2	Texas A&M
Hunt, Ron (T)	6-6	274	22	2	Oregon
Fairchild, Greg (G-T-C)	6-4	258	23	2	Tulsa
(T)—Tackle		(G)—Guard		(C)—Center	

The Bengals claim Holland and Mayes are among the league's finest tackles. Shinners does solid work as the senior messenger guard. Bujnoch won the junior position as a rookie. The best of the guards is anchor man Lapham. Johnson has been the starting center since the team was formed. These starters are big, powerful, but not too fast—and they allowed 37 quarterback sacks in 1976. Maybe they were concentrating too hard on making the running game go. Hunt will probably develop, but Fairchild may not. PERF. QT.: 2.

KICKERS	Ht	Wt	Age	Exp	College
Bahr, Chris (Pk)	5-9	170	24	2	Penn State
McInally, Pat (P)	6-5	200	24	2	Harvard

(Pk)—Placekicker   (P)—Punter

Bahr was just over .500 as a rookie field-goaler. The Bengals say they are happy with McInally's punting. PERF. QT.: 3.

DEFENSE

FRONT LINEMEN	Ht	Wt	Age	Exp	College
Bacon, Coy (E)	6-4	270	35	10	Jackson State
Burley, Gary (E)	6-3	262	24	2	Pittsburgh
Carpenter, Ron (T)	6-5	265	29	8	North Carolina State
Brown, Bob (T)	6-5	280	37	13	Arkansas AM&N
Kollar, Bill (T)	6-4	256	24	4	Montana
Johnson, Ken (E)	6-6	262	30	7	Indiana

(E)—End   (T)—Tackle

Is former Ram and Charger Bacon a one-year wonder? He isn't Paul Brown's type of player and he is 35 years old. In a postponed rookie debut, Burley improved on the work of the departed Sherman White. Carpenter, the "stay-home" tackle, anchors this unit. Brown may finally have had it. Kollar, hurt much of '76, could challenge. Johnson could find his roster spot taken by a fresh face. PERF. QT.: 2.

LINEBACKERS	Ht	Wt	Age	Exp	College
Williams, Reggie (O)	6-1	230	22	2	Dartmouth
Harris, Bo (O)	6-3	228	24	3	Louisiana State
LeClair, Jim (M)	6-3	237	26	6	North Dakota
Pritchard, Ron (O)	6-1	226	30	9	Arizona State
Devlin, Chris (O)	6-2	228	23	3	Penn State
Cameron, Glenn (M)	6-1	230	24	3	Florida
Kuhn, Ken (O)	6-1	225	23	1	Ohio State

(O)—Outside Linebacker   (M)—Middle Linebacker

Rookie Williams was one of the NFL's most pleasant surprises in 1976. Harris blossomed in his soph season. LeClair is now near the equal of Bill Bergey, who departed three years ago. The retooling the Bengals started in this department a few campaigns ago is now complete, and it was for the better. Pritchard, now that he's lost his job, wants out. Devlin and Cameron are next on the development program. Kuhn, a prospect, makes a delayed rookie appearance. PERF. QT.: 2.

CORNERBACKS	Ht	Wt	Age	Exp	College
Parrish, Lemar	5-10	180	29	8	Lincoln
Riley, Ken	5-11	183	30	9	Florida A&M
Perry, Scott	6-0	185	23	2	Williams

The Bengals led the AFC in pass defense. It was no accident. Parrish and Riley are as good a tandem as plays in the NFL. Perry has a future, but he can't figure on much playing time. PERF. QT.: 1.

SAFETIES	Ht	Wt	Age	Exp	College
Casanova, Tom (S)	6-2	194	27	6	Louisiana State
Cobb, Marvin (W)	6-0	185	24	3	Southern California
Morgan, Melvin (S-W)	5-11	175	24	2	Mississippi Valley
(S)—Strong-side			(W)—Weak-side or "Free" Safety		

Casanova made the Pro Bowl last season after his finest work as a pro. Cobb does a good job, too. He'd better, with the swift young Morgan pushing him hard. PERF. QT.: 2.

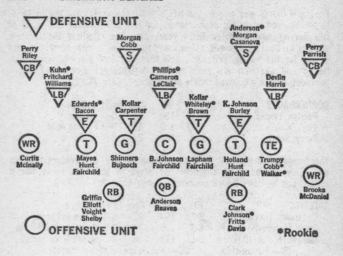

DEFENSIVE UNIT

Perry
Riley
CB

Kuhn
Pritchard
Williams
LB

Morgan
Cobb
S

Phillips
Cameron
LeClair
LB

Anderson
Morgan
Casanova
S

Devlin
Harris
LB

Perry
Parrish
CB

Edwards
Bacon
E

Kollar
Carpenter
T

Kollar
Whiteley
Brown
T

K. Johnson
Burley
E

WR
Curtis
McInally

T
Mayes
Hunt
Fairchild

G
Shinners
Bujnoch

C
B. Johnson
Fairchild

G
Lapham
Fairchild

T
Holland
Hunt
Fairchild

TE
Trumpy
Cobb
Walker

WR
Brooks
McDaniel

RB
Griffin
Elliott
Voight
Shelby

QB
Anderson
Reaves

RB
Clark
Johnson
Fritts
Davis

OFFENSIVE UNIT

*Rookie

1977 DRAFT SELECTIONS

1A	Edwards, Eddie	DE	6-4	242	Miami, Fla.
1B	Whitley, Wilson	DT	6-2	268	Houston
1C	Cobb, Mike	TE	6-5	241	Michigan State
2	Johnson, Pete	FB	6-1	248	Ohio State
3	Voight, Mike	RB	6-0	210	North Carolina
4A	Walker, Rick	TE	6-4	226	UCLA
4B	Wilson, Mike	T	6-5	255	Georgia
4C	Anderson, Jerry	S	6-0	187	Oklahoma
5	Phillips, Ray	LB	6-4	225	Nebraska
6	Dunlven, Tommy	QB	6-2	211	Texas Tech
7A	Breeden, Louis	DB	6-0	190	N. C. Central
7B	Corbett, Jim	TE	6-4	228	Pittsburgh
8	St. Victor, Jose	G	6-4	245	Syracuse
9	Zacahary, Willie	WR	6-1	185	Central St., Ohio
10	Bialik, Bob	P	6-0	195	Hillsdale
11A	Parrish, Joel	G	6-3	242	Georgia
11B	Allen, Carl	DB	6-0	186	So. Mississippi
12	Percival, Alex	WR	6-3	180	Morehouse

The Bengals drafted two of the quickest pursuers in football in the first round in Edwards and Whitley. They'll combine with Burley to provide one of the quickest lines in football some day. Cobb fills the hole caused by Bruce Coslet's retirement. If Boobie wants to "go on vacation," as he tends to do at times, Johnson can take his job away. He'll team with his college mate, Griffin. Voight is the type of runner the Bengals like, straight-ahead and hard. Wilson and Parrish signed in Canada before the draft. They'll probably return to help some day. The Bengals gambled that Anderson will come back from a knee injury. Phillips has a chance. PERF. QT.: 1.

American Conference • Central Division

PITTSBURGH STEELERS

Prediction: Second

Maybe someone in Pittsburgh should introduce Chuck Noll to Terry Bradshaw.

The Steelers win on defense, most of the time, but every now and then they need major help from their offense. When they played Oakland in the AFC championship game last season, they were minus super fullback Franco Harris and reliable halfback Rocky Bleier. Both had been hurt in the previous playoff game against Baltimore. To compensate for their absence, Coach Noll made significant alterations in his offense.

After seven seasons of exposure to quarterback Bradshaw's intellect, he should have known he wasn't dealing with one of the giant thinkers of our time. But whether because of lack of a grasp of the new offense or lack of execution, the attack plan died with a resounding thud.

Starting anew in 1977, the Steelers still have plenty of talent on hand to make a run at regaining their crown—as long as Harris and most of his colleagues stay healthy and Noll overcomes the temptation to outcoach himself.

Franco had another terrific year, rushing for 1128 yards, and Bleier, who is supposed to be around for his blocking and receiving, gained 1036.

Bradshaw missed six starts because of injury, but when the Steelers bombed the Colts in the first play-off game he went 14-of-18 for 264 yards and three touchdowns. In familiar surroundings, he is still one of the league's most dangerous quarterbacks, and he runs his offense, when it is intact, with sure-handedness.

Spearheading that offense for the Steelers is their gem of an offensive line.

Mike Webster takes over at center full-time from retired Ray Mansfield, with versatile Gerry Mullins at one guard and Jim Clack and Sam Davis fighting over the other. Jon Kolb and Gordon Gravelle are seasoned tackles. Behind the starters are such impressive reserves as Ray Pinney and Jim Files (hurt throughout his inaugural campaign) and a pack of hungry rookies.

If there are offensive changes, they are likely to happen in the receiving department.

Larry Brown is the tight end of record and Randy Grossman plays a lot, but huge Bennie Cunningham is the favorite to win the job in his second pro season. Lynn Swann is one of the NFL's most dangerous deep receivers on one side, while Frank Lewis tries to beat off John Stallworth on the other.

Behind Harris and Bleier are Frenchy Fuqua, Reggie Harrison, Jack Deloplaine and Mike Collier—a combination of journeymen vets and untested youngsters.

Down the stretch in 1976, when they had to win every week to make the playoffs, the Steelers' defense racked up five shutouts and had eight games in which the opposition did not score a touchdown. There is little reason to believe this unit will collapse in '77.

Joe Greene came back strongly from his 1975 arm injury late in the season. His tackle partner, Ernie Holmes, beat an off-season drug rap to remain eligible.

The ends, L.C. Greenwood and Dwight White, are no less hostile than they used to be. Steve Furness, John Banaszak and young Gary Dunn provide backup strength.

The major alteration in the Steel Curtain platoon in 1977 will be at outside linebacker, where Andy Russell retired after a dozen seasons. Replacing him will be no small task. Loren Toews has been getting ready for four years, but the Steelers will miss Russell's direction and leadership.

Toews will have good companions. Jack Lambert is the popular choice for All-Pro middle linebacker and Jack Ham is literally an automatic All-Pro on the strong-side.

The major problem there is depth. Marv Kellum is the only other experienced backer of consequence on the roster. To shore up this area, Pittsburgh made New Mexico's Robin Cole its first draft choice, and selected Dennis Winston of Arkansas on the fifth round.

The cornerbacks, Mel Blount and J.T. Thomas, rank among the best at their position in the NFL. The same goes for the safeties, Glen Edwards and Mike Wagner. The subs, corner Jimmy Allen and safety Donnie Shell, can step in and play.

Roy Gerela had just a fair year as a placekicker, but he was nagged by injuries. At 39, Bobby Walden should think about retiring, but 22 of his punts landed inside the 20-yard line in '76.

The schedule is not easy. The Steelers play eight of their first 10 games against teams that had winning records last year. They are in the same conference as the powerful Cincinnati Bengals, and they have a tougher set of opponents than their major rival's. But, count on it: Pittsburgh will be in contention for a postseason spot in 1977.

1976 RECORD (11-5)

28	Oakland	31	14	Miami		3
31	Cleveland	14	32	Houston		16
27	New England	30	7	Cincinnati		3
6	Minnesota	17	42	Tampa Bay		0
16	Cleveland	18	21	Houston		0
23	Cincinnati	6		(Playoff)		
27	New York Giants	0	40	Baltimore		14
23	San Diego	0		(AFC Championship)		
45	Kansas City	0	7	Oakland		24

PASSING

	Atts	Comps	Yds	Lgst	TDs	Ints	Pct
Bradshaw	192	92	1177	50	10	9	47.9
Kruczek	85	51	758	64	0	3	60.0

SCORING

	TDs†	PATs	FGs	Total
Harris	14†	0	0	84
Gerela	0	40	14	82
Bleier	5	0	0	30
Harrison	4	0	0	24
Three tied with	3	0	0	18

RUSHING

	Atts	Yds	TDs	Lgst	Avg
Harris	289	1128	14†	30	3.9
Bleier	220	1036	5	28	4.7
Harrison	54	235	4	27	4.4
Bradshaw	31	219	3	17	7.1

RECEIVING

	Recs	Yds	TDs	Lgst	Avg
Swann	28	516	3	47	18.4
Bleier	24	294	0	32	12.3
Harris	23	151	0	39	6.6
Lewis	17	306	1	64	18.0
Grossman	15	181	1	35	12.1

INTERCEPTIONS

	Ints	Yds	TDs	Lgst	Avg
Edwards	6	95	0	55	15.8
Blount	6	75	0	28	12.5
Four tied with 2					

SYMBOL †—Conference leader

1977 SCHEDULE

Home: Sept. 19—San Francisco; Sept. 25—Oakland; Oct. 17—Cincinnati; Oct. 23—Houston; Nov. 13—Cleveland; Nov. 20—Dallas; Dec. 4—Seattle.

Away: Oct. 2—Cleveland; Oct. 9—Houston; Oct. 30—Baltimore; Nov. 6—Denver; Nov. 27—New York Jets; Dec. 10—Cincinnati; Dec. 18—San Diego.

OFFENSE

QUARTERBACKS	Ht	Wt	Age	Exp	College
Bradshaw, Terry	6-3	210	28	8	Louisiana Tech
Kruczek, Mike	6-0	196	24	2	Boston College
Graff, Neil	6-3	200	27	4	Wisconsin

Bradshaw seemed to regress in '76, but part of that was due to injuries. Kruczek started several games under heavy wraps. We'll hear more of him in the future. Graff doesn't count. PERF. QT.: 2.

RUNNING BACKS	Ht	Wt	Age	Exp	College
Harris, Franco	6-2	230	27	6	Penn State
Bleier, Rocky	5-11	210	31	9	Notre Dame
Fuqua, John	5-11	200	29	9	Morgan State
Harrison, Reggie	5-11	220	27	4	Cincinnati
Deloplaine, Jack	5-10	205	23	2	Salem, W. Va.
Collier, Mike	5-11	200	23	2	Morgan State

Franco, healthy, is awesome. And in big games he's even better than that. Bleier is vital in this fullback-oriented offense. He blocks, runs, catches. When they were hurt in the playoffs, the attack died. So the search is on for reserves. Of the subs listed, Deloplaine is the most interesting. Fuqua may be about used up. Harrison isn't the answer. Collier is iffy. PERF. QT.: 2.

RECEIVERS	Ht	Wt	Age	Exp	College
Lewis, Frank (W)	6-1	196	30	7	Grambling
Swann, Lynn (W)	6-0	180	25	4	Southern California
Cunningham, Bennie (T)	6-4	255	22	2	Clemson
Stallworth, John (W)	6-2	185	25	4	Alabama A&M
Bell, Theo (W)	5-11	180	23	2	Arizona
Brown, Larry (T)	6-4	230	28	7	Kansas
Grossman, Randy (T)	6-1	215	23	4	Temple
Pough, Ernie (W)	6-1	174	25	2	Texas Southern
Garrett, Reggie (W)	6-1	175	26	3	Eastern Michigan
Leak, Curtis (W)	5-11	180	23	1	Johnson C. Smith

(W)—Wide Receiver　　　(T)—Tight End

If the Steelers can prevent Swann from becoming punchy and Lewis and Stallworth from falling victim to nagging leg injuries, they may get production from their passing game to equal 1975's. Last year Swann led the team in catches with 28, 21 less than '75—and he had eight less TDs than in the previous season. Cunningham, a young stallion, should start. Bell has speed and promise. Brown could be used as trade bait if Cunningham comes through; Grossman is a competent backup. Pough, like Bell, is talented. Garrett missed 1976 with injury and had back surgery in the off-season. He's not likely to come back. Leak is a longshot. PERF. QT.: 2.

INTERIOR LINEMEN	Ht	Wt	Age	Exp	College
Kolb, Jon (T)	6-3	262	30	9	Oklahoma State
Gravelle, Gordon (T)	6-5	255	28	6	Brigham Young
Davis, Sam (G)	6-1	250	33	11	Allen
Mullins, Gerry (G)	6-3	240	28	7	Southern California
Webster, Mike (C)	6-1	245	25	4	Wisconsin
Pinney, Ray (T-C)	6-4	240	23	2	Washington
Clack, Jim (G-C)	6-3	250	29	7	Wake Forest
Files, Jim (G-C)	6-2	246	24	1	McNeese State

(T)—Tackle   (G)—Guard   (C)—Center

This is one of the NFL's most underrated lines. Kolb is solid, as is Gravelle, who was hurt late last year. Davis is aging, but he's still useful. Mullins had to play tackle when Gravelle was hurt. Gerry is also used as a tight end in the Steelers' short-yardage offense. If they left him at guard, he could be one of the league's finest. Webster is another capable performer. Pinney is promising. Clack is about ready to move ahead of Davis. Files, hurt in his rookie camp, makes his debut—and it's anxiously awaited. PERF. QT.: 2.

KICKERS	Ht	Wt	Age	Exp	College
Gerela, Roy (Pk)	5-10	190	29	9	New Mexico State
Walden, Bobby (P)	6-1	197	39	14	Georgia

(Pk)—Placekicker   (P)—Punter

Gerela did not have his typical year in '76, but injuries can be blamed. Walden, as he has for eons, punted well. PERF. QT.: 3.

DEFENSE

FRONT LINEMEN	Ht	Wt	Age	Exp	College
Greenwood, L.C. (E)	6-6	245	30	9	Arkansas AM&N
White, Dwight (E)	6-4	255	28	7	East Texas State
Greene, Joe (T)	6-4	275	30	9	North Texas State
Holmes, Ernie (T)	6-3	260	29	6	Texas Southern
Banaszak, John (E)	6-4	232	27	3	Eastern Michigan
Furness, Steve (T)	6-4	255	26	6	Rhode Island
Dunn, Gary (T)	6-3	240	24	2	Miami, Fla.

(E)—End   (T)—Tackle

Oakland murdered this group in the AFC title game last season, and that could be the inspiration for these guys to reclaim their title. Greenwood can be ferocious, and some experts say White is even better.

Greene started playing up to his reputation late in '76. Holmes beat another legal rap, and the last time he did that he had a super year. Banaszak is a good one. Furness could start for most clubs. Dunn has promise but can't get playing time. PERF. QT.: 1.

LINEBACKERS	Ht	Wt	Age	Exp	College
Ham, Jack (O)	6-1	225	28	7	Penn State
Toews, Loren (O)	6-3	222	25	5	California
Lambert, Jack (M)	6-4	220	25	4	Kent State
Kellum, Marv (M-O)	6-2	225	25	4	Wichita State
Humphrey, Al (O)	6-3	225	24	1	Tulsa
Blankenship, Greg (O)	6-0	208	23	2	Hayward State

(O)—Outside Linebacker   (M)—Middle Linebacker

Ham is the ever-efficient All-Pro. Toews is the heir-designate to the retired Andy Russell's job but the youngster is by no means fully tested. Lambert is just as wild a head-hunter as ever. Kellum is the only serviceable sub, so the search is on for reserves. Humphrey, a '75 draft who went to the WFL and CFL, was hurt in training camp last year. Blankenship isn't the answer. PERF. QT.: 2.

CORNERBACKS	Ht	Wt	Age	Exp	College
Thomas, J.T.	6-2	196	26	5	Florida State
Blount, Mel	6-3	200	29	9	Southern
Allen, Jimmy	6-2	194	25	4	UCLA

Everyone knows you can't run on the Steelers, so the opposition tries to throw. Thomas and Blount keep demonstrating that route isn't easy, either. Allen can play if needed. PERF. QT.: 1.

SAFETIES	Ht	Wt	Age	Exp	College
Wagner, Mike (S)	6-1	210	29	7	Western Illinois
Edwards, Glen (W)	6-0	185	30	7	Florida A&M
Shell, Donnie (S-W)	5-11	195	25	4	South Carolina State

(S)—Strong-side   (W)—Weak-side or "Free" Safety

Both Wagner and Edwards have cornerbacks' speed. Both are hitters, both are smart. With Shell, another sub who can play, in reserve, this is one of the team's best fortified positions. PERF. QT.: 1.

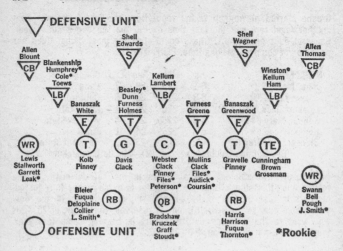

DEFENSIVE UNIT

Allen Blount — **CB**
Blankenship
Humphrey•
Cole•
Toews — **LB**
Shell Edwards — **S**
Banaszak White — **E**
Beasley Dunn Furness Holmes — **T**
Kellum Lambert — **LB**
Furness Greene — **T**
Banaszak Greenwood — **E**
Shell Wagner — **S**
Winston• Kellum Ham — **LB**
Allen Thomas — **CB**

OFFENSIVE UNIT

WR — Lewis Stallworth Garrett Leak•
T — Kolb Pinney
G — Davis Clack
C — Webster Clack Pinney Files• Peterson•
G — Mullins Clack Files• Audick• Coursin•
T — Gravelle Pinney
TE — Cunningham Brown Grossman
WR — Swann Bell Pough J. Smith•

RB — Bleier Fuqua Deloplaine Collier L. Smith•
QB — Bradshaw Kruczek Graff Stoudt•
RB — Harris Harrison Fuqua Thornton•

•**Rookie**

1977 DRAFT SELECTIONS

1	Cole, Robin	LB	6-2	220	New Mexico
2	Thornton, Sid	RB	5-11	233	N. W. Louisiana
3A	Beasley, Tom	DT	6-5	235	Virginia Tech
3B	Smith, Jim	WR	6-3	200	Michigan
4A	Peterson, Ted	C	6-3	245	Eastern Illinois
4B	Smith, Laverne	RB	6-0	190	Kansas
4C	Audick, Dan	G	6-3	235	Hawaii
5A	Stoudt, Cliff	QB	6-5	207	Youngstown
5B	Coursin, Steve	G	6-1	258	South Carolina
5C	Winston, Dennis	LB	6-1	228	Arkansas
6	Harris, Paul	LB	6-3	204	Alabama
7	Frisch, Randy	DT	6-4	250	Missouri
8	August, Phil	WR-DB	6-3	195	Miami
9	Kelly, Roosevelt	TE	6-3	214	Eastern Kentucky
10A	Cowans, Al	DB	6-0	190	Florida
10B	LaCrosse, Dave	LB	6-3	205	Wake Forest
11	West, Lou	DB	5-11	167	Cincinnati
12	Stephens, Jim	TE	6-2	233	Florida

With Andy Russell retired, the Steelers had to protect themselves at line-backer, so they took Cole, a swift stinger. Thornton is a low-slung power runner. Beasley should be ready when older gents on the front four are ready for retirement. The Smiths could be steals. Some scouts projected both to be selected on the first round. Jim should help on kick returns right away, but he needs to develop concentration as a receiver. Laverne has speed and wiggles, although his hands are suspect. Peterson and Audick each stand a chance, as does Stoudt, a big strong quarterback, like Bradshaw. Coursin and Winston also can make the big roster. **PERF. QT.: 2.**

HOUSTON OILERS

Prediction: Third

Can Dan Pastorini find happiness in Houston?

Can Houston find happiness with Dan Pastorini as its quarterback?

The answers to these questions probably will tell the story of the Oilers' 1977 season. This team needs the reluctant quarterback at his very best in order to reverse its backslide of 1976.

Pastorini spent a large part of the winter telling the Oilers and almost everyone else how he didn't want to play for them any more. The NFL rumor mill had him going to the Los Angeles Rams or one of a variety of other clubs.

Nothing materialized. Pastorini wanted to go to Los Angeles and the Rams would have welcomed him. But where would that have left the Oilers?

They need Dante, as long as he possesses a good attitude and mental sharpness, for at least three reasons. One is that their running game is second rate. Another is that their offensive line is third rate. A third is that their defense isn't quite as formidable as it was when the Oilers went 10-4 two seasons ago.

Last year they started out of the gate with a rush. After the first month they had a 4-1 record. They finished 5-9.

John Hadl did a lot of the quarterbacking late in the season. He's a good man to have on the roster. But he is 37 years old, too old to start for a team like the Oilers. If a resurgence is to take place in Houston, Pastorini must lead it.

The Oilers are the thinnest team in the sharply competitive Central Division of the American Conference. They must have superior quarterbacking to keep up with Pittsburgh, Cincinnati and Cleveland. And remember, the Browns passed them in the standings last year.

Ronnie Coleman is, by far, the best running back the Oilers have. He finished 14th in AFC rushing with 684 yards. But he is not the game-breaker type. The fullback, Don Hardeman, is a tough, rugged bocker, but he doesn't have the quickness to be the bread-and-butter power runner the Oilers thought he would be when they drafted him in the first round two years ago. To give Coleman a more productive partner, the Oilers used a pair of third-round picks to draft fullbacks, Maryland's hard-knocking Tim Wilson and Rob Carpenter of Miami of Ohio.

The receiving was largely a one-man show last year. That man was Ken Burrough, who caught 51 passes, seven for touchdowns. It was a mistake to play Billy "White Shoes" Johnson opposite him. Regular duty just wore Johnson down so that he was less effective on kickoff and punt returns.

The answer might be to switch Mike Barber from tight end to wide receiver. Barber was the Oilers' highest draft pick last year, a second-round choice, but got hurt just as the season started. He has loads of speed and not much blocking ability. If they do switch him, John Sawyer, a tough blocker, will be the starting tight end.

The first two draft picks for 1977 were offensive linemen. Both, Missouri tackle Morris Towns and Penn State guard George Reihner, could start.

The incumbent line lists 34-year-old Elbert Drungo and Greg Sampson at tackles, Ed Fisher and Conway Hayman at guards with Carl Mauck, probably the best of the lot, at center.

The three-man defensive front that carried the Oilers for better than a season and a half is now altered. Tody Smith departed and in his place at end is Al Burton, who has a lot of trouble keeping up with his two star linemates, end Elvin Bethea and nose tackle Curley Culp.

The linebacking is still first rate, particularly on the outside, where All-Pro Robert Brazile and Ted Washington reside. Gregg Bingham and Steve Kiner are veterans in the middle, but one could be pushed by Tim Rossovich, who made a comeback last year. Art Stringer, a rookie who spent last season on the injured reserve list, could come back to upgrade the linebacker reserves.

The secondary is one of the team's soundest areas. Zeke Moore is in his 11th pro season and is just as cantankerous as ever. Young Greg Stemrick could push Willie Alexander, who has been around for seven seasons, to the bench. Regardless of who starts alongside Moore, this department will be a strong one.

Mike Weger, signed after he played out his option in Detroit, steadies things at free safety. C. L. Whittington is a savage at strong-side safety.

Skip Butler is turning into one of the more reliable placekickers. He went 16 for 27 in field goals last year. Quarterback Pastorini handled Houston's punting duties in 1976. He didn't do a very good job, and the search is on for a replacement.

1976 RECORD (5-9)

20	Tampa Bay	0	14	Baltimore	38
13	Buffalo	3	7	Cleveland	21
13	Oakland	14	27	Cincinnati	31
31	New Orleans	26	16	Pittsburgh	32
17	Denver	3	20	Atlanta	14
27	San Diego	30	10	Cleveland	13
7	Cincinnati	27	0	Pittsburgh	21

PASSING

	Atts	Comps	Yds	Lgst	TDs	Ints	Pct
Pastorini	309	167	1795	67	10	10	54.0
Hadl	113	60	634	69	7	8	53.1

SCORING

	TDs	PATs	FGs	Total
Butler	0	24	16	72
Burrough	7	0	0	42
Coleman	6	0	0	36
B. Johnson	4	0	0	24
Willis	3	0	0	18

RUSHING

	Atts	Yds	TDs	Lgst	Avg
Coleman	171	684	2	39	4.0
Willis	148	542	2	44	3.7
Hardeman	32	114	1	21	3.6
Dawkins	31	61	1	7	2.0

RECEIVING

	Recs	Yds	TDs	Lgst	Avg
Burrough	51	932	7	69	18.3
B. Johnson	47	495	4	40	10.5
Coleman	40	247	3	19	6.2
Willis	32	255	1	42	8.0
Alston	19	174	1	29	9.2
Sawyer	18	208	1	53	11.6

INTERCEPTIONS

	Ints	Yds	TDs	Lgst	Avg
Whittington	5	103	0	50	20.6
Bingham	2	18	0	15	9.0

1977 SCHEDULE

Home: Sept. 18—New York Jets; Oct. 9—Pittsburgh; Oct. 16—Cleveland; Nov. 6—Chicago; Nov. 27—Kansas City; Dec. 4—Denver; Dec. 18—Cincinnati.

Away: Sept. 25—Green Bay; Oct. 2—Miami; Oct. 23—Pittsburgh; Oct. 30—Cincinnati; Nov. 13—Oakland; Nov. 20—Seattle; Dec. 11—Cleveland.

OFFENSE

QUARTERBACKS	Ht	Wt	Age	Exp	College
Pastorini, Dan	6-3	205	28	7	Santa Clara
Hadl, John	6-1	215	37	16	Kansas
Foote, Jim	6-2	210	25	3	Delaware Valley

Pastorini is wearing out his welcome. He rarely plays up to his ability, but the team's hopes rest with him. Hadl, good for occasional stints, is no starter. Foote is a hanger-on. PERF. QT.: 3.

RUNNING BACKS	Ht	Wt	Age	Exp	College
Coleman, Ronnie	5-11	198	26	4	Alabama A&M
Hardeman, Don	6-2	235	25	3	Texas A&I
Willis, Fred	6-0	205	29	7	Boston College
Dawkins, Joe	6-2	220	29	8	Wisconsin
Taylor, Altie	5-10	200	29	9	Utah State
Rodgers, Willie	6-1	210	28	6	Kentucky State
Johnson, Al	6-0	200	27	6	Cincinnati

There are no first-echelon runners here. Coleman, the best of the lot, is an honest player. Hardeman is a tough, rugged guy, but he just doesn't have the footwork to help big. Willis is an injury-prone journeyman. Dawkins and Taylor no longer have big-league ability, though the former may scrape by for another year. Rodgers comes off the injury list. He's never been a major contributor. Johnson has had his chances and hasn't delivered. PERF. QT.: 4.

RECEIVERS	Ht	Wt	Age	Exp	College
Burrough, Ken (W)	6-3	210	29	8	Texas Southern
Johnson, Billy (W)	5-9	170	25	4	Widener
Sawyer, John (T)	6-2	230	24	3	So. Mississippi
Barber, Mike (T-W)	6-3	225	23	1	Louisiana Tech
Alston, Mack (T)	6-3	230	30	8	Maryland State
Thomas, Earl (W)	6-3	215	28	7	Houston
Darby, Al (W)	6-5	225	22	2	Florida

(W)—Wide Receiver   (T)—Tight End

Burrough had another big year in '76. The Oilers say he will catch in traffic now, but there are doubters. "White Shoes" can't be used as a regular and still be a kick return ace. Sawyer gives his all, but it isn't enough. Barber was injured and missed his rookie season. He can catch and run, but will he block if he plays tight end? Alston isn't much. Thomas could lift the entire offense if he plays back to his St. Louis days. Darby isn't the answer. PERF. QT.: 4.

INTERIOR LINEMEN	Ht	Wt	Age	Exp	College
Drungo, Elbert (T)	6-5	265	34	9	Tennessee State
Sampson, Greg (T)	6-6	270	26	6	Stanford
Fisher, Ed (G)	6-3	250	28	4	Arizona State
Hayman, Conway (G)	6-3	260	28	5	Delaware
Mauck, Carl (C)	6-4	250	30	9	Southern Illinois
Hunt, Kevin (T)	6-5	260	28	7	Doane
Havig, Dennis (G)	6-3	251	28	7	Colorado
Lou, Ron (C)	6-2	242	26	5	Arizona State

(T)—Tackle   (G)—Guard   (C)—Center

The Oilers finished last in the AFC in ground gaining in 1976, and these guys have to take much of the blame. They do a better job of protecting the passer, though. At 34, Drungo has about had it. Sampson never became the stud they thought he'd be. Both guards would have trouble finding work elsewhere. Mauck, however, is solid. The problem is that the reserves—all of them—are no better than any of the starters, and the Oilers seem reluctant to trade any defensive talent in exchange for help in this area. PERF. QT.: 4.

KICKERS	Ht	Wt	Age	Exp	College
Butler, Skip (Pk)	6-0	200	29	8	Texas-Arlington
Pastorini, Dan (P)	6-3	205	28	7	Santa Clara

(Pk)—Placekicker   (P)—Punter

Butler's kicking is vital to a team like this that doesn't have much offensive punch. Pastorini is a fair punter, at best. PERF. QT.: 3.

DEFENSE

FRONT LINEMEN	Ht	Wt	Age	Exp	College
Bethea, Elvin (E)	6-2	255	31	10	North Carolina A&T
Burton, Al (E)	6-5	265	25	2	Bethune-Cookman
Culp, Curley (T)	6-1	265	30	10	Arizona State
Little, John (T-E)	6-3	250	30	8	Oklahoma State
Owens, Joe (E)	6-3	255	30	8	Alcorn

(E)—End   (T)—Tackle

Bethea is, justifiably, an established star. Burton started often as a rookie but had trouble keeping up with the vets. It is said that Culp, like Pastorini, has just about worn out his welcome in Houston. That's hard to figure, because he and the team had their best days together. Little and Owens are below average. PERF. QT.: 2.

LINEBACKERS

	Ht	Wt	Age	Exp	College
Brazile, Robert (O)	6-4	238	24	3	Jackson State
Washington, Ted (O)	6-1	245	29	5	Mississippi Valley
Bingham, Gregg (M)	6-1	230	26	5	Purdue
Kiner, Steve (M)	6-1	225	30	7	Tennessee
Rossovich, Tim (M)	6-4	240	31	9	Southern California
Benson, Duane (O)	6-2	225	32	11	Hamline
Thompson, Ted (M)	6-1	220	24	3	Southern Methodist
Stringer, Art (O)	6-1	223	23	1	Ball State

(O)—Outside Linebacker　　　(M)—Middle Linebacker

It's only the third pro season for Brazile, and NFLers are already calling him the best in the league. Washington is underrated; he's a superb blitzer. Bingham is a sound player. Kiner's career got off to a rocky start, but he's found a home here and keeps improving. Rossovich, another comeback kid, plays excellently in the four-linebacker formation. Benson provides savvy and toughness, but age is rapidly overcoming him. Thompson is another competent player, though the least of this group. Stringer, hurt in his rookie year, is highly regarded. PERF. QT.: 1.

CORNERBACKS

	Ht	Wt	Age	Exp	College
Moore, Zeke	6-3	195	33	11	Lincoln
Alexander, Willie	6-3	195	27	7	Alcorn
Stemrick, Greg	5-11	185	25	3	Colorado State
Akili, Samaji Adi	6-1	187	25	4	New Mex. Highlands

Moore is still at the top of the game; he's a real head-hunter. Alexander is also a classy player, though young Stemrick will give him the fight of his life for the first-string job. Akili, formerly known as Sam Williams, won't make it. PERF. QT.: 2.

SAFETIES

	Ht	Wt	Age	Exp	College
Whittington, C.L. (S)	6-1	200	25	4	Prairie View
Weger, Mike (W)	6-2	200	31	10	Bowling Green
Reinfeldt, Mike (W-S)	6-2	195	24	2	Wisc.-Milwaukee
Walker, Donnie (S)	6-2	180	26	3	Central State, Ohio

(S)—Strong-side　　　(W)—Weak-side or "Free" Safety

Whittington is a savage hitter who is just coming into his own. Weger, signed after playing out his option in Detroit, stabilized the entire secondary. Reinfeldt is a former Raider prospect; in his case, Oakland let one get away. Walker is a camp body. PERF. QT.: 2.

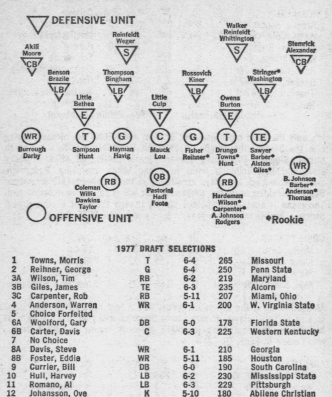

DEFENSIVE UNIT

Akili
Moore
CB

Reinfeldt
Weger
S

Walker
Reinfeldt
Whittington
S

Stemrick
Alexander
CB

Benson
Brazile
LB

Thompson
Bingham
LB

Rossovich
Kiner
LB

Stringer●
Washington
LB

Little
Bethea
E

Little
Culp
T

Owens
Burton
E

WR
Burrough
Darby

T
Sampson
Hunt

G
Hayman
Havig

C
Mauck
Lou

G
Fisher
Reihner●

T
Drungo
Towns●
Hunt

TE
Sawyer
Barber●
Alston
Giles●

RB
Coleman
Willis
Dawkins
Taylor

QB
Pastorini
Hadl
Foote

RB
Hardeman
Wilson●
Carpenter●
A. Johnson
Rodgers

WR
B. Johnson
Barber●
Anderson●
Thomas

OFFENSIVE UNIT   ●Rookie

1977 DRAFT SELECTIONS

1	Towns, Morris	T	6-4	265	Missouri
2	Reihner, George	G	6-4	250	Penn State
3A	Wilson, Tim	RB	6-2	219	Maryland
3B	Giles, James	TE	6-3	235	Alcorn
3C	Carpenter, Rob	RB	5-11	207	Miami, Ohio
4	Anderson, Warren	WR	6-1	200	W. Virginia State
5	Choice Forfeited				
6A	Woolford, Gary	DB	6-0	178	Florida State
6B	Carter, Davis	C	6-3	225	Western Kentucky
7	No Choice				
8A	Davis, Steve	WR	6-1	210	Georgia
8B	Foster, Eddie	WR	5-11	185	Houston
9	Currier, Bill	DB	6-0	190	South Carolina
10	Hull, Harvey	LB	6-2	230	Mississippi State
11	Romano, Al	LB	6-3	229	Pittsburgh
12	Johansson, Ove	K	5-10	180	Abilene Christian

The Oilers moved to build up one of the NFL's flabbiest offensive lines with Towns and Reihner, both of whom may start immediately. Reihner also played defense in college. Wilson and/or Carpenter may give Hardeman a battle for the fullback assignment. Giles could displace a veteran as a TE reserve. The lack of quality at wide receiver gives Anderson a chance. **PERF. QT.: 4.**

CLEVELAND BROWNS

Prediction: Fourth

Of the 13 National Football League teams that won more games than they lost in 1976, the Cleveland Browns' record was the most fragile.

The Browns won nine games last year. The aggregate margin of victory in five of those contests was 16 points. None of the 13 winning teams scored as few points as Cleveland. None of them gave up as many points as the Browns. None of them scored less than they gave up, as Cleveland did.

Just one year previously the Browns were a 3-11 team. Could they slip back into that kind of morass again? Followers of the team will have some indication after the first four games of the season; in them the Browns will confront some of the strongest teams in the NFL. They start against the Cincinnati Bengals, followed by New England, Pittsburgh and the champion Oakland Raiders.

For all intents and purposes, the Browns are now in the hands of Brian Sipe, who was the club's 13th draft choice five years ago and who hung around Cleveland Stadium for four seasons without attracting much attention. Until last year.

Then he ousted Mike Phipps from the starting quarterback job, threw for 2113 yards, a 57.1 completion percentage and 17 touchdowns. When the season was over the Browns traded Phipps to Chicago, leaving Sipe in total command of the team's offense.

While Sipe's background may not be too impressive, he not only had a big year throwing the ball, but he demonstrated that he could direct a running game.

Greg Pruitt, the Browns' ace, ran for an even 1000 yards in 209 carries, and unheralded fullback Cleo Miller ran for another 613. The Browns' brass hopes that 1976's No. 1 draftee, Mike Pruitt, will push Miller this season. Mike P. has more skills than Miller, and if he can harness them he probably would help Greg P. to greater heights.

Sipe has some formidable targets for his passes, too.

Reggie Rucker always seems to finish among the top catchers in the NFL. Paul Warfield will be playing his final season as a pro, but he's still dangerous. Oscar Roan, the tall tight end, is employed almost as a third wide receiver, something on the line of Richard Caster of the New York Jets.

The Browns' offensive line is none too formidable. Tackle Doug Dieken is solid, but the other linemen seem far from the Pro Bowl. First-stringer Barry Darrow and former starter Gerry Sullivan are seasoned tackles, but not stars. Often-injured Pete Adams was hurt again in the off-season, jeopardizing his career, so young Henry Sheppard will be at one guard with Chuck Hutchison, who missed last season due to an injury, at the other. The center is Cincinnati castoff Tom DeLeone.

Don Cockroft had a so-so year as a placekicker, 15 of 28 field goals, but that average may go up since he will be relieved of his punting chores by rookie Tom Skladany, the Ohio Stater who is reputed to be in the Ray Guy class. Cockroft averaged 38.9 yards on his punts last year, close to the bottom of the AFC standings.

The Cleveland defensive unit puzzles Coach Forrest Gregg. At one point down the stretch of the season it was allowing opponents just eight points a game for the five contests leading to the season finale. Then Kansas City, not a potent team, creamed them for 39.

With that game in mind, the Browns made a middle linebacker, Robert Jackson of Texas A&M, their No. 1. draft choice. He is virtually certain to be an instant starter for them. The rookie will be flanked by Gerald Irons, who had a first-class season after coming from Oakland in a trade, and Charlie Hall, who is considerably underrated. And if Jackson makes it, one of the previous MLB incumbents, Bob Babich and Dick Ambrose, is likely to be used in a trade.

After two seasons, Tony Peters is nearly in the class of his fellow cornerback, Clarence Scott. They are backed by a savvy veteran, former Patriot Ron Bolton.

The Browns' defense pulled together last season when Thom Darden came back from a 1975 knee injury and played free safety in All-Pro style. With strong safety Neal Craig traded to St. Louis the way is open for either Terry Brown or Bill Craven. A pair of rookies, Oliver Davis from Tennessee State and Bill Armstrong from Wake Forest, may also figure there.

The big need in the line is for Mack Mitchell to play end as he was supposed to when he was a premium pick in the draft of '75. He hasn't played well. The other end, Joe Jones, is strictly a fill-in. The strength is at tackle, where All-Pro Jerry Sherk holds forth alongside veteran Earl Edwards now that Walter Johnson has been released.

The team will have to play much better than it did last year to equal its 1976 mark, and that is unlikely to happen against this season's tougher set of opponents.

1976 RECORD (9-5)

38	New York Jets	17	6	Cincinnati		21
14	Pittsburgh	31	21	Houston		7
13	Denver	44	24	Philadelphia		3
24	Cincinnati	45	24	Tampa Bay		7
18	Pittsburgh	16	17	Miami		13
20	Atlanta	17	13	Houston		10
21	San Diego	17	14	Kansas City		39

PASSING

	Atts	Comps	Yds	Lgst	TDs	Ints	Pct
Sipe	312	178	2113	52	17	14	57.1
Phipps**	37	20	146	23	3	0	54.1
Mays	20	9	101	21	0	1	45.0

SCORING

	TDs	PATs	FGs	Total
Cockroft	0	27	15	72
Rucker	8	0	0	48
Warfield	6	0	0	36
G. Pruitt	5	0	0	30
Miller	4	0	0	24
Roan	4	0	0	24

RUSHING

	Atts	Yds	TDs	Lgst	Avg
G. Pruitt	209	1000	4	64	4.8
Miller	153	613	4	21	4.0
Poole	78	356	1	26	4.6
M. Pruitt	52	138	0	18	2.7

RECEIVING

	Recs	Yds	TDs	Lgst	Avg
Rucker	49	676	8	45	13.8
G. Pruitt	45	341	1	27	7.6
Warfield	38	613	6	37	16.1
Miller	16	145	0	38	9.1
Roan	15	174	4	23	11.6

INTERCEPTIONS

	Ints	Yds	TDs	Lgst	Avg
Darden	7	73	0	21	10.4
Scott	4	11	0	5	2.8
Bolton	3	76	1	39	25.3
Babich	2	29	0	21	14.5

SYMBOL **—Traded

1977 SCHEDULE

Home: Sept. 26—New England; Oct. 2—Pittsburgh; Oct. 9—Oakland; Oct. 30—Kansas City; Nov. 6—Cincinnati; Nov. 27—Los Angeles; Dec. 11—Houston.

Away: Sept. 18—Cincinnati; Oct. 16—Houston; Oct. 23—Buffalo; Nov. 13—Pittsburgh; Nov. 20—New York Giants; Dec. 4—San Diego; Dec. 18—Seattle.

QUARTERBACK
Ken Stabler
Oakland Raiders

AFC ALL-STARS/OFFENSE

RUNNING BACK
Franco Harris
Pittsburgh Steelers

RUNNING BACK
O.J. Simpson
Buffalo Bills

WIDE RECEIVER
Charlie Joiner
San Diego Padres

WIDE RECEIVER
Isaac Curtis
Cincinnati Bengals

AFC ALL-STARS/OFFENSE

TIGHT END
Dave Casper
Oakland Raiders

CENTER
Dave Dalby
Oakland Raiders

TACKLE
Leon Gray
New England
Patriots

TACKLE
Art Shell
Oakland Raiders

AFC ALL-STARS/OFFENSE

GUARD
Joe DeLamielleure
Buffalo Bills

GUARD
Gene Upshaw
Oakland Raiders

PLACEKICKER
Jim Turner
Denver Broncos

PUNTER
Ray Guy
Oakland Raiders

AFC ALL-STARS/DEFENSE

END
L.C. Greenwood
Pittsburgh Steelers

END
John Dutton
Baltimore Colts

TACKLE
Jerry Sherk
Cleveland Browns

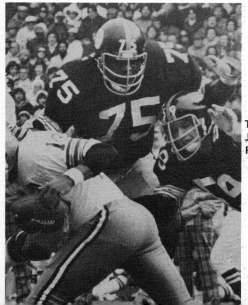

TACKLE
Joe Greene
Pittsburgh Steelers

AFC ALL-STARS/DEFENSE

OUTSIDE LINEBACKER
Phil Villapiano
Oakland Raiders

OUTSIDE LINEBACKER
Jack Ham
Pittsburgh Steelers

AFC ALL-STARS/DEFENSE

MIDDLE LINEBACKER
Jack Lambert
Pittsburgh Steelers

CORNERBACK
Mike Haynes
New England
Patriots

CORNERBACK
Ken Riley
Cincinnati Bengals

AFC ALL-STARS/DEFENSE

**STRONG-SIDE
SAFETY**
George Atkinson
Oakland Raiders

FREE SAFETY
Thom Darden
Cleveland Browns

OFFENSE

QUARTERBACKS	Ht	Wt	Age	Exp	College
Sipe, Brian	6-1	190	28	4	San Diego State
Mays, Dave	6-1	204	28	2	Texas Southern

How did the Browns win nine with Sipe, who won the job from Mike Phipps by default? Former WFLer Mays hasn't had a chance. PERF. QT.: 4.

RUNNING BACKS	Ht	Wt	Age	Exp	College
Pruitt, Greg	5-10	190	26	5	Oklahoma
Miller, Cleo	5-11	202	24	4	Arkansas AM&N
Pruitt, Mike	6-0	214	23	2	Purdue
Poole, Larry	6-1	195	25	3	Kent State
Duncan, Brian	6-0	201	25	2	Southern Methodist

Greg P. comes off his finest pro season. He's a multi-talented star. But where is his help? Miller is a journeyman, at best, and not a power runner. Mike P. had a disappointing rookie year. Poole has some moments, but not too many. Duncan is no answer. Look for a trade to beef up this area. PERF. QT.: 3.

RECEIVERS	Ht	Wt	Age	Exp	College
Warfield, Paul (W)	6-0	188	34	13	Ohio State
Rucker, Reggie (W)	6-2	190	29	8	Boston University
Roan, Oscar (T)	6-6	214	25	3	Southern Methodist
Holden, Steve (W)	6-2	194	26	5	Arizona State
Logan, Dave (W)	6-4	226	23	2	Colorado
Feacher, Ricky (W)	5-10	174	23	2	Mississippi Valley
Lefear, Billy (W)	5-11	197	27	5	Henderson State
Parris, Gary (T)	6-2	226	27	5	Florida State

(W)—Wide Receiver   (T)—Tight End

Warfield is no longer a superstar, but he's still dangerous. The big guy now is Rucker, who always finishes high in the rankings. Roan is known for his catching, not his blocking. The coaches would like to see Holden come on enough to give some rest to Warfield. They haven't given up on Logan, either (he may also be the team's third quarterback). Feacher is valued mostly as a kick returner, as is Lefear, who missed last season because of injury. Parris is a reserve type who could be pushed off the roster. PERF. QT.: 2.

INTERIOR LINEMEN	Ht	Wt	Age	Exp	College
Dieken, Doug (T)	6-5	252	28	7	Illinois
Darrow, Barry (T)	6-7	260	27	4	Montana
Sheppard, Henry (G)	6-6	246	24	2	Southern Methodist
Hutchison, Chuck (G)	6-3	250	28	6	Ohio State

INTERIOR LINEMEN (Contd.)	Ht	Wt	Age	Exp	College
DeLeone, Tom (C)	6-2	248	27	6	Ohio State
Sullivan, Gerry (C-T)	6-4	250	25	4	Illinois
Adams, Pete (G)	6-4	260	26	3	Southern California
Jackson, Bob (G)	6-5	245	24	3	Duke
Dennis, Al (G)	6-4	250	26	3	Grambling

(T)—Tackle   (G)—Guard   (C)—Center

No All-Pros are present, but there's a deep pool of experienced players. Dieken is the best of the bunch. Darrow does an adequate job. Sheppard moves up to starting status; he could develop. Hutchison, who missed '76 due to an injury, is counted on to come back. DeLeone has been helpful since coming from Cincinnati. Sullivan has been a starter, but the line is better with him in a relief role. Adams was hurt again, this last time in the off-season, and that may signal the end of an injury-wracked career. Jackson, too, has started, but not effectively. Dennis is excess baggage. PERF. QT.: 3.

KICKERS	Ht	Wt	Age	Exp	College
Cockroft, Don (Pk-P)	6-1	195	32	10	Adams State
Roder, Mirro (Pk)	6-1	218	33	3	None

(Pk)—Placekicker   (P)—Punter

Cockroft had a sub-par season both as punter and placekicker. It is unlikely, though, that ex-Bear Roder will challenge. PERF. QT.: 3.

DEFENSE

FRONT LINEMEN	Ht	Wt	Age	Exp	College
Mitchell, Mack (E)	6-8	245	25	3	Houston
Jones, Joe (E)	6-6	250	29	7	Tennessee State
Sherk, Jerry (T)	6-5	250	29	8	Oklahoma State
Edwards, Earl (T)	6-7	256	31	9	Wichita
St. Clair, Mike (E)	6-5	245	23	2	Grambling

(E)—End   (T)—Tackle

The big disappointment here is Mitchell. Instead of being a star he's less than a journeyman. Jones isn't dependable, either. Sherk is simply terrific, one of the best. Edwards tries to replace the departed Walter Johnson. They are about equal, considering Johnson's recent decline. St. Clair can't cut it. PERF. QT.: 3.

LINEBACKERS	Ht	Wt	Age	Exp	College
Irons, Gerald (O)	6-2	230	30	8	Md.-Eastern Shore
Hall, Charlie (O)	6-4	230	28	7	Houston
Babich, Bob (M)	6-2	231	30	8	Miami, Ohio

LINEBACKERS (Contd.)	Ht	Wt	Age	Exp	College
Ambrose, Dick (M)	6-0	235	24	3	Virginia
Garlington, John (O)	6-1	221	31	10	Louisiana State
Graf, Dave (O)	6-3	215	24	3	Penn State

(O)—Outside Linebacker   (M)—Middle Linebacker

Irons was a brilliant pickup from Oakland. He upgraded the Browns by a ton. Hall is a solid, though underrated, vet. Both players can move and protect against the pass. Babich and Ambrose have shifted in and out of the starting job. Garlington is experienced and versatile. Graf, a college end, may show a lot of improvement now that he's acclimated to his new position. PERF. QT.: 3.

CORNERBACKS	Ht	Wt	Age	Exp	College
Scott, Clarence	6-0	180	28	7	Kansas State
Peters, Tony	6-2	192	24	3	Oklahoma
Bolton, Ron	6-2	170	27	6	Norfolk State

Scott remains one of the classy corners in the NFL. Peters could approach his partner's standards this season. Bolton, who came from New England, is a steady vet. PERF. QT.: 2.

SAFETIES	Ht	Wt	Age	Exp	College
Brown, Terry (S)	6-2	205	30	8	Oklahoma State
Darden, Thom (W)	6-2	193	27	5	Michigan
Craven, Bill (S-W)	5-11	190	25	2	Harvard

(S)—Strong-side   (W)—Weak-side or "Free" Safety

Brown gets a chance after the trade of Neal Craig. He may not be up to it. Darden, back from injury, stabilized the entire defense. He's as good as there is. Craven has promise. PERF. QT.: 3.

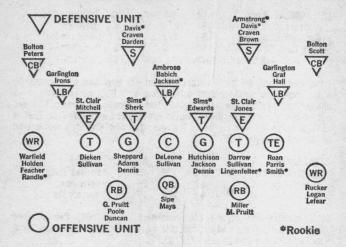

DEFENSIVE UNIT

Armstrong•
Davis•
Craven
Brown

Davis•
Craven
Darden

Bolton
Peters
CB

Bolton
Scott
CB

Garlington
Irons
LB

Garlington
Graf
Hall
LB

Ambrose
Babich
Jackson•
LB

St. Clair
Mitchell
E

Sims•
Sherk
T

Sims•
Edwards
T

St. Clair
Jones
E

WR

Warfield
Holden
Feacher
Randle•

Dieken
Sullivan
T

Sheppard
Adams
Dennis
G

DeLeone
Sullivan
C

Hutchison
Jackson
Dennis
G

Darrow
Sullivan
Lingenfelter•
T

Roan
Parris
Smith•
TE

WR

Rucker
Logan
Lefear

RB

G. Pruitt
Poole
Duncan

QB

Sipe
Mays

RB

Miller
M. Pruitt

OFFENSIVE UNIT   •Rookie

1977 DRAFT SELECTIONS

1	Jackson, Robert	LB	6-2	228	Texas A&M
2	Skladany, Tom	P-K	6-0	190	Ohio State
3	No Choice				
4A	Davis, Oliver	S	6-2	189	Tennessee State
4B	Sims, Mickey	DT	6-5	270	S. Carolina State
5	No Choice				
6	No Choice				
7A	Randle, Kenny	WR	6-0	185	So. California
7B	Smith, Blaine	TE	6-5	237	Purdue
7C	Lingenfelter, Bob	T	6-7	282	Nebraska
8	Armstrong, Bill	S	6-4	205	Wake Forest
9	Brown, Daryl	DB	5-9	185	Tufts
10	Burkett, Tom	T	6-5	280	North Carolina
11	Nash, Charles	WR	5-10	173	Arizona
12	Tierney, Leo	C	6-3	240	Georgia Tech

The Browns look upon Jackson and Skladany as instant starters. Jackson has an open road in the middle unless he has enormous difficulty adjusting to pro ball. Skladany will make Cockroft strictly a placekicker. Sims, too, can win a starting berth, especially now that Walter Johnson has been released. If he's not needed at tackle, the rookie will be tried at end. Davis has a good shot at making the club in a reserve capacity. Cleveland has a lot of sleepers, too—quality youngsters who just may develop quickly enough to help. Randle is in this category; so is Smith, who could also get shots at defensive end or linebacker; so is Lingenfelter, if he shows some agility; and so is Armstrong, especially with Neal Craig having been traded. PERF. QT.: 3.

OAKLAND RAIDERS

Prediction: First

Once the last Super Bowl ended, it seemed that everyone immediately stopped talking about it. It must have been that Oakland's victory over Minnesota was so emphatic that there was nothing over which football fans could argue.

"I talked about it all winter and spring," kidded big John Madden, the Raider coach. "I could have talked about it forever. I loved it.

"The best thing was that people stopped asking me when we were ever going to win the big one. Now they ask me if we're going to win two straight."

The Raiders may not win two straight, as their fellow American Conference teams, Pittsburgh and Miami, did, but they'll come close.

No one has better firepower nor more versatility than Oakland. A fair tip-off on how strong the defending champs will be comes in the second game of the season when they meet their bitter rivals, the Steelers, in Pittsburgh.

The Raiders' schedule is not as cushy as usual this year. They play four winning teams from out of their division: Pittsburgh, Cleveland, Los Angeles and Minnesota—the last two in succession. But their closest rivals in the AFC's Western Division, San Diego and

Denver, play even tougher schedules. The Raiders should be into the playoffs on a pass, as if they weren't good enough to make it into the post-season hoopla on their own ability.

The Raiders simply can beat a team too many ways.

Take their quarterbacking. Not since Sammy Baugh played has there been such an accurate passer in the NFL as Kenny Stabler. Stabler completed 66.7 per cent of his passes last year for 2737 yards and 27 touchdowns. He led the conference in overall rating, percentage and TDs, and he was playing hurt for a third of the season.

For receivers Stabler has the best tight end in the league, Dave Casper; the most threatening deep receiver, Cliff Branch; and the Most Valuable Player in the Super Bowl, Fred Biletnikoff.

Casper caught 10 touchdowns passes, Branch led the AFC with 12 and Biletnikoff took seven catches into the end zone.

When the Raiders want to run the ball, as they did against the Vikings, they use just about anyone and aim him right over the left side, behind All-Pro tackle Art Shell and guard Gene Upshaw.

They had a 1000-yard rusher, fullback Mark van Eeghen, who is even more treasured for his blocking, and such other reliable ball carriers as Clarence Davis, Pete Banaszak, Carl Garrett plus a horde of etcs. who get the job done in fine style.

Their center, Dave Dalby, is the most underrated in football, guard George Buehler is superb and tackle John Vella is good enough to keep one of the best young linemen in the NFL, Henry Lawrence, on the bench.

Defensively, Madden's big decision will be to stick

with the Raiders' new three-man front with four line-backers or return to the standard four-man line he used before a plague of injuries wiped out his linemen. Odds are he'll stick to the alignment that worked so well last year, the 3-4.

In the three-man front, huge Dave Rowe is the nose tackle, flanked by reliable Otis Sistrunk and a re-habilitated John Matuszak. Having end Horace Jones and tackle Art Thoms back from sick bay allows Mad-den additional flexibility and increases the quality of his reserve force.

The four-man linebacking crew in the Super Bowl was devastating. Regulars Phil Villapiano, Monte John-son and Ted Hendricks were joined in the big game—and through the regular season—by Willie Hall, who is another retread job.

Hall figures to make Madden's decision of 3-4 vs. 4-3 for him. Willie was so outstanding that the Raiders may not be able to afford to let him sit.

Ordinarily, this would be gold watch presentation time for Willie Brown, the 36-year-old cornerback. But Willie looked like a mere youth streaking down the sidelines for a touchdown with that 75-yard interception in the Super Bowl. Neal Colzie may have to do more watching in 1977 because Skip Thomas is solid on the other side.

Everyone knows the Raiders don't play safeties. They employ assassins, Jack Tatum on the weak side and George Atkinson on the strong side. That's why an-other quality safety, Charles Phillips, will sit again.

The punter, Ray Guy, is the best in the NFL, no matter what the statistics say. Errol Mann was the placekicker for half the season and in the Super Bowl, but Fred Steinfort should boot him off the roster if the sophomore's groin injury is fully healed.

1976 RECORD (16-1)

31	Pittsburgh	28	26	Philadelphia	7
24	Kansas City	21	49	Tampa Bay	16
14	Houston	13	35	Cincinnati	20
17	New England	48	24	San Diego	0
27	San Diego	17		(Playoff)	
17	Denver	10	24	New England	21
18	Green Bay	14		(AFC Championship)	
19	Denver	6	24	Pittsburgh	7
28	Chicago	27		(Super Bowl)	
21	Kansas City	10	32	Minnesota	14

PASSING

	Atts	Comps	Yds	Lgst	TDs	Ints	Pct
Stabler†	291	194	2737	88†	27†	17	66.7†
Rae	65	35	417	37	6	1	53.8
Humm	5	3	41	29	0	0	60.0

SCORING

	TDs	PATs	FGs	Total
Branch	12	0	0	72
Casper	10	0	0	60
Mann•	0	35	8	59
Biletnikoff	7	0	0	42
Banaszak	5	0	0	30
Steinfort	0	16	4	28

RUSHING

	Atts	Yds	TDs	Lgst	Avg
van Eeghen	233	1012	3	21	4.3
Davis	114	516	3	31	4.5
Banaszak	114	370	5	15	3.2
Garrett	48	220	1	17	4.6

RECEIVING

	Recs	Yds	TDs	Lgst	Avg
Casper	53	691	10	30	13.0
Branch	46	1111	12†	88†	24.2
Biletnikoff	43	551	7	32	12.8
Davis	27	191	0	17	7.1
van Eeghen	17	173	0	21	10.2
Banaszak	15	74	0	20	4.9

INTERCEPTIONS

	Ints	Yds	TDs	Lgst	Avg
Johnson	4	40	0	22	10.0
Brown	3	25	0	22	8.3
Thomas	2	26	0	14	13.0
Hall	2	17	0	12	8.5
Tatum	2	0	0	0	0.0

SYMBOLS †—Conference leader
•—Combined Detroit-Oakland record

1977 SCHEDULE

Home: Sept. 18—San Diego; Oct. 16—Denver; Nov. 6—Seattle; Nov. 13—Houston; Nov. 28—Buffalo; Dec. 11—Minnesota; Dec. 18—Kansas City.

Away: Sept. 25—Pittsburgh; Oct. 3—Kansas City; Oct. 9—Cleveland; Oct. 23—New York Jets; Oct. 30—Denver; Nov. 20—San Diego; Dec. 4—Los Angeles.

OFFENSE

QUARTERBACKS	Ht	Wt	Age	Exp	College
Stabler, Ken	6-3	215	31	8	Alabama
Rae, Mike	6-0	190	26	2	Southern California
Humm, David	6-2	185	25	3	Nebraska

The question now seems to be: Should Stabler be ranked among the all-time great quarterbacks? He's the most accurate passer since Sammy Baugh. Rae is a comer. Humm has talent, too. PERF. QT.: 1.

RUNNING BACKS	Ht	Wt	Age	Exp	College
Davis, Clarence	5-10	195	28	7	Southern California
van Eeghen, Mark	6-2	225	25	4	Colgate
Banaszak, Pete	6-0	210	33	12	Miami, Fla.
Hubbard, Marv	6-1	235	31	8	Colgate
Garrett, Carl	5-10	205	30	9	New Mex. Highlands
Kunz, Terry	6-1	215	24	2	Colorado

Davis, spectacular in the Super Bowl, has always been underrated. Blocking is van Eeghen's main attribute, despite the 1012 yards he gained in '76. He could be one of the NFL's coming stars. Banaszak still knows the way to the end zone. Hubbard gives it another try after almost two seasons of injury. Garrett can still play. Kunz has potential. Some speed is needed here. PERF. QT.: 2.

RECEIVERS	Ht	Wt	Age	Exp	College
Biletnikoff, Fred (W)	6-1	190	34	13	Florida State
Branch, Cliff (W)	5-11	170	29	6	Colorado
Casper, Dave (T)	6-4	230	25	4	Notre Dame
Siani, Mike (W)	6-2	195	27	6	Villanova
Bradshaw, Morris (W)	6-1	195	24	4	Ohio State
Kwalick, Ted (T)	6-4	225	30	9	Penn State
Jennings, Rick (W)	5-9	180	24	2	Maryland
Bankston, Warren (T)	6-4	235	30	9	Tulane

(W)—Wide Receiver   (T)—Tight End

Biletnikoff was the Super Bowl MVP, but he'll still be pressed this year by Siani and maybe the speedy Bradshaw. Branch is dynamite; he's highly respected by defensive backs. Last year was Casper's first as a starter. He could be the All-Pro tight end for the next decade. Siani was hurt part of last year, but he has talent. Bradshaw's only catch was a 25-yard TD, but the Raiders think highly of him. Kwalick hasn't paid dividends yet. Jennings is primarily a kick returner. Bankston helps in many ways. PERF. QT.: 1.

INTERIOR LINEMEN	Ht	Wt	Age	Exp	College
Shell, Art (T)	6-5	275	30	10	Md.-Eastern Shore
Vella, John (T)	6-4	260	27	6	Southern California
Upshaw, Gene (G)	6-5	255	32	11	Texas A&I
Buehler, George (G)	6-2	270	30	9	Stanford
Dalby, Dave (C)	6-3	250	26	6	UCLA
Lawrence, Henry (T)	6-4	270	25	4	Florida A&M
Medlin, Dan (G)	6-4	255	27	4	North Carolina State
Sylvester, Steve (C-T)	6-4	260	24	3	Notre Dame

(T)—Tackle   (G)—Guard   (C)—Center

Shell may be the best tackle in the entire NFL. Vella Is tough, almost mean, and talented. Upshaw, even at 32, is a force to be reckoned with. Buehler may be unnoticed by fans, but he's tremendous. Dalby is among the league's most underrated players; once he gets known, he'll be recognized as the equal of Miami's Jim Langer. Lawrence would be starting on any other team in the league, and he may even force his way in here. Medlin and Sylvester benefit from Oakland's careful nurturing program. PERF. QT.: 1.

KICKERS	Ht	Wt	Age	Exp	College
Steinfort, Fred (Pk)	5-11	180	25	2	Boston College
Guy, Ray (P)	6-3	195	27	5	So. Mississippi
Mann, Errol (Pk)	6-0	205	36	10	North Dakota

(Pk)—Placekicker   (P)—Punter

Say bye-bye to Mann when Steinfort gets well. Fred should blossom now that living-legend George Blanda is no longer looking over his shoulder. Guy is simply the best punter in pro ball. PERF. QT.: 3.

DEFENSE

FRONT LINEMEN	Ht	Wt	Age	Exp	College
Matuszak, John (E)	6-7	270	26	5	Tampa
Sistrunk, Otis (E)	6-4	270	29	6	None
Rowe, Dave (T)	6-7	270	32	11	Penn State
Jones, Horace (E)	6-4	260	28	6	Louisville
Thoms, Art (T)	6-5	250	30	8	Syracuse
McMath, Herb (E-T)	6-4	250	22	2	Morningside
Philyaw, Charles (E)	6-9	270	23	2	Texas Southern

(E)—End   (T)—Tackle

Did Matuszak really find himself after rejections by Houston, Kansas City and even Washington? He sure played well after joining the Raiders in '76. Sistrunk is steady on every play, inspired upon occasion. Rowe, another retread, filled the middle well. Jones and Thoms come back from injury to give Coach Madden welcome reinforcements. McMath is an overgrown linebacker, but a player. Philyaw could turn into a permanent disappointment. PERF. QT.: 3.

LINEBACKERS	Ht	Wt	Age	Exp	College
Villapiano, Phil (O)	6-2	225	28	7	Bowling Green
Hendricks, Ted (O)	6-7	220	29	9	Miami, Fla.
Johnson, Monte (M)	6-5	240	25	5	Nebraska
Hall, Willie (M-O)	6-2	225	27	5	Southern California
Barnes, Rodrigo (O)	6-1	215	27	5	Rice
Bonness, Rik (M)	6-3	220	23	2	Nebraska
Rice, Floyd (O)	6-3	225	28	7	Alcorn

(O)—Outside Linebacker   (M)—Middle Linebacker

This gang produced big plays by the bundle. Vet Villapiano is just as fiery now as when he was a rookie. Hendricks isn't as consistent as he was in his All-Pro days, but his help is undeniable. Johnson is solid in the middle. Hall turned into a golden find; he's another of the Raiders' reclamation projects. So is Barnes, who helped when called on. Young Bonness is projected as a future star by Raider brass. Rice could be pushed by a young prospect. PERF. QT.: 1.

CORNERBACKS	Ht	Wt	Age	Exp	College
Brown, Willie	6-1	210	36	15	Grambling
Thomas, Skip	6-1	205	27	6	Southern California
Colzie, Neal	6-2	205	24	3	Ohio State

At 36, Brown should be thinking of retirement. Instead, he plays like a colt. Thomas is fine, and he's young enough to get even better. Colzie could play regularly for most teams. PERF. QT.: 1.

SAFETIES	Ht	Wt	Age	Exp	College
Atkinson, George (S)	6-0	185	30	10	Morris Brown
Tatum, Jack (W)	5-11	205	28	6	Ohio State
Phillips, Charles (W-S)	6-2	215	24	3	Southern California

(S)—Strong-side   (W)—Weak-side or "Free" Safety

Meet Mr. Hyde and Mr. Hyde. Nobody wants to run pass patterns at Atkinson and Tatum. Phillips is still another on this team who could play regularly for most NFL clubs. PERF. QT.: 1.

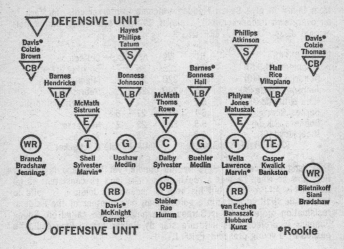

DEFENSIVE UNIT

Davis•
Colzie
Brown
CB

Barnes
Hendricks
LB

McMath
Sistrunk
E

Hayes•
Phillips
Tatum
S

Bonness
Johnson
LB

McMath
Thoms
Rowe
T

Barnes•
Bonness
Hall
LB

Phillips
Atkinson
S

Philaw
Jones
Matuszak
E

Hall
Rice
Villapiano
LB

Davis•
Colzie
Thomas
CB

OFFENSIVE UNIT

WR
Branch
Bradshaw
Jennings

T
Shell
Sylvester
Marvin•

G
Upshaw
Medlin

C
Dalby
Sylvester

G
Buehler
Medlin

T
Vella
Lawrence
Marvin•

TE
Casper
Kwalick
Bankston

WR
Biletnikoff
Siani
Bradshaw

RB
Davis•
McKnight
Garrett

QB
Stabler
Rae
Humm

RB
van Eeghen
Banaszak
Hubbard
Kunz

•Rookie

1977 DRAFT SELECTIONS

1	No Choice				
2A	Davis, Mike	CB	6-2	199	Colorado
2B	McKnight, Ted	RB	6-2	218	Minnesota-Duluth
3	No Choice				
4	Marvin, Mickey	T	6-4	270	Tennessee
5A	Hayes, Lester	S	6-2	208	Texas A&M
5B	Barnes, Jeff	LB	6-3	235	California
6	No Choice				
7	Martini, Rick	WR	6-2	185	California-Davis
8	Robiskie, Terry	RB	6-1	215	Louisiana State
9	No Choice				
10	No Choice				
11	No Choice				
12A	Martin, Rod	LB	6-1	195	So. California
12B	Benirshke, Rolf	K	6-1	170	California-Davis

The Raiders love those far-out picks. Boss Al Davis always looks for another like Monte Johnson. Davis will break in slowly, an Oakland custom. McKnight was the small-college ground-gaining champion. He could find a lot of work with the champs, to violate the established precedent. Marvin has jumbo size, which the Raiders love. Hayes is not the cerebral type but he hits in the manner of Tatum and Atkinson. Barnes has a chance. **PERF. QT.: 4.**

DENVER BRONCOS

Prediction: Second

The Denver Broncos should find out about themselves between October 16 and November 6 this season. Between those dates they play their arch-rivals, the Oakland Raiders, twice, plus games against Cincinnati and Pittsburgh.

Last year the Broncos won nine games, but their coach, John Ralston, was fired because he didn't make the playoffs. If he doesn't get through this autumn's four-game gauntlet, Red Miller, Ralston's successor, is likely to get more than his ration of heat from the impatient Bronco fans. And the new coach also has Dallas, St. Louis and Baltimore on his first schedule.

Miller was an NFL assistant for 17 seasons. He was an offensive line coach with the first Boston Patriots, Buffalo, Denver, St. Louis, Baltimore and New England before landing in the Bronco hot seat. He's well prepared for his debut as a head coach, but he's not being allowed to break in easy.

Miller will operate with a new quarterback, Craig Morton, whom the Broncos got in a trade for Steve Ramsey. Morton was dismal in his three seasons with the New York Giants.

If Morton doesn't have at least something left, Miller will be left with two kiddies—Craig Penrose and Norris

Weese—and another questionable veteran, former Tampa Bay quarterback Steve Spurrier. Penrose is a pocket passer who had a couple of encouraging games as a rookie. Weese is a scrambler who played in the WFL. Spurrier spent years in San Francisco before being traded to the expansion Buccaneers.

The Broncos have good receivers. Riley Odoms is right there with the finest tight ends. Haven Moses will average a touchdown every three or four catches, and Rick Upchurch, best known as the man who returned four punts for touchdowns last year, can be an exciting deep receiver. Former WFL star Jack Dolbin also bids for regular work.

Otis Armstrong bounced back from his '75 injury to compile a 1008-yard season. He carries the ball twice as much as the Bronc fullback, whose identity may be changed this year. Jon Keyworth filled that role for the last several seasons, but Lonnie Perrin did enough impressive things as a rookie to earn a big shot at the job in 1977.

Denver's offensive line is still in a state of growth. It may not grow fast enough for Morton, since Bronco quarterbacks were sacked 48 times last year.

Last year's No. 1 draftee, Tom Glassic, won a job at guard. The Broncos traded with Green Bay for Bill Bain and started him at tackle. Huge Claudie Minor moved over to play right tackle for the first time. Ex-defensive lineman Phil Olsen started at center for the first time. Paul Howard, an experienced guard, missed all last season due to injury, but Miller hopes he'll be back to play regularly.

Miller, an old offensive line coach himself, hired one of his former All-Pro charges, ex-Cardinal Ken Gray, to school this young line.

Defensively, the Broncos played a three-man front

with four linebackers out of necessity last year when Lyle Alzado, Paul Smith and a bright rookie, Brison Manor, got hurt. It went so well that Denver may stick with it.

In this "Oklahoma" setup, Rubin Carter plays nose tackle, with Barney Chavous and, it is hoped, Alzado at his sides.

Linebacking is the reason defensive coordinator Joe Collier is leaning toward the "Oklahoma" as the standard defense for his team. It is among the strongest departments on the club. The right side is a fortress, with underrated Tom Jackson on the outside and Randy Gradishar alongside him. Joe Rizzo plays the other inside position, backed by former Jet Godwin Turk, with Bob Swenson on the outside.

Louie Wright is developing into one of the bright young cornerbacks in the NFL. The other side is manned by Steve Foley, who wrested the job away from Calvin Jones last year. Veteran Bill Thompson is one safety, but with John Rowser waived, the other spot is open. Bernard Jackson, acquired from Cincinnati, or 1976 rookie Kurt Knoff, who sat out the year with a college knee injury that didn't respond to treatment, will compete for the slot alongside Thompson.

Jim Turner is still a reliable placekicker, but Billy Van Heusen hasn't had a good punting season in a couple of years, and he doesn't figure to return for this campaign.

The draft brought at least three players who will help. Boston College's Steve Schindler may push Howard for the right guard spot. Rob Lytle, the Michigan All-America, is a capable backup for Armstrong. And Billy Bryan of Duke could insert himself into the center picture, which could be jumbled for most of training camp.

1976 RECORD (9-5)

7	Cincinnati	17	6	Oakland	19
46	New York Jets	3	48	Tampa Bay	13
44	Cleveland	13	17	San Diego	0
26	San Diego	0	14	New York Giants	13
3	Houston	17	14	New England	38
10	Oakland	17	17	Kansas City	16
35	Kansas City	26	28	Chicago	14

PASSING

	Atts	Comps	Yds	Lgst	TDs	Ints	Pct
Ramsey*	270	128	1931	71	11	13	47.4
Penrose	36	16	265	41	3	3	44.4
Weese	47	24	314	43	1	6	51.1

SCORING

	TDs	PATs	FGs	Total
Turner	0	36	15	81
Moses	7	0	0	42
Armstrong	6	0	0	36
Upchurch	6	0	0	36
Odoms	5	0	0	30
Keyworth	4	0	0	24

RUSHING

	Atts	Yds	TDs	Lgst	Avg
Armstrong	247	1008	5	31	4.1
Keyworth	122	349	3	13	2.9
Weese	23	142	0	20	6.2
Perrin	37	118	2	14	3.2
Kiick	31	114	1	19	3.7

RECEIVING

	Recs	Yds	TDs	Lgst	Avg
Armstrong	39	457	1	36	11.7
Odoms	30	477	3	47	15.9
Moses	25	498	7	71	19.9
Keyworth	22	201	1	31	9.1
Dolbin	19	354	1	40	18.6
Upchurch	12	340	1	59	28.3

INTERCEPTIONS

	Ints	Yds	TDs	Lgst	Avg
T. Jackson	7	136	1	46	19.4
Rowser**	4	104	2‡	41	26.0
Foley	4	95	0	34	23.8
Gradishar	3	44	1	31	14.7

Two tied with 2

SYMBOLS   *—Traded
           **—Waived
           ‡—Tied for conference lead

1977 SCHEDULE

Home: Sept. 18—St. Louis; Sept. 25—Buffalo; Oct. 9—Kansas City; Oct. 30—Oakland; Nov. 6—Pittsburgh; Nov. 27—Baltimore; Dec. 11—San Diego.

Away: Oct. 2—Seattle; Oct. 16—Oakland; Oct. 23—Cincinnati; Nov. 13—San Diego; Nov. 20—Kansas City; Dec. 4—Houston; Dec. 18—Dallas.
BUFFALO..BILLS

OFFENSE

QUARTERBACKS	Ht	Wt	Age	Exp	College
Morton, Craig	6-4	210	34	13	California
Penrose, Craig	6-3	222	24	2	San Diego State
Weese, Norris	6-1	195	26	2	Mississippi
Spurrier, Steve	6-1	205	32	11	Florida

Steve Ramsey wasn't much, but does Morton have anything left? He was a resounding flop with the Giants. Penrose will be the man someday, but probably not this year. Weese is an interesting scrambler. Spurrier fights for his pro life. PERF. QT.: 3.

RUNNING BACKS	Ht	Wt	Age	Exp	College
Armstrong, Otis	5-10	196	26	5	Purdue
Keyworth, Jon	6-3	230	26	4	Colorado
Perrin, Lonnie	6-1	222	25	2	Illinois
Kiick, Jim	5-11	215	31	8	Wyoming
Franckowiak, Mike	6-3	220	24	3	Central Michigan
Jenkins, Darrell	6-2	235	25	1	San Jose State

Armstrong came back from his '75 injury to crack the 1000-yard barrier, but it wasn't the kind of season he enjoyed in '74 when he unseated O.J. as the ground-gaining king. Keyworth will be pushed hard by Perrin, who showed promise as a rookie. Kiick hasn't got much left. Franckowiak is progressing slowly, maybe too slowly. Jenkins is a prospect who was waived by San Francisco. PERF. QT.: 3.

RECEIVERS	Ht	Wt	Age	Exp	College
Moses, Haven (W)	6-2	208	31	10	San Diego State
Upchurch, Rick (W)	5-10	170	25	3	Minnesota
Odoms, Riley (T)	6-4	230	27	6	Houston
Dolbin, Jack (W)	5-10	180	28	3	Wake Forest
Schultz, John (W)	5-10	182	24	2	Maryland
Brown, Boyd (T)	6-4	216	25	4	Alcorn
Van Heusen, Billy (W)	6-1	200	31	10	Maryland

(W)—Wide Receiver   (T)—Tight End

Moses averaged almost 20 yards on his 25 catches and scored seven TDs—a satisfactory performance. Upchurch almost has to play regularly on the basis of his 28.3-yard average, even if it was only for a dozen catches. And he also had an incredible four touchdowns on punt returns. Odoms remains one of the NFL's top tight ends, a well-rounded player. Dolbin is the only first-class sub. The others could find themselves unemployed in '77. PERF. QT.: 2.

INTERIOR LINEMEN	Ht	Wt	Age	Exp	College
Bain, Bill (T)	6-4	270	25	3	Southern California
Minor, Claudie (T)	6-4	280	26	4	San Diego State
Glassic, Tom (G)	6-4	254	23	2	Virginia
Howard, Paul (G)	6-3	260	26	4	Brigham Young
Olsen, Phil (C)	6-4	260	29	7	Utah State
Parrish, Scott (T)	6-6	265	24	2	Utah State
Goodman, Harvey (G-T)	6-4	260	24	2	Colorado
Maples, Bobby (C)	6-3	250	34	13	Baylor
DuLac, Bill (G)	6-4	260	26	3	Eastern Michigan

(T)—Tackle   (G)—Guard   (C)—Center

Coach Miller's background is mostly as an offensive line coach. Maybe he can cure what ails the Broncos; they allowed 48 sacks last year. One problem was the presence of three green players—former Packer Bain, rookie Glassic and ex-defensive lineman Olsen—and one player at a new position—Minor at right tackle instead of his accustomed left side. They can all get better, though Olsen is the most subject to challenge. If Howard can return from a back injury that cost him all of '76, that could help to stabilize things. The reserve strength here isn't very encouraging at all. PERF. QT.: 4

KICKERS	Ht	Wt	Age	Exp	College
Turner, Jim (Pk)	6-2	205	36	14	Utah State
Van Heusen, Billy (P)	6-1	200	31	10	Maryland

(Pk)—Placekicker   (P)—Punter

Turner turned in a sparkling 15 for 21 in the field goal department. Van Heusen is on the way out. PERF. QT.: 3.

DEFENSE

FRONT LINEMEN	Ht	Wt	Age	Exp	College
Chavous, Barney (E)	6-3	252	26	5	S. Carolina State
Alzado, Lyle (E)	6-3	252	28	6	Yankton
Carter, Rubin (T)	6-0	256	24	3	Miami, Fla.
Smith, Paul (E)	6-3	256	32	10	New Mexico
Grant, John (T-E)	6-3	235	27	5	Southern California
Manor, Brison (E)	6-4	248	25	1	Arkansas

(E)—End   (T)—Tackle

Chavous had his best pro year. Alzado missed virtually all of '76, but the Broncos expect him to return to his usual ferocious form. Carter started to resemble Curley Culp late last season. Only a miraculous return from injury by Smith could force the team back into the standard four-man front. Grant is versatile, useful. Manor was a touted rookie before injury hit. PERF. QT.: 3.

LINEBACKERS	Ht	Wt	Age	Exp	College
Swenson, Bob (O)	6-3	220	24	3	California
Jackson, Tom (O)	5-11	220	26	5	Louisville
Gradishar, Randy (M)	6-3	233	25	4	Ohio State
Rizzo, Joe (M-O)	6-1	220	26	4	Merchant Marine
Turk, Godwin (M)	6-2	230	26	4	Southern
Baska, Rich (M)	6-3	225	25	2	UCLA
Evans, Larry (O)	6-2	216	24	2	Mississippi College

(O)—Outside Linebacker   (M)—Middle Linebacker

This is the most improved unit on the team. Swenson contributes, and he'll get even better. Jackson is short, but the Broncos think he's one of the league's most valuable players. His seven intercepts led AFC linebackers in '76. Gradishar looked like the enforcer he was in his Ohio State days. Rizzo came out of nowhere to play superbly. Turk was a Jet failure, but the Broncos think he's rehabilitated. Baska, Evans are promising. PERF. QT.: 1.

CORNERBACKS	Ht	Wt	Age	Exp	College
Wright, Louie	6-2	195	24	3	San Jose State
Foley, Steve	5-11	185	23	2	Tulane
Jones, Calvin	5-7	169	26	5	Washington

Wright justified his selection in the first round of the draft two years ago. Foley stepped in and played well after Jones was hurt last year. The tiny one plays hard, though. PERF. QT.: 2.

SAFETIES	Ht	Wt	Age	Exp	College
Thompson, Bill (S-W)	6-1	200	30	9	Maryland State
Jackson, Bernard (W)	6-0	178	26	6	Washington State
Knoff, Kurt (S-W)	6-3	188	23	1	Kansas
Poltl, Randy (W)	6-3	190	25	4	Stanford

(S)—Strong-side   (W)—Weak-side or "Free" Safety

There's a scramble here. Thompson figures to start at one safety position. Jackson, from Cincinnati, could muscle his way in as a starter here or at corner. If Knoff can shake his knee injury, he's in the running, too. Poltl is expendable. PERF. QT.: 3.

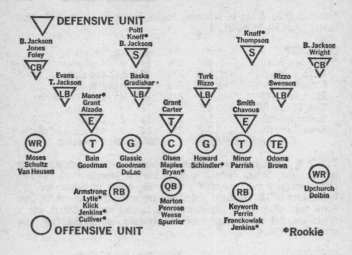

DEFENSIVE UNIT

B. Jackson
Jones
Foley
CB

Poitl
Knoff*
B. Jackson
S

Knoff*
Thompson
S

B. Jackson
Wright
CB

Evans
T. Jackson
LB

Baska
Gradishar
LB

Turk
Rizzo
LB

Rizzo
Swenson
LB

Manor*
Grant
Alzado
E

Grant
Carter
T

Smith
Chavous
E

WR
Moses
Schultz
Van Heusen

T
Bain
Goodman

G
Glassic
Goodman
DuLac

C
Olsen
Maples
Bryan*

G
Howard
Schindler*

T
Minor
Parrish

TE
Odoms
Brown

WR
Upchurch
Dolbin

Armstrong
Lytle*
Klick
Jenkins*
Culliver*
RB

QB
Morton
Penrose
Weese
Spurrier

RB
Keyworth
Perrin
Franckowiak
Jenkins*

OFFENSIVE UNIT

*Rookie

1977 DRAFT SELECTIONS

1	Schindler, Steve	G	6-3	260	Boston College
2	Lytle, Rob	RB	6-1	195	Michigan
3	No Choice				
4	Bryan, Bill	C	6-2	244	Duke
5	No Choice				
6	No Choice				
7	Swider, Larry	P	6-2	193	Pittsburgh
8	Culliver, Calvin	RB	6-0	197	Alabama
9	Jackson, Charles	DT-G	6-2	229	Washington
10	Middlebrook, Orna	WR	6-3	185	Arkansas State
11	Heck, Phil	LB	6-3	230	California
12	Levenhagen, Scott	TE	6-4	215	Western Illinois

The Broncos had success with Glassic last year so they went for another guard, Schindler, in Round 1 and moved again to upholster the line with Bryan. Lytle is their second halfback type. Swider has a chance to win the punting job. Culliver did not figure to be available in the eighth round. He has possibilities. PERF. QT.: 3.

SAN DIEGO CHARGERS

Prediction: Third

The Chargers have been trying to upgrade themselves for the last few years, making moves that make sense. It may pay off with a winning record in 1977. They may even leapfrog over Denver into second place.

The most significant changes this year were the trade with Los Angeles for quarterback James Harris and the signing of Johnny Rodgers out of the Canadian League.

Rodgers, the former Heisman Trophy winner, was the Chargers' No. 1 draftee four seasons ago, but he had soured on the U.S. at the time and signed in Montreal. He is going to give the U.S. another chance this year, and the Chargers may be the beneficiaries. Not only does he give them another excellent speed receiver, but he is one of the most dangerous punt and kick returners in football.

San Diego also traded with Cincinnati for a veteran possession receiver, Chip Myers. The season before, they dealt with the Bengals for Charlie Joiner, who gave them a super season. With Joiner on one side, Rodgers on the other and underrated Pat Curran at tight end, San Diego will make any pass defense nervous.

And with the acquisition of Harris, the Chargers' quarterbacking picture seems to be clarified. Dan Fouts improved last year, but he still didn't look like a passer who could put the Chargers into the playoffs.

One reason for Fouts' improvement was the guidance of Bill Walsh, the team's offensive coordinator. But Walsh left to become the head coach at Stanford this year. His successor, Max Coley, helped make Denver one of the league's high-scoring teams a couple of years ago, but now with Harris present it's not a Fouts-or-nothing situation, and the team will benefit.

It will be interesting, too, to see how Coley will use Joe Washington, last year's No. 1 draft pick who never got to play due to a knee injury. The ex-Oklahoma cyclone can do just about everything Rodgers can do with the ball, plus run from scrimmage.

Washington may be the ultimate utility man, since Ricky Young gained 802 yards and averaged five yards a carry last year. Young relegated former rookie whiz Don Woods to a secondary offensive role.

The Chargers could stand some sharper fullbacking. Bo Matthews blocks all right, but his hands leave something to be desired and he's not much when carrying the ball.

Coach Tommy Prothro decided to draft a center, Bob Rush of Memphis State, in the first round since he had an antique, former Detroit All-Pro Ed Flanagan, playing the position. Rush will start, unless Flanagan has more left than is generally thought.

Prothro used another top rookie, Don Macek, as a starting guard last year, and he did all right. The other guard, Doug Wilkerson, is considered among the NFL's best. Russ Washington, another frequent All-Pro, keeps one tackle in good hands, but the other side is trouble, unless former WFLer Booker Brown can snap back from his '76 illness. Billy Shields played the position in his absence.

The Chargers allowed 46 quarterback sacks last year. If they are to do any leapfrogging, that figure will have to be cut down considerably.

Field-goaling has been a Charger trouble spot for several seasons, and even with the addition of ex-Cowboy Toni Fritsch, the record was a mere .500 in '76.

The Chargers finished next-to-last among all 28 NFL teams in pass defense last year. Two years ago they used high draft picks to name three defensive linemen, but last year the sum total of their sacks was 23, one of the lowest in the league.

Prothro has to get more production out of tackles Louie Kelcher and Gary Johnson. Johnson was supposed to be a certain eventual All-Pro. He hasn't come close yet. Fred Dean is super swift for an end, but his lack of heft—he weighs only 219—is a considerable handicap. The Chargers traded for huge Leroy Jones from the Rams last year. He may pay dividends after a year of experience as the other starting end.

San Diego's linebacking has been in a state of constant change for years. The best news was some sound play from Woodrow Lowe, the stubby rookie from Alabama. Strong-sider Don Goode never has delivered as promised. Tom Graham is a journeyman in the middle.

Mike Williams showed some signs of developing as a cornerback, and Chris Fletcher is an underrated free safety, but Danny Colbert and Tom Hayes don't seem to be the answer at the other corner, and Mike Fuller, the strong safety, may be most valuable as a punt returner. A huge rookie, Keith King of Colorado State, may push Fuller for his safety job.

Cliff Olander, a fifth-round draft pick, could win the punting assignment from Jeff West, the former Cardinal. West was barely adequate over the last half of '76, when he was employed in San Diego.

1976 RECORD (6-8)

30	Kansas City	16	0	Pittsburgh	23
23	Tampa Bay	0	21	Baltimore	37
43	St. Louis	24	0	Denver	17
0	Denver	26	34	Buffalo	13
17	Oakland	27	20	Kansas City	23
30	Houston	27	13	San Francisco (OT)	7
17	Cleveland	21	0	Oakland	24

PASSING

	Atts	Comps	Yds	Lgst	TDs	Ints	Pct
Fouts	359†	208†	2535	81	14	15	57.9
Longley	24	12	130	28	2	3	50.0

SCORING

	TDs	PATs	FGs	Total
Joiner	7	0	0	42
Young	5	0	0	30
Fritsch	0	11	6	29
Wersching	0	14	4	26
Three tied with	4	0	0	24

RUSHING

	Atts	Yds	TDs	Lgst	Avg
Young	162	802	4	46	5.0
Woods	126	450	3	24	3.6
Morris	50	256	2	30	5.1
Scarber	61	236	1	14	3.9
Matthews	46	199	3	42	4.3

RECEIVING

	Recs	Yds	TDs	Lgst	Avg
Joiner	50	1056	7	81	21.1
Young	47	441	1	33	9.4
Woods	34	224	1	34	6.6
Curran	33	349	1	29	10.6
Scarber	14	96	1	13	6.9

INTERCEPTIONS

	Ints	Yds	TDs	Lgst	Avg
Goode	6	82	0	27	13.7
Williams	4	76	0	35	19.0
Graham	3	55	0	25	18.3
Hayes	2	37	1	37	18.5

SYMBOL †—Conference leader

1977 SCHEDULE

Home: Oct. 2—Cincinnati; Oct. 16—New England; Oct. 23—Kansas City; Nov. 13—Denver; Nov. 20—Oakland; Dec. 4—Cleveland; Dec. 18—Pittsburgh.

Away: Sept. 18—Oakland; Sept. 25—Kansas City; Oct. 9—New Orleans; Oct. 30—Miami; Nov. 6—Detroit; Nov. 27—Seattle; Dec. 11—Denver.

OFFENSE

QUARTERBACKS	Ht	Wt	Age	Exp	College
Harris, James	6-4	210	30	8	Grambling
Fouts, Dan	6-3	204	26	5	Oregon
Longley, Clint	6-1	195	25	4	Abilene Christian

Harris, despite good stats, never won respect in L.A. Fouts improved greatly last year, but he hasn't shown he's a playoff quarterback. Longley did zilch after coming from Dallas. PERF. QT.: 3.

RUNNING BACKS	Ht	Wt	Age	Exp	College
Young, Ricky	6-2	193	23	3	Jackson State
Matthews, Bo	6-4	230	25	4	Colorado
Woods, Don	6-1	210	26	4	New Mexico
Washington, Joe	5-10	184	23	2	Oklahoma
Scarber, Sam	6-2	232	29	3	New Mexico
Morris, Mercury	5-10	192	30	9	West Texas State

Young, ninth in AFC rushing in '76, established himself as a solid, dangerous runner. Matthews is only so-so. Woods, a super rookie in 1974, has difficulty getting playing time. They will have to find a place for Washington, the swifty who watched his rookie season from the bench because of a bad knee. Scarber does well in his infrequent chances. Morris' work doesn't equal his pay. PERF. QT.: 3.

RECEIVERS	Ht	Wt	Age	Exp	College
Rodgers, Johnny (W)	5-10	180	26	1	Grambling
Joiner, Charlie (W)	5-11	185	29	9	Nebraska
Curran, Pat (T)	6-3	238	31	9	Lakeland
Myers, Chip (W)	6-6	205	32	10	Northwest Oklahoma
Dorsey, Larry (W)	6-1	195	24	2	Tennessee State
Owens, Artie (W)	5-10	170	24	2	West Virginia
McDonald, Dwight (W)	6-2	187	26	3	San Diego State
Garrison, Gary (W)	6-1	194	33	11	San Diego State
Bradley, Chuck (T)	6-6	235	26	3	Oregon
(W)—Wide Receiver			(T)—Tight End		

This is the most improved part of the Chargers, and with Harris throwing, it could be dynamite. Rodgers may not get A in deportment, but he can play. Joiner did well enough to deserve All-Pro; he averaged 21.1 yards on 50 catches. Curran is qualified for the NFL all-underrated team; he is a solid blocker and a dependable catcher. Myers, from the Bengals, is savvy. Dorsey and the ultra-quick Owens have promising futures. McDonald is in danger of losing his job. So is Garrison, who missed most of last season with injuries. Bradley is adequate as Curran's understudy. PERF. QT.: 1.

INTERIOR LINEMEN	Ht	Wt	Age	Exp	College
Washington, Russ (T)	6-7	285	30	10	Missouri
Shields, Billy (T)	6-7	260	24	3	Georgia Tech
Macek, Don (G)	6-3	253	23	2	Boston College
Wilkerson, Doug (G)	6-3	262	30	8	N. Carolina Central
Flanagan, Ed (C)	6-3	245	33	13	Purdue
Brown, Booker (T)	6-2	257	24	2	Southern California
Perretta, Ralph (G-C)	6-2	252	24	3	Purdue
Singleton, Ron (T)	6-7	245	25	2	Grambling
Aiu, Charles (G)	6-2	248	23	2	Hawaii

(T)—Tackle   (G)—Guard   (C)—Center

Only Tampa Bay and Denver allowed more quarterback sacks than San Diego in '76 AFC play. If the passing attack is to really improve, this unit will have to do much better. Washington made the Pro Bowl again. The jury is still out on Shields. Macek progressed; he made the All-Rookie team, but he needs more schooling. Wilkerson is one of the top guards in the NFL. Flanagan is not a top center any more. Brown missed 1976 because of illness; it is hoped he can take Shields' starting job. Reserves Perretta, Singleton and Aiu are not the stuff that playoff hopes are built on. PERF. QT.: 3.

KICKERS	Ht	Wt	Age	Exp	College
Fritsch, Toni (Pk)	5-7	195	32	6	None
West, Jeff (P)	6-2	220	24	3	Cincinnati
Wersching, Ray (Pk)	5-10	222	27	5	California

(Pk)—Placekicker   (P)—Punter

Fritsch didn't improve the Chargers' kicking after he joined the team. West didn't help much, either, when he came aboard. Wersching, the man unseated by Fritsch, gets another chance. PERF. QT.: 4.

DEFENSE

FRONT LINEMEN	Ht	Wt	Age	Exp	College
Dean, Fred (E)	6-3	219	25	3	Louisiana Tech
Jones, Leroy (E)	6-8	245	26	2	Norfolk State
Kelcher, Louie (T)	6-5	282	24	3	Southern Methodist
Johnson, Gary (T)	6-2	262	25	3	Grambling
Lee, John (E)	6-2	247	24	2	Nebraska
DeJurnett, Chuck (T)	6-4	270	25	2	San Jose State

(E)—End   (T)—Tackle

Dean is among the lightest defensive ends in pro ball, and the Chargers may not be able to play him much longer. Jones, acquired from the Rams last year, could help out. Kelcher and Johnson just haven't lived up to what the Chargers expected of them. Lee and DeJurnett are not the answers, either. This is a make-or-break year for this young contingent. PERF. QT.: 4.

LINEBACKERS	Ht	Wt	Age	Exp	College
Goode, Don (O)	6-2	225	26	4	Kansas
Lowe, Woodrow (O)	6-0	227	23	2	Alabama
Graham, Tom (M)	6-2	235	27	6	Oregon
Horn, Bob (M)	6-3	235	23	2	Oregon State
Middleton, Rick (O)	6-2	234	25	4	Ohio State
Preston, Ray (O)	6-0	223	23	2	Syracuse

(O)—Outside Linebacker   (M)—Middle Linebacker

Patience is wearing thin with Goode. Lowe made some contributions as a rookie. Graham is no better than mediocre. Horn will get a shot at the middle job now that he's had a year to acclimate himself. Middleton did little after his arrival from New Orleans. Preston is not highly rated. This is one of the team's weakest areas, which becomes even worse when it plays behind a bad line. PERF. QT.: 5.

CORNERBACKS	Ht	Wt	Age	Exp	College
Williams, Mike	5-10	181	23	3	Louisiana State
Hayes, Tom	6-1	198	31	7	San Diego State
Stringert, Hal	5-11	185	25	3	Hawaii
Colbert, Danny	5-11	176	26	4	Tulsa

Williams is starting to look like the first-round draft shoice the Chargers named two years ago. Hayes is a journeyman. Stringert, also the back-up at the safety spots, is a former WFLer. Colbert has some good games, some bad ones. PERF. QT.: 3.

SAFETIES	Ht	Wt	Age	Exp	College
Fuller, Mike (S)	5-9	195	24	3	Auburn
Fletcher, Chris (W)	5-11	189	28	8	Temple

(S)—Strong-side   (W)—Weak-side or "Free" Safety

Fuller is a hitter and one of the league's most exciting punt returners. Fletcher is a solid vet. PERF. QT.: 2.

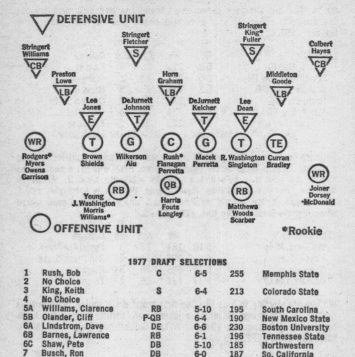

DEFENSIVE UNIT

Stringert
Williams
CB

Stringert
Fletcher
S

Stringert
King*
Fuller
S

Colbert
Hayes
CB

Preston
Lowe
LB

Horn
Graham
LB

Middleton
Goode
LB

Lee
Jones
E

DeJurnett
Johnson
T

DeJurnett
Kelcher
T

Lee
Dean
E

WR

T

G

C

G

T

TE

Rodgers*
Myers
Owens
Garrison

Brown
Shields

Wilkerson
Aiu

Rush*
Flanagan
Perretta

Macek
Perretta

R. Washington
Singleton

Curran
Bradley

WR

RB

QB

RB

Young
J. Washington
Morris
Williams*

Harris
Fouts
Longley

Matthews
Woods
Scarber

Joiner
Dorsey
*McDonald

OFFENSIVE UNIT

*Rookie

1977 DRAFT SELECTIONS

1	Rush, Bob	C	6-5	255	Memphis State
2	No Choice				
3	King, Keith	S	6-4	213	Colorado State
4	No Choice				
5A	Williams, Clarence	RB	5-10	195	South Carolina
5B	Olander, Cliff	P-QB	6-4	190	New Mexico State
6A	Lindstrom, Dave	DE	6-6	230	Boston University
6B	Barnes, Lawrence	RB	6-1	196	Tennessee State
6C	Shaw, Pete	DB	5-10	185	Northwestern
7	Busch, Ron	DB	6-0	187	So. California
8	No Choice				
9	Washington, Gene	WR	5-9	169	Georgia
10	Townsend, Curtis	LB	6-0	225	Arkansas
11	No Choice				
12	Stansik, Jim	TE	6-4	246	Eastern Michigan

Rush will be the successor to aging Flanagan. He may start immediately. King might relieve Fuller at strong safety so that Fuller can concentrate on his kick return specialties. Williams has some talent, but it's hard to see where he fits with this team. Olander is viewed as a punter, not a quarterback, here. PERF. QT.: 5.

KANSAS CITY CHIEFS

Prediction: Fourth

The Kansas City Chiefs were full of hope when they upset Cleveland, 39-14, on the final day of the 1976 season. It was a fast finish for a team that was beleaguered most of the year. They won two of their last three games. Their last two defeats were by a total of four points to strong clubs, the Cincinnati Bengals and Denver Broncos.

So what do they get as a reward in 1977? A schedule that could well turn out to be the toughest in the NFL in 1977.

Kansas City's opponents won 88 games and lost 66 last year. The Chiefs play eight games against teams that had winning records last season.

KC isn't ready for that sort of action. The Chiefs were the second-worst defensive team in the league last year, the worst in the AFC. They had one of the poorest offensive rushing records and their ranking of second in the NFL in passing is a misleading statistic.

The passing record was compiled with the help of a ton of dinky, dump-off passes. MacArthur Lane, the aged fullback, led the NFL with 66 receptions.

Mike Livingston, the 31-year-old quarterback, played better than he had in his entire career. He had a 332-yard day in an upset victory over Washington. But he is not the type of field general to build your dreams on.

Lane doesn't have many days left as a fullback, either, but his 29-year-old halfback partner, Ed Podolak, played surprisingly well in the last month of the season.

Podolak's late production was vital, since the Chiefs are getting tired of waiting for Woody Green, once thought to be a future star, to stay healthy and produce. To make sure they are well protected against another disappointing season by Green, they drafted Tony Reed of Colorado in the second round, and he could even challenge for a starting job before the season gets too old. But behind Lane there is nothing of certified quality.

The Chiefs' receiving corps is thin, too, but promising.

The star is tight end Walter White, whom the Chiefs claimed two years ago from Pittsburgh. Henry Marshall made the All-Rookie team after he broke into the KC lineup at the start of the season, while Larry Brunson did satisfactory work.

Billy Masters used to share the tight end job with White, but he had a spinal disc operation in the off-season so Andre Samuels of Bethune-Cookman was drafted as insurance.

The offensive line could see some big changes. Rod Walters, last year's No. 1 draft choice, was given a bit of starting duty at guard last year, but now he'll be aimed at Jim Nicholson's tackle assignment. Matt Herkenhoff, a WFL escapee, did well in his first shot at the other tackle. Charlie Getty, the former tackle, satisfied Coach Paul Wiggin as a starting guard. His partner is Tom Condon. The one constant is center Jack Rudnay. The reserves are far from overwhelming.

Jan Stenerud can still kick field goals. He did it 21 times last year. Punter Jerrel Wilson is another veteran who gets his job done in fine style.

The Chiefs' defensive statistics are depressing: 27th out of 28 NFL teams in total defense; 27th against the rush; 24th against the pass; and only 22 sacks. Those are unmitigated disaster numbers.

The Chiefs have to start rebuilding somewhere. They elected to start at cornerback, with one of the best players eligible for the NFL draft this year, Baylor's Gary Green.

Green is almost a sure starter, whether he is slotted into the job of 34-year-old Emmitt Thomas or that of Kerry Reardon. Another youngster, second-year pro Tim Collier, may be Green's partner.

Green's emergence, especially, would give Wiggin an aggressive secondary, and if Collier wins a job it will be a young one, to boot. Gary Barbaro won the weak safety job last year as a rookie and Tim Gray, who came from St. Louis in a trade, did well as the starting strong safety.

The line is a mess. The only dependable vet is end Wilbur Young. Tackle Keith Simons had a so-so rookie year. The rest of the available players are just so many bodies scrambling to stay in pro football.

Jimbo Elrod probably will be installed as the No. 1 middle linebacker again. He played there as a rookie until he was injured, then Willie Lanier resumed his old duties.

Jim Lynch and Billy Andrews, who have been around a long time, are the incumbent outside backers but rookie Tom Howard of Texas Tech could win a job before the snow starts to fall.

There is little depth anywhere, but Wiggin can't fix everything at once.

1976 RECORD (5-9)

16	San Diego	30	28	Tampa Bay	19
21	Oakland	24	0	Pittsburgh	45
17	New Orleans	27	10	Oakland	21
17	Buffalo	50	24	Cincinnati	27
33	Washington	30	23	San Diego	20
20	Miami (OT)	17	16	Denver	17
26	Denver	35	39	Cleveland	14

PASSING

	Atts	Comps	Yds	Lgst	TDs	Ints	Pct
Livingston	338	189	2682	57	12	13	55.9
Adams	71	36	575	49	3	4	50.7
Nott	10	4	46	23	0	1	40.0

SCORING

	TDs	PATs	FGs	Total
Stenerud	0	27	21†	90
White	7	0	0	42
Lane	6	0	0	36
Podolak	5	0	0	30
Reamon**	5	0	0	30
Two tied with	3	0	0	18

RUSHING

	Atts	Yds	TDs	Lgst	Avg
Lane	162	542	5	20	3.3
Podolak	88	371	5	22	4.2
Green	73	322	1	27	4.4
Reamon**	103	314	4	14	3.0

RECEIVING

	Recs	Yds	TDs	Lgst	Avg
Lane	66†	686	1	44	10.4
White	47	808	7	41	17.2
Brunson	33	656	1	57	19.9
Marshall	28	443	2	31	15.8
Masters	18	269	3	30	14.9

INTERCEPTIONS

	Ints	Yds	TDs	Lgst	Avg
Reardon	5	26	0	22	5.2
Gray	4	19	0	11	4.8
Lanier	3	28	0	14	9.3
Barbaro	3	27	0	16	9.0
Three tied with 2					

SYMBOLS **—Traded
† —Conference leader

1977 SCHEDULE

Home: Sept. 25—San Diego; Oct. 3—Oakland; Oct. 16—Baltimore; Nov. 6—Green Bay; Nov. 20—Denver; Dec. 4—Cincinnati; Dec. 11—Seattle.

Away: Sept. 18—New England; Oct. 9—Denver; Oct. 23—San Diego; Oct. 30—Cleveland; Nov. 13—Chicago; Nov. 27—Houston; Dec. 18—Oakland.

OFFENSE

QUARTERBACKS	Ht	Wt	Age	Exp	College
Livingston, Mike	6-4	211	31	10	Southern Methodist
Adams, Tony	6-0	198	27	3	Utah State
Nott, Mike	6-3	200	25	2	Santa Clara

The Chiefs seem happy with Livingston. He had his first good year as a starter, throwing for 2682 yards and a 55.9 per cent completion mark. But he's 31, and the bench is zilch. PERF. QT.: 3.

RUNNING BACKS	Ht	Wt	Age	Exp	College
Lane, MacArthur	6-1	220	35	10	Utah State
Podolak, Ed	6-1	205	29	9	Iowa
Green, Woody	6-1	205	26	4	Arizona State
McNeil, Pat	5-9	208	23	2	Baylor
Harrison, Glynn	5-11	191	23	2	Georgia
Jennings, J.J.	6-1	220	25	1	Rutgers

Lane and Podolak? That's almost a 65-year-old running back tandem. Lane led the league with 66 receptions, but most of them were dump-off jobs, and how far can you go with a 35-year-old fullback. Podolak can no longer do it for a full season. Green probably will never play as advertised. McNeil and Harrison haven't showed anything. Jennings went down with a summer injury. PERF. QT.: 4.

RECEIVERS	Ht	Wt	Age	Exp	College
Marshall, Henry (W)	6-2	205	23	2	Missouri
Brunson, Larry (W)	5-11	180	28	4	Colorado
White, Walter (T)	6-3	218	26	3	Maryland
Masters, Billy (T)	6-5	240	33	11	Louisiana State
Pearson, Barry (W)	5-11	185	27	6	Northwestern
Williams, Lawrence (W)	5-10	173	23	2	Texas Tech

(W)—Wide Receiver   (T)—Tight End

Marshall showed enough to make the Chiefs feel he can be a solid major leaguer. Brunson was satisfactory, but he's not in the top rank. White is light for a TE, but he's a good one, possibly the most dangerous catcher on the team. Masters used to split duty with White, but the vet's back injury may end his career. Pearson is adequate in reserve. Williams returns kicks. PERF. QT.: 3.

INTERIOR LINEMEN	Ht	Wt	Age	Exp	College
Nicholson, Jim (T)	6-6	275	27	4	Michigan State
Herkenhoff, Matt (T)	6-4	255	26	2	Minnesota
Condon, Tom (G)	6-3	240	24	4	Boston College
Getty, Charlie (G)	6-4	260	25	4	Penn State

INTERIOR LINEMEN (Contd.)	Ht	Wt	Age	Exp	College
Rudnay, Jack (C)	6-3	240	29	8	Northwestern
Walters, Rod (T)	6-3	258	23	2	Iowa
Ane, Charlie (C)	6-1	233	25	3	Michigan State
Olsen, Orrin (C-G)	6-1	245	24	2	Brigham Young
Beisler, Randy (G)	6-5	244	32	11	Indiana

(T)—Tackle   (G)—Guard   (C)—Center

This line is still fermenting. Nicholson's job is subject to challenge. Herkenhoff was a pleasant surprise after his return from the WFL. Condon moved in to start after '76 began and performed adequately. Getty and Rudnay are superior players; Rudnay is one of the best centers in the league. Walters moves from guard to tackle to take on Nicholson. Rod started a few games at guard last year after being drafted No. 1. He has great ability, but he's not a quick learner. Ane and Olsen just fill in. Beisler probably can't come back from a two-year neck injury at this advanced stage of his career. PERF. QT.: 3.

KICKERS	Ht	Wt	Age	Exp	College
Stenerud, Jan (Pk)	6-2	187	33	11	Montana State
Wilson, Jerrel (P)	6-2	222	35	15	So. Mississippi

(Pk)—Placekicker   (P)—Punter

Stenerud led the AFC in field goals made. Wilson finished among the leading punters. These are two old-reliables. PERF. QT.: 1.

DEFENSE

FRONT LINEMEN	Ht	Wt	Age	Exp	College
Young, Wilbur (E)	6-6	290	28	7	William Penn
Paul, Whitney (E)	6-3	220	23	2	Colorado
Simons, Keith (T)	6-3	254	23	2	Minnesota
Wolf, James (T)	6-3	250	25	3	Prairie View
Maddox, Bob (E)	6-5	250	28	4	Frostburg State
Lohmeyer, John (E)	6-4	229	26	4	Emporia State
Lee, Willie (T)	6-5	249	27	2	Bethune-Cookman
Estes, Lawrence (T-E)	6-6	250	30	6	Alcorn
Magrum, Bud (T)	6-4	255	28	1	Colorado

(E)—End   (T)—Tackle

The Chiefs finished very, very close to the bottom of the NFL in virtually every defensive statistic. What more is there to say? Only Young, the seven-year vet, commands any respect around the league. It's not only that there's no record of accomplishment among these players, but it's hard to find reason for hope for improvement. Many of them are on the small side, some are past the age of being called prospects. Paul

Is too small, but he at least plays hard. Simons is at least young. But the others have very little to recommend them. Coach Wiggin will try magic and the waiver lists. PERF. QT.: 5.

LINEBACKERS	Ht	Wt	Age	Exp	College
Lynch, Jim (O)	6-1	225	31	11	Notre Dame
Andrews, Billy (O)	6-0	220	32	11	Southeast Louisiana
Elrod, Jimbo (M)	6-0	209	23	2	Oklahoma
Lanier, Willie (M)	6-1	245	32	11	Morgan State
Rozumek, Dave (O)	6-2	212	23	2	New Hampshire
Werner, Clyde (O)	6-3	230	29	7	Washington

(O)—Outside Linebacker   (M)—Middle Linebacker

The Chiefs need a heavy injection of youth here. Lynch and Andrews are well past their primes, and the former is even considering retirement. Elrod took the middle job away from Lanier, then was hurt and lost for the season. Jimbo is not big, but Wiggin loves him. Lanier is another who is thinking of packing it in. Rozumek at least is youthful. Werner has leg problems. PERF. QT.: 5.

CORNERBACKS	Ht	Wt	Age	Exp	College
Thomas, Emmitt	6-2	192	34	12	Bishop
Reardon, Kerry	5-11	180	28	7	Iowa
Collier, Tim	5-11	166	23	2	East Texas State
Taylor, Steve	6-3	204	23	2	Kansas

Thomas isn't the corner he was a few seasons ago. Reardon is fairly dependable, but the coaches feel he would be a better four-position reserve than a starter. Collier will hit anything that moves. Taylor is a safety candidate. PERF. QT.: 3.

SAFETIES	Ht	Wt	Age	Exp	College
Gray, Tim (S)	6-1	200	24	3	Texas A&M
Barbaro, Gary (W)	6-4	198	23	2	Nicholls State
Bograkos, Steve (W)	5-11	171	23	1	Central Michigan

(S)—Strong-side   (W)—Weak-side or "Free" Safety

Gray was a major asset after he came from the Cardinals. Barbaro overcame a small school background. Bograkos may stick for lack of spear-carriers. PERF. QT.: 2.

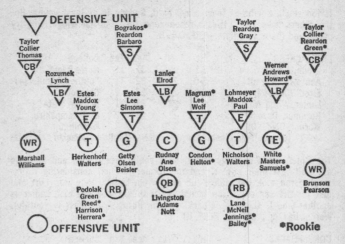

1977 DRAFT SELECTIONS

1	Green, Gary	CB	5-11	184	Baylor
2	Reed, Tony	RB	5-11	197	Colorado
3	Howard, Tom	LB	6-1	210	Texas Tech
4A	Bailey, Mark	RB	6-3	237	Cal St.-Long Beach
4B	Samuels, Andre	TE	6-4	230	Bethune-Cookman
4C	Helton, Darius	G	6-2	260	N. Carolina Central
4D	Harris, Eric	DB	6-3	187	Memphis State
5	No Choice				
6A	Burleson, Rick	DE	6-5	240	Texas
6B	Herrera, Andre	RB	6-0	197	Southern Illinois
7	Golub, Chris	S	6-3	200	Kansas
8A	Olsonoski, Ron	LB	6-3	235	St. Thomas
8B	Smith, Waddell	WR	6-2	162	Kansas
9A	Glanton, Derrick	DE	6-6	246	Bishop
9B	Green, Dave	T	6-4	263	New Mexico
10	Vitali, Mark	QB	6-5	209	Purdue
11	Mitchell, Maurice	WR	5-11	185	No. Michigan
12	Burks, Ray	LB	6-2	217	UCLA

Green was one of the best picks in the draft, an instant starter who should help an already-improved secondary. Reed is insurance against Woody Green's penchant for disappointing. The youngster, a fine receiver coming out of the backfield, could even push his way into the starting lineup. Howard gets a big chance to start with the Chiefs' linebacking in decrepit condition. Bailey could be the heir to the aging MacArthur Lane. Samuels stands a chance, especially because Masters' back is so bad. Helton's opportunity comes from the lack of quality reserves on the offensive line. Harris went to Canada; when he comes back to the NFL, he'll be a good one. A dark horse to watch is Herrera, a youngster with talent. PERF. QT.: 2.

SEATTLE SEAHAWKS

Prediction: Fifth

Seattle had the second pick in the 1977 NFL draft. Tampa Bay had selected first and taken Ricky Bell.

This meant, of course, that Tony Dorsett was ready for the plucking.

Suddenly, Seattle traded its pick to Dallas for the right to swap first-round choices and for three of Dallas' second-round selections, one of which was traded back to the Cowboys a few hours later for wide receiver Duke Fergerson. Then the Seahawks traded their own second choice to Los Angeles for center Geoff Reece and the Rams' second-round draft slot.

Now, the two sides of the blockbuster transaction.

"A running back wouldn't do us much good now," says Seahawk Coach Jack Patera. "By the time we're ready to contend, he could be burned out. I believe you have to strengthen the basics—the lines, the overall defense—and then get the flash."

Perfectly acceptable.

"Tony Dorsett might be another O.J. Simpson," says Tex Schramm, the general manager of the Cowboys. "You can't afford not to try to get him for your team."

Even more acceptable.

But the Seahawks chose to take the extra choices. With the first one, they picked guard Steve August of Tulsa, who was rated no higher than seventh at his position in any of the scouting pools.

In the second round, they named offensive tackle Tom Lynch of Boston College, followed by the selection of two middle linebackers, Terry Beeson of Kansas and Pete Cronan of Boston College.

"We were pleased," said Patera. "We got at least three starters with our picks plus Fergerson and Reece, both of whom could start."

Oh, well, it is hoped that the fans up in the Northwest will buy the rationale.

In other respects, the Seahawks finished their first season in far better shape than the other expansionists in Tampa. They found some legitimate stars-to-be, such as QB Jim Zorn, RB Sherman Smith, WR Steve Largent, DT Steve Niehaus, LB Sammy Green. Now they must whip their lines into shape and start moving the ball better on the ground.

Zorn was fine, a young Tarkenton type who runs and throws and provides leadership. Smith showed in his nine starting assignments that he is going to be a workhorse back, but he isn't enough by himself and there isn't a lot else there. The wide receivers are Largent and Sam McCullum, but Sam may lose his job to Fergerson because of a severe knee problem, while Steve Raible and fourth-round rookie Larry Seivers apply additional pressure.

The tight end is Ron Howard, but maybe only until camp opens and 6-5, 233-pound Charles Waddell, former North Carolina basketballer, takes over. He was hurt and missed all of '76, as did Fergerson.

August and Bob Penchion should be the guards, Lynch and Norm Evans or Nick Bebout the tackles, and Fred Hoaglin, Reece, Art Kuehn and rookie John Yarno will fight for the center job. At the moment,

Don Testerman has the other running spot alongside Smith, but such rookies as Tony Benjamin and David Sims will supply heated competition.

The defensive line needed some help and got it via trade, when Patera sent middle linebacker Ed Bradley to San Francisco for tackle-end Bill Sandifer. He and rookie end Dennis Boyd should win regular jobs, along with last year's super freshman tackle, Niehaus. That leaves the other tackle holdover, Richard Harris, and such as Bob Lurtsema, Dave Tipton and Carl Barisich as reserves.

Mike Curtis and Ken Geddes are the holdover outside linebackers, but both are going to be hard-pressed by such as Randy Coffield, Ken Hutcherson and Sammy Green. Greg Collins, the nominal starter with Bradley departed, will almost certainly lose the job in the middle to Beeson or Cronan.

The secondary didn't get any trade or draft help, but it wasn't bad. On the corners are Rolly Woolsey and Eddie McMillan, both backed up by Ernie Jones. Dave Brown is the free safety, Al Matthews the strong safety, and Lyle Blackwood, Steve Preece and Don Dufek are in reserve.

Zorn is the key to the offense. He threw 439 times last season to lead the league by 80 attempts; he hit 208 for 2571 yards and 12 TDs. He was the team's second-highest ground gainer, too, with 246 yards in 52 carries. His favorite pass-catcher was Largent, a rookie taken from the Oilers on summer waivers, who caught 54 passes for 705 yards.

More yards out of those paid to carry the ball, some more effective blocking and some tougher defense can make the Seahawks an almost respectable team. But how hard it must have been to pass up Dorsett. And how much will Patera come to regret that decision?

1976 RECORD (2-12)

24	St. Louis	30	6	Los Angeles	45
7	Washington	31	30	Atlanta	13
21	San Francisco	37	21	Minnesota	27
13	Dallas	28	27	New Orleans	51
20	Green Bay	27	16	New York Giants	28
13	Tampa Bay	10	7	Chicago	34
14	Detroit	41	10	Philadelphia	27

PASSING

	Atts	Comps	Yds	Lgst	TDs	Ints	Pct
Zorn	439†	208	2571	80	12	27	47.4
Munson	37	20	295	44	1	3	54.1

SCORING

	TDs	PATs	FGs	Total
Leypoldt•	0	22	8	46
Smith	5	0	0	30
Largent	4	0	0	24
McCullum	4	0	0	24
McKinnis	4	0	0	24
Zorn	4	0	0	24

RUSHING

	Atts	Yds	TDs	Lgst	Avg
Smith	119	537	4	53	4.5
Zorn	52	246	4	19	4.7
Testerman	67	246	1	16	3.7
Nelson	52	173	1	25	3.3
McKinnis	46	105	4	14	2.3

RECEIVING

	Recs	Yds	TDs	Lgst	Avg
Largent	54	705	4	45	13.1
Howard	37	422	0	30	11.4
Smith	36	384	1	34	10.7
McCullum	32	506	4	72	15.8
Testerman	25	232	1	25	9.3
McKinnis	13	148	0	22	11.4

INTERCEPTIONS

	Ints	Yds	TDs	Lgst	Avg
Brown	4	70	0	33	17.5
Woolsey	4	19	0	13	4.8
Matthews	3	60	1	40	20.0
Curtis	2	40	0	26	20.0

SYMBOLS †—Conference leader (NFC in 1976)
•—Combined Buffalo-Seattle record

1977 SCHEDULE

Home: Sept. 18—Baltimore; Oct. 2—Denver; Oct. 16—Tampa Bay; Oct. 30—Buffalo; Nov. 20—Houston; Nov. 27—San Diego; Dec. 18—Cleveland.

Away: Sept. 25—Cincinnati; Oct. 9—New England; Oct. 23—Miami; Nov. 6—Oakland; Nov. 13—New York Jets; Dec. 4—Pittsburgh; Dec. 11—Kansas City.

OFFENSE

QUARTERBACKS	Ht	Wt	Age	Exp	College
Zorn, Jim	6-2	200	24	2	Cal Poly-Pomona
Munson, Bill	6-2	205	36	14	Utah State
Myer, Steve	6-2	188	23	2	New Mexico

Zorn showed real Pro Bowl potential as last year's major surprise. Munson was acquired from Detroit strictly as bench strength and quasi-coach. While Zorn plays and learns, Myer sits and learns. PERF. QT.: 3.

RUNNING BACKS	Ht	Wt	Age	Exp	College
Smith, Sherman	6-4	217	22	2	Miami, Ohio
Testerman, Don	6-2	230	24	2	Clemson
McKinnis, Hugh	6-1	219	29	5	Arizona State
Nelson, Ralph	6-2	195	23	3	None
Ross, Oliver	6-0	210	27	5	Alabama A&M

Smith, who became the team's workhorse, has strength but no real speed. Testerman was a waiver pickup who stuck, which is no guarantee now. McKinnis has some power but doesn't do standout work often enough. Nelson is simply a retread without much hope of sticking this year. Ross isn't much, either. PERF. QT.: 4.

RECEIVERS	Ht	Wt	Age	Exp	College
Largent, Steve (W)	5-11	184	22	2	Tulsa
McCullum, Sam (W)	6-2	203	24	4	Montana State
Howard, Ron (T)	6-4	225	26	4	Seattle
Fergerson, Duke (W)	6-1	193	23	1	San Diego State
Waddell, Charles (T)	6-5	233	24	1	North Carolina
Raible, Steve (W)	6-2	195	23	2	Georgia Tech
McMakin, John (T)	6-3	225	26	6	Clemson

(W)—Wide Receiver   (T)—Tight End

Largent, a clever waiver-list find, showed moves, finesse and intelligence. McCullum is a fine athlete, but he had serious off-season knee surgery. Howard won the tight end job in '76, but much more is hoped for by the Seahawks. Fergerson, hurt as a Dallas rookie, has speed. He returns kicks, also. Waddell, also a '76 injury case, could win Howard's job. Raible was a rookie with good hands and speed; he, too, could challenge. McMakin will have to be lucky to stick. PERF. QT.: 3.

INTERIOR LINEMEN	Ht	Wt	Age	Exp	College
Evans, Norm (T)	6-5	250	34	12	Texas Christian
Bebout, Nick (T)	6-5	260	26	5	Wyoming
Penchion, Bob (G)	6-6	252	28	6	Alcorn
Newton, Bob (G)	6-4	260	28	7	Nebraska

INTERIOR LINEMEN (Contd.)	Ht	Wt	Age	Exp	College
Hoaglin, Fred (C)	6-4	250	33	12	Pittsburgh
Reece, Geoff (C)	6-4	247	25	2	Washington State
Jolley, Gordon (T)	6-5	245	28	6	Utah
Demarie, John (G)	6-3	248	32	11	Louisiana State
Coder, Ron (G)	6-3	250	23	2	Penn State
Simonson, Dave (T)	6-6	248	25	4	Minnesota
Kuehn, Art (C)	6-3	255	24	2	UCLA

(T)—Tackle   (G)—Guard   (C)—Center

Evans was the team's top lineman and may have been its only good one. Bebout, a former Falcon, has good size but not many credentials. Penchion has always had potential but must continue to improve. Newton is adequate, but he's not starting caliber on most lines. Hoaglin is a veteran who could be moved to the Hawks' bench. Reece, from Los Angeles, could be the one to demote Hoaglin. Jolley will need a big break just to stick around again. DeMarie is a versatile vet, and that should keep him on this team. Coder played some and didn't do badly, but he isn't the answer. Simonson is in over his head. Kuehn has the heaviest competition on the line at his position and would be a surprise to make the roster. PERF. QT.: 5.

KICKERS	Ht	Wt	Age	Exp	College
Leypoldt, John (Pk)	6-2	230	31	7	None
Engles, Rick (P)	5-10	170	23	2	Tulsa

(Pk)—Placekicker   (P)—Punter

Leypoldt is a journeyman whose performance proved to be adequate. Engles is competent, no problem. PERF. QT.: 3.

DEFENSE

FRONT LINEMEN	Ht	Wt	Age	Exp	College
Sandifer, Bill (T-E)	6-6	260	25	4	UCLA
Lurtsema, Bob (E-T)	6-6	250	35	11	Western Michigan
Niehaus, Steve (T)	6-4	270	22	2	Notre Dame
Harris, Richard (T)	6-5	258	29	7	Grambling
Barisich, Carl (T-E)	6-4	255	26	5	Princeton
Tipton, Dave (E)	6-6	246	28	7	Stanford

(E)—End   (T)—Tackle

Sandifer never did it in San Francisco, but he'll be a helpful starter here. Lurtsema brought experience and familiarity with Coach Patera's system to the Hawks in '76. Rookie Niehaus was a genuine prize; he played well with great strength. Harris has always been overrated and proved that as an expansion-team starter. Barisich is a fill-in at best.

Tipton started most of '76, but they hope he won't in '77. PERF. QT.: 4.

LINEBACKERS	Ht	Wt	Age	Exp	College
Geddes, Ken (O)	6-3	235	29	7	Nebraska
Curtis, Mike (O)	6-2	232	34	13	Duke
Collins, Greg (M)	6-3	227	24	3	Notre Dame
Green, Sammy (O)	6-2	228	22	2	Florida
Coffield, Randy (O)	6-3	215	23	2	Florida State
Hutcherson, Ken (O)	6-0	225	25	2	Livingston

(O)—Outside Linebacker   (M)—Middle Linebacker

This is Seattle's strong point. Geddes plays well; he has good range, speed. Curtis will be challenged; he has slowed down a lot. Collins is a heavy hitter, but not Ed Bradley's replacement. Green was an impressive rookie who has his eye on a starting position. Coffield is another youngster who showed ability and may be of value. Hutcherson was hurt all year, but he's a good one. PERF. QT.: 2.

CORNERBACKS	Ht	Wt	Age	Exp	College
McMillan, Eddie	6-0	190	25	5	Florida State
Woolsey, Rolly	6-1	182	24	3	Boise State
Jones, Ernie	6-3	180	24	2	Miami, Fla.

McMillan plays with intelligence and has been a regular for a long time. Woolsey could face a challenge, although he, too, played with élan. Jones is versatile. PERF. QT.: 3.

SAFETIES	Ht	Wt	Age	Exp	College
Matthews, Al (S)	5-11	190	29	8	Texas A&I
Brown, Dave (W)	6-1	190	24	3	Michigan
Blackwood, Lyle (S-W)	6-0	190	26	5	Texas Christian
Preece, Steve (W-S)	6-1	195	30	9	Oregon State
Dufek, Don (S)	6-0	195	23	2	Michigan

(S)—Strong-side   (W)—Weak-side or "Free" Safety

Matthews won a starting berth and played with skill. Brown, once a Pittsburgh No. 1 choice, should continue to improve. Blackwood has the ability to play both safety spots and cornerback, too, if necessary. Preece was a handy performer in Los Angeles, but can he help playing behind this group? Dufek has physical limitations. PERF. QT.: 3.

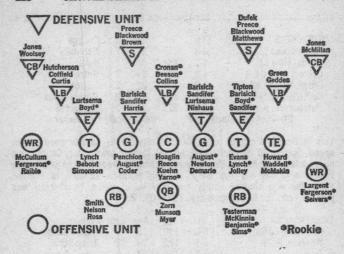

1977 DRAFT SELECTIONS

1	August, Steve	G	6-4	243	Tulsa
2A	Lynch, Tom	T	6-5	260	Boston College
2B	Beeson, Terry	LB	6-2	240	Kansas
2C	Cronan, Pete	LB	6-2	243	Boston College
3	Boyd, Dennis	DE	6-6	245	Oregon State
4A	Yarno, John	C	6-5	245	Idaho
4B	Selvers, Larry	WR	6-4	204	Tennessee
5	No Choice				
6	Benjamin, Tony	RB	6-3	214	Duke
7	Sims, David	RB	6-3	219	Georgia Tech
8	No Choice				
9	Adzick, George	DB	6-4	196	Minnesota
10	Adkins, Sam	QB	6-4	214	Wichita State
11	Westbeld, Bill	T	6-7	250	Dayton
12	Wilson, I. V.	DT	6-4	260	Tulsa

August had better make it, and big, since he was the important choice received for the right to draft Tony Dorsett. The youngster's forte is pass blocking. Lynch, Beeson or Cronan and Boyd all figure to start, and Yarno may have been the best of the thin crop of collegiate centers. Selvers was rated higher than a fourth-rounder, and a lot of scouts liked Sims and Benjamin. PERF. QT.: 2.

SUPER FEATURES, ROUND-BY-ROUND DRAFT SELECTIONS, STATISTICAL REFERENCE SECTION

MARCHING LEFT
TO VICTORY

There is no truth at all to the rumor that the NFL owners tried to pass a five-year moratorium on further Minnesota appearances in the Super Bowl. Such a proposal would never have a chance. The owners of the AFC teams would unanimously reject it.

The Vikings, who play in a weak division and win it annually without breaking a sweat, handled Washington and then a silly Los Angeles team (which should have won by two touchdowns) and found themselves in Pasadena on the morning of January 9 to meet Oakland in Super Bowl XI.

Better they should have conducted the game by mail, or via the procedure known as unconditional surrender.

The Vikings lost their fourth Super Bowl in as many tries, and were never really in danger of ending their streak. No team has made four Super Bowl appearances. Obviously, no team has lost that many, either.

But this was the worst of all. In their first three tries—against Kansas City, Miami and Pittsburgh—the Vikings looked as if they had at least a semblance of a chance. But Oakland allowed no such gestures of bravado. The Raiders simply snuffed out the Vikings' multi-faceted offense (Chuck Foreman running the ball or Fran Tarkenton throwing the ball) and erased the Vikings' fearsome defense, and when the smoke cleared and the rubble was swept away, the score was 32-14.

It was never that close.

Oakland, which finally realized the potential that had produced a frustrating decade of near-misses, never allowed the Vikings to get into the game.

"Our offense did everything we hoped it would be able to do," said Coach John Madden, the burly, bulky young man who is referred to by his players as The Pink Elephant.

The easy victory was Oakland's 13th in a row, and the final season record was 16-1. Not bad for a team that lost a busload of regulars to injury, and finally had to go with a 3-4 defense just because there weren't four healthy or playable linemen. The survivors of training camp were veterans Otis Sistrunk and Dave Rowe, who had spent nine years toiling in obscurity, and rookies Charles Philyaw and Herb McMath. Then John Matuszak, the problem child of the '70s, was picked up on waivers.

In the post-Super Bowl locker room, Madden tried not to be nasty, but it didn't work. "We had tougher games in the AFC than we had today," he said. He was perfectly justified in his opinion. The Raiders had had to get past the rampaging Steelers in the AFC championship game, and although Pittsburgh running backs Franco Harris and Rocky Bleier sat on the bench mending, the victory was still an upset.

Indeed, Madden might have had a tougher game if he coached the Raiders against a Big Eight team on January 9.

The Oakland offense—lefthanded because its quar-

terback, Ken Stabler, is and because of the quality
of the linemen on that side—reaped yardage in record-
setting clusters. The 429 yards gained was a Super
Bowl record. So was the 266 yards gained rushing.
Clarence Davis, the erratic halfback who was one of
Oakland's dubious links going into the game, re-
sponded to taunting with 137 yards in 16 carries, an
incredible 8.6 per carry. Mark van Eeghen, who played
at Colgate, of all places, added 73 yards in 18 trips.
Each of them surpassed Minnesota's rushing yardage,
71.

But there was more. Lord, were there stars for the
Raiders!

Stabler, the lefthanded scalpel, completed 12 of 19
passes for 180 yards. Wide receiver Fred Biletnikoff,
who was named the game's MVP, caught four of them
for 79 yards and twice was tripped up at the 1-yard
line. Tight end Dave Casper, who could have been the
MVP, caught four short passes and turned them into
70 yards' worth of ground, as well as a touchdown.

And the blocking. Left guard Gene Upshaw and left
tackle Art Shell might have been considered more
carefully for the MVP designation, too. They wiped
out the two most important Viking defenders, end Carl
Eller and tackle Alan Page.

Nothing yet has been said about the Oakland defense, which neutralized Foreman's efforts and frus-
trated Tarkenton and rose up to make big plays when
nothing less would suffice.

It was more a unit achievement than a case of
specific individuals playing well, and it is therefore
difficult to single out one player. Cornerback Willie
Brown returned an interception 75 yards for a touchdown. Linebackers Ted Hendricks, Phil Villapiano,
Monte Johnson and Willie Hall combined to register

23 tackles, one sack, one interception and a monstrously important fumble recovery.

But it was that lefthanded offense that buried the Vikings, and the first drive of the game, although it climaxed with an unsuccessful field goal, showed the Vikings the sort of troubles they would have all day.

The first two plays were slants to the left. Having established that, Stabler faked a handoff to Davis and wheeled to his right, finding Casper on the sideline and throwing a pass that became a 25-yard gain. Then Davis took a handoff, after a fake to van Eeghen going left, and gained four around right end.

Already, the Vikings were scrambling, so Stabler called a draw for Davis, who naturally broke to his left, and when he cleared through an Upshaw block, he gained 20 yards. That took the ball to the Minnesota 12 in just five plays (which gained 54 yards).

The script was written.

Perhaps the most unique aspect of that first quarter, in light of the final count, was that it was scoreless. But the Vikings had their only chance and blew it. Badly.

Having made their own breaks all season by blocking 14 kicking attempts (punts and field goals), the Vikings brought the total to 15 with five minutes left in the quarter when linebacker Fred McNeill crashed through to register the first-ever block on Oakland punter Ray Guy.

The ball was recovered by McNeill, too, on the Raiders' 3. No defense could hold the Vikings in four downs from there, right?

Wrong.

Foreman hit the middle and picked up a yard.

Brent McClanahan hit the middle and was waffled by Villapiano, the headhunter. McClanahan was rendered unconscious, the ball fell from his limp fingers and Hall captured it on the 2.

And do you know what? The Raiders drove from there to the Vikings' 7 and took an early second quarter lead when Errol Mann (another waiver pickup) kicked a 24-yard field goal.

It began.

On the next series, Stabler hit five of five passes on a 64-yard march capped by a one-yard TD toss to Casper. That made it 10-0. On the next drive, Stabler took his team 35 yards in just five plays, following a 25-yard punt return by Neal Colzie. Pete Banaszak, one of four Raiders to have played in Super Bowl II, crashed over right guard (George Buehler) from the 1. The PAT was wide to the right, but it was 16-0, which is how the half ended.

Mann made it 19-0 with a 40-yarder, but then, with 47 seconds left in the third quarter, the Vikings finally got on the scoreboard. Aided by a running-into-the-punter flag on Hendricks, the Vikings moved a total of 68 yards, capped by Tarkenton's eight-yard TD pass to rookie wide receiver Sammie White.

And it was 19-7.

And then the Raiders ran away. Hall intercepted a Tarkenton pass on the Raider 31 and took it to the 47 early in the fourth quarter. Three plays later Stabler hit Biletnikoff for 48 yards to the one. Then Banaszak ran it over for his second TD and Mann added the point-after.

That made it 26-7. On the Vikings' next series, Tarkenton was plucked again. This time it was Brown, the 37-year-old, 14-year veteran, and he shed his years with each step as he outdistanced the Viking for a 75-yard TD return.

That put it up to 32-7.

Nothing else mattered, not even a TD pass from sub QB Bob Lee to tight end Stu Voigt with 25 seconds remaining in the game. The 103,424 paid customers had seen enough. Not even Woody Hayes had managed to embarrass himself so totally on this same Rose Bowl turf.

And the Vikings knew it.

Page had nothing to say. Neither did Eller.

"They just totally dominated us," said Tarkenton. "The Raiders played extremely well and made us play badly."

Coach Bud Grant—variously referred to as Iron Eyes or Son of Grey Eagle—was testy. "Is Oakland the best team in pro football? I'd be crazy if I didn't think so. They are a great team and they played a great game and they won."

Tarkenton added that "we didn't play well at all and I have absolutely no answers as to why. We'll have to look for an AFC team we can beat when we come back to the Super Bowl again."

Like the Jets? It's a pick-'em.

There was one Viking hero, however. Middle linebacker Jeff Siemon, who made 15 tackles, sat on his stool in the locker room looking exactly like a man who had just run 20 miles with a piano on his back. "We were on the field too much," he said. "Nobody should have to make that many tackles."

At least not a guy playing on a Super Bowl team.

"TOO GOOD TO BE TRUE"

Soldier Field is called Payton Place.

His locker underneath the ancient stadium is called Payton's Space.

His unique style of running is called Payton's Pace.

He has excited the football-hungry fans of Chicago in a manner unlike anyone since Gale Sayers.

His name is Walter Payton, and there is very little he cannot do with a football in his hands.

"Walter is . . . well, he's the closest thing I've seen to Sayers," says Coach Jack Pardee, who once spent his Sunday afternoons with the Rams and Redskins trying to tackle Sayers. "He has the impossible speed Gale had, the kind that doesn't look so fast until you try to catch him."

Walter Payton, then, is somebody special. More than that. He may become incomparable. He is entering only his third NFL year, and he's only 23, and barring injury he can look forward to another decade of heroism.

Payton is only 5-10½. But he weighs 204 pounds. So he's not just another small man trying to stay whole in a big man's game. Walter's legs are out of proportion to the rest of his body. They are heavily muscled and resemble pistons when he drives for extra ground.

Payton was drafted on the first round in 1975, the fourth player chosen (behind Steve Bartkowski, Randy White and Ken Huff, none of whom has approached his success). The college was Jackson State. In Mississippi. But there was nothing resembling the dark horse or the sleeper about Payton. He had been labeled the best running back in that draft, and that has proved to be absolutely correct.

Indeed. He finished his four-year Jackson State career with 3563 yards gained—a 6.1-yard per carry average—and 66 touchdowns. He even kicked five field goals and 53 extra points, and emerged as the leading scorer in NCAA history. Oh, yes: He had a 14-for-19 passing record (474 yards, four TDs) and punted 27 times for a 39-yard average.

In 1976, Walter won the NFC's rushing title with 1390 yards in 311 carries. He entered the final game of the season with a chance to beat out O.J. Simpson for league rushing honors, but he failed. He finished 113 yards behind Simpson, and he refers to that effort now as "the worst day of my life."

By way of explanation, he says, "All season it had been building, this thing between me and O.J. I wanted it very badly [to beat out Simpson], and when that last game came around, I was tight. I had a lead on Simpson but he had a great last game and I didn't. It was just so disappointing. I couldn't even look back at the game as a victory, because we lost [to Denver]."

True, the Bears lost that game. The loss riveted their season record at 7-7, a dramatic upswing from the 4-10 of a year before. And Payton was, hands down, NFC Player of the Year.

"The honors were great," he said. "Being in the Pro Bowl and making the All-Pro teams were great, too. But we didn't win enough games. Look, seven games was better than four, but if you view it another way, we lost as many as we won. I can't accept that as being anywhere near good enough. Our problem was newness, I think, and a lack of confidence in ourselves. One of these days we are all going to realize, at the same time, just how good we can be. When that happens, the winning will be easier."

Payton is the sort of runner—as was Sayers—to whom team improvement can be directly linked. In 1975, his rookie year, he led the Bears in rushing, but it was a far more realistic performance than had been expected by the team. He had some injuries and he made some mistakes and he wound up with 679 yards in 196 carries, certainly not bad but . . .

"Walter was pressing," says Pardee, who was also a rookie in 1975 (in the NFL as a coach after serving hard time as a coach in the WFL). "So much was expected of him . . . all the stories and attention and interviews . . . it just affected him the wrong way. He tried too hard."

But there were flashes. One of his touchdown runs as a rookie came against New Orleans in the final game of the season. It was a 54-yarder in which he either broke or eluded seven separate tackles. And in that game his combined yardage (134 yards rushing, 104 on two kickoff returns, 62 on five receptions) of 300 established an NFC high for the year.

More amazing, perhaps, was his season total of 679 yards when it is broken down. He missed one game. In two others he was held to zero net yards. He gained all of two yards in still another. Which means, of course, that he gained 677 yards in 10 games.

Which ain't bad at all.

"Walter came to us out of the College All-Star

camp with a bruised elbow," says Pardee, "and he missed the entire preseason schedule. He needed that time. Mostly he needed the pro team experience."

He got that in his first season, and then came 1976.

Payton had seven games of more than 100 yards, including such lofty totals as 183 (vs. Seattle), 148 (vs. San Francisco), 145 (vs. Los Angeles) and 141 (vs. Minnesota). In the Minnesota game, he also had a 58-yard TD jaunt called back by penalty.

"Payton was one of the few guys we created a defensive game plan around," said Viking middle linebacker Jeff Siemon. "It is unusual for us to do that, especially for a guy in his second year. But the man is just too tough. He can go different directions in a split second. He just can't be nailed head-on very often."

Pardee, savoring the accomplishments of his 23-year-old superstar, dropped an unsettling hint to the rest of the NFL. "Walter didn't play nearly as good as he can," the coach said. "Just wait until he gets more confidence. And there are still things he must learn." With that said, it must be stated that the Bears' coaches and executives are fond of saying that Payton is "too good to be true."

He reads the Bible daily, and is deeply religious. He is married to his college sweetheart and is never happier than when he is at home. He finished his college curriculum in three and a half years, majoring in special education, and is now working toward a Master's degree in electronic communications.

"Football won't last forever for me," he says. "I have to establish a sound family life and a sound professional career in something else."

But not for a while, fans. Walter Payton has a lot more running to do before he can rest.

THE BEST OF THE BEST

For the "ordinary" good ball carrier, a 100-yard game in the National Football League is a helluva day. For O.J. Simpson it is routine.

The standards the Juice has set for himself since he turned pro in 1969 are so high now that it takes a sensational game for O.J. to rise above his norm. But he has enough of those sensational days to remain consistently in the headlines.

When he lines up to start the 1977 season, he will trail only the great Jim Brown in career ground gaining. Brown ran for 12,312 yards. O.J. has 9626 yards.

With two more years left in his career, Simpson will undoubtedly have more great games. But up to now, these are nine of his best:

Oct. 29, 1972 . . . War Memorial Stadium, Buffalo: What to do? The Bills are playing the Pittsburgh Steelers with Joe Greene, L.C. Greenwood and other defensive stars. Buffalo's only lineman of quality is rookie guard Reggie McKenzie.

Coach Lou Saban's answer is to use an unbalanced line, a rarity in pro football. It works. O.J. gets 189 yards, including the longest run from scrimmage in the NFL in the last 26 years, a 94-yard touchdown.

But a Steeler rookie named Franco Harris is almost as good and Pittsburgh wins, 38-21.

yards to win his first NFL rushing title with 1251 yards.

Sept. 16, 1973 . . . Scheafer Stadium, Foxboro, Mass.:

Buffalo, which hasn't had a winning season since 1966, finished the preseason with a winless record, 0-6. But Coach Lou Saban kept telling his players, "Don't worry, we're building a running attack that will get us victories."

This is the test, the season opener.

Early in the first quarter, guard Reggie McKenzie leads a sweep. He blocks a linebacker and Simpson cuts outside the block and runs 80 yards for a touchdown. It sets the tone of the afternoon.

Simpson carries 29 times for 250 yards, breaking Willie Ellison's NFL single-game record by three yards. The Bills win, 31-13, and also break their team record for rushing with 360 yards as the Pats are so concerned with stopping O.J. that fullback Larry Watkins gains 105 yards, mostly on counter plays.

Dec. 9, 1973 . . . Rich Stadium, Orchard Park, N.Y.:

Five minutes before kickoff the snow starts and doesn't stop for a half hour. Few can see. Fewer can hold their footing.

O.J. Simpson can still run.

He averages 10 yards on 22 carries for his second 200-yard game of the season, 219 to be exact, against New England as the Bills win, 37-13. The only thing that stops him from gaining more are a couple of slippery spots in which he falls after long runs.

Dec. 16, 1973 . . . Shea Stadium, Queens, N.Y.:

It's just a week after his 219-yard day against the Pats. He's just 61 yards away from Jim Brown's single-season NFL record, 1863 yards set in 1963.

The record falls on Simpson's eighth carry of the day, a six-yard cut through the muddy, soggy turf of Shea. It doesn't stop there. He carries 34 times for 200 yards to become the first 2000-yard runner in history and the Bills end the season on a winning note.

Sept. 28, 1975 . . . Three Rivers Stadium, Pittsburgh:

These are the world champions, the Pittsburgh Steelers. No one runs on them, right? The week before, they opened the season by allowing San Diego to come no closer than the Steelers' 42-yard line.

O.J. Simpson destroys them. He slips through their middle, he turns their end. He bounces off a pileup, fakes All-Pro linebacker Jack Ham off his feet and races 88 yards down the sidelines for a touchdown.

When the final gun sounds, he has 227 yards and Buffalo has a 30-21 upset victory.

Oct. 12, 1975 . . . Memorial Stadium, Baltimore:

The Juice has had games in which he gained more ground. This day he finishes with 159 yards. But some of that was the toughest of the day when he carries seven times in the winning touchdown drive as Buffalo wins a wild game, 38-31.

Nov. 17, 1975 . . . Riverfront Stadium, Cincinnati:

It's Ken Anderson, the brilliant Cincinnati quarterback, vs. O.J. on Monday night football. The Bills' pass defense can't stop Anderson. The Bengals' rush defense can't stop Simpson.

O.J. carries only 17 times for 197 yards. Late in the game, when Cincinnati leads, 30-24, the Bills abandon Simpson for almost a full quarter in an effort to catch up via the pass. The abandonment costs the Juice Jim Brown's record for most 200-yard games in a season —and possibly costs the Bills the game as they lose, 33-24.

Nov. 25, 1976 . . . The Silverdome, Pontiac, Mich.:

It's Thanksgiving Day, a traditional football feast in the Detroit area. The Lions lead the NFL in defense. Only one runner pierced them for 100 yards all season.

The Bills, who are battered and injured, have only one offensive cannon—Simpson. They fire it.

The Lions are stacked in what amounts to a seven-man front against a team it knows can't throw the football. Still, Simpson rips them. He almost breaks free on a 36-yard run. Then he does break free for a 48-yard touchdown gallop. Suddenly he has his fifth 200-yard game, an all-time NFL record.

Even the Lions' fans cheer for him as he takes aim at his own record. He gets it, and more, finishing with 273 yards in 29 carries, even though his team is never really close to winning the contest.

Dec. 5, 1976 . . . Orange Bowl, Miami:

The Dolphins have defeated the Bills 13 consecutive times, and they will make it 14 today. For a brief moment, though, O.J. gives Buffalo hope, racing 75 yards down the sideline for a touchdown.

At halftime, Miami is back on top, but the Juice, who has 121 yards at intermission, roars for 19, 9, 16. He's almost ignored by his own play-callers in the last quarter, but he still finishes with his sixth 200-yard game.

And remember, he's got two more seasons to play. Don't tune out yet.

VERSATILE ATTACKERS

Style, trademark, modus operandi—call it what you like; Super Bowl winners usually are endowed with a certain something that stamps their individuality.

With the Miami Dolphins it was ball control. The Dolphins' style was to sit on the ball for large measures of time, bludgeoning their way downfield as they ate up the clock. By the time they got to the end zone, the opposition would look at the scoreboard to find themselves not only in arrears but with most of the quarter eaten up.

That's what happened to the Minnesota Vikings in Houston during Super Bowl VIII.

The Dolphins kept giving the ball to Larry Csonka. He would run through a huge hole created by guard Bob Kuechenberg, who was probably the best man on the field that day, and center Jim Langer. By the time the Vikings made contact with him, Csonka would be two or three yards past the line of scrimmage. His power would get him three or four more yards.

It was demoralizing for the Vikings. It was also effective for the Miamis. It did two things:

1. It gave the Dolphins' defensive unit a great deal of rest. With that rest, they were able to perform above their usual capabilities.

2. It allowed quarterback Bob Griese to hoard his passes. Griese doesn't like to throw all that much. He's more effective when his running game is plowing through a defense and he can use as few as 10 or 12 passes, all of which are thrown off play-action, when the defense has to respect the run.

The Pittsburgh Steelers were far more primitive.

"What we do," said defensive end Dwight White when the Steelers were preparing to line up for Super Bowl IX, "is hope the offense doesn't screw up too much and put us in a hole. If they don't, eventually we'll get them the ball in good field position and get us some points."

It was an exaggeration, but not by much.

The Pittsburgh theme was really a variation on Miami's. The Steelers played it conservatively on offense, using their running game with Franco Harris doing wiggly things behind one of the NFL's more underrated offensive lines. But the biggest reason the Steelers succeeded in their Super Bowl season was that their defense, led by L.C. Greenwood and Joe Greene, completely stymied the running game of just about every opponent. The Vikings, for instance, produced just 17 yards rushing in Super IX.

When a team can't run with reasonable success against Pittsburgh and must throw more than it wants to, then it's tee-off time for L.C., Mean Joe and their colleagues.

That brings us to the reigning champions, the Oakland Raiders.

The Raiders are unlike any of the Super Bowl contestants of the last few years. They are far harder to label. As Kenny Stabler, their cool quarterback, points out, "We like to pass, we're basically a passing team, but we'll take whatever they give us."

That was the story of Super Bowl XI last January.

The Raiders took a long, long look at the Vikings' game films and decided that this was going to be great fun. The teams hadn't met in a regular-season game since opening day of the 1973 season. But the films provided enough familiarity for the Raiders to feel contempt. What the Raiders saw was an invitation to run the ball.

"We knew all week we were going to win," said Phil Villapiano, the cocky linebacker, in the Raiders' dressing room after Oakland's 32-14 victory.

"The hardest part was waiting all week to go to the Rose Bowl to do it. If the Vikings don't believe it, we'll play 'em Tuesday and do it again."

One Oakland star, who is not as bold as Villapiano, requested anonymity when he pointed out, "The films showed us there were only three solid tacklers on Minnesota's defensive unit and none of them are in the secondary."

So Oakland decided, "Why pass a lot when it's so easy to run?"

And, when Oakland runs, it runs behind its left guard, Gene Upshaw, and left tackle, Art Shell.

It was behind them that Oakland netted most of its Super Bowl record 266 yards rushing. The Raider strategists had sized up a fantastic mismatch: the 285-pound Shell vs. 39-year-old Jim Marshall, who the Raiders suspected weighed closer to 220 than his program weight of 240.

Shell embarrassed Marshall. The veteran not only didn't make a tackle, he didn't even have an assist in an area where most of the action took place.

But if the Raiders get into Super Bowl XII, as they well may, don't count on seeing a repeat of that offensive strategy.

"If we have to throw 35 or 40 passes to win," says Stabler, "we'll do it."

Oakland's principal offensive tactic can be summed up in one word: Attack.

"We go for the scoreboard right from the start," says Tom Flores, the receiver coach. "We don't stray from our philosophy."

The Oakland defense is an adjunct to the offensive philosophy. It is not as overpowering as the Steelers' bunch, but its philosophy is "Hit, hit and then hit some more!"

Carrying that philosophy to its ultimate conclusion are the two headhunting safeties, George Atkinson and Jack Tatum, and linebackers Ted Hendricks, Willie Hall, Monte Johnson and Villapiano.

Hall got to play when a deluge of injuries hit the Oakland defensive line. Things were so bad that Coach John Madden changed the basic formation from a normal four-man front with three linebackers to a 3-4. It was another display of Oakland's versatility, its trademark, and the new alignment gave Hall a chance to play. He and Villapiano might have turned the Super Bowl around with a crushing play in the first quarter.

The Vikings had become the first team in Ray Guy's professional career to block one of his punts. Minneota had the ball, first and goal on the Oakland 3. Two plays later the Raiders had possession again on Hall's recovery of a fumble caused by Villapiano.

"I came in low, behind their tight end, Stu Voigt, and the tackle, Ron Yary," said Villapiano. "My helmet went right into Brent McClanahan's stomach. I knew he coughed it up when he said something unprintable."

Versatility, a trademark.

"HEADY ... TOUGH ... WILD"

It was, without any question, the most bizarre incident of the 1976 football season.

The Baltimore Colts, who had finished the previous campaign with 10 consecutive victories to capture the Eastern Division championship of the American Football Conference, were tinkering and experimenting in their final preseason contest in Detroit. The tinkering probably cost them the game.

No big deal. Only an exhibition.

No big deal, that is, to anyone except the Colts' owner, Robert Irsay.

Irsay burst into the Colt dressing room after the game and launched into a tirade, berating players and ridiculing the head coach, Ted Marchibroda, in front of his squad. He promised to hire a "consultant" coach for Marchibroda, who had been named the AFC's Coach of the Year the previous season.

The general manager of the team, Joe Thomas, backed Irsay against Marchibroda. The following day, less than a week before the season opened, Marchibroda resigned. The team was without a coach for two days.

Total chaos yawned at one of the most promising franchises in football. The situation was in shambles.

What saved the season, and possibly the very future of the team, was a lanky, toothy young quarterback named Bertram Hays Jones.

"I think I can serve as spokesman for my teammates," said Jones, holding his own press conference at a time when the team was almost rudderless, "because financially I'm in a secure position to do so.

"I don't know if it was Robert Irsay speaking or whiskey speaking the other night, but Ted Marchibroda built this team.

"He was the carpenter. You don't just throw lumber down in front of a lot and then expect a house to go up. It has to be built, and Marchibroda did our building.

"If he doesn't return, I'll finish out the year with the Colts, but next season I expect to be elsewhere."

Less than 24 hours later, Marchibroda not only was back as coach, but he had firmer control of the football operation than ever before.

As for Jones, he had new status on his team. Before, he had been just one of the leaders. Now he was the undisputed commander. He then demonstrated that he knew how to use, not abuse, leadership. After Marchibroda came back, Jones made another statement, a healing one:

"This isn't just Ted Marchibroda's team or Robert Irsay's or [then General Manager] Joe Thomas' team," he said. "I think all three mules are pulling in the same direction now. It's a combination of the three."

There are less tactless diplomats in important jobs with the State Department. But don't get the idea that Bert Jones is a politician, a guy who talks his way into prominence. Most of the time, Jones speaks with his arm.

In the opening game of the year, against a New

England team that would be the surprise of '76, the Colts won, 27-13, on the strength of two clutch touchdown passes from Bert to Glenn Doughty. The following week, in a key early season game against the Bengals, a touted passing duel between Bert and Cincinnati's highly skilled Ken Anderson, Bert was the winner, 28-27, with touchdown passes of 68, 22 and 65 to Roger Carr over three different defensive backs.

A few weeks later against the pretender to the AFC-Eastern throne, Miami, it was a day to run the ball but Bert still completed 11 passes for 177 yards and raced seven yards for a touchdown in a 28-14 victory.

During a season in which Oakland's Ken Stabler was as solid a quarterback as anyone could imagine, Jones outpolled him by 26 votes in balloting for the Associated Press' Most Valuable Player Award in the NFL.

No wonder they are referring to Bert as "The Franchise" in Baltimore these days.

Jones was bred to play football. His father, William (Dub) Jones, was a star with the Cleveland Browns of the late '40s and '50s. He once scored six touchdowns in one game against the Chicago Bears, a record that still stands.

"I used to go to training camp with my dad when he became a coach with the Browns," remembers Jones. "I shagged kicks for Lou Groza, washed uniforms, polished shoes, stuff like that. The best part was when I got to warm up with the quarterbacks, Frank Ryan and Jim Ninowski, before the games. They taught me the technique of passing a football."

He learned well. In high school at Ruston, La., he was a superior player. Recruited by Louisiana State, he was among the nation's top college stars.

The Colts traded veteran defensive end Billy Newsome plus a fourth-round draft choice to New Orleans for the Saints' No. 1 choice, the second pick in the entire 1973 draft. Baltimore heard that the first team to make its selection, Houston, would take defensive lineman John Matuszak. The Oilers did as expected, to the outright joy of the Colts.

Jones wasn't an instant hero. He completed only 39.8 per cent of his passes and had three times as many interceptions, 12, as he did touchdown passes, four, when he was a rookie. He improved in his second year, but not by a lot.

It was in 1975 that Jones virtually exploded. That was the year when the Colts pulled the greatest turnaround in NFL history. They had finished dead last in the AFC East in '74 with a 2-12 record. After five weeks of play in '75 they were 1-4, losers of four games in a row after an opening win.

Then Jones almost picked up his team by the bootstraps. The Colts won nine straight. During the last 10 games, Bert had only four interceptions. His season's completion percentage, 59, established a Colt record. That might be the most amazing thing of all, since Johnny Unitas preceded him as "The Franchise."

The pivotal game in the '75 season may have been the meeting with the Bills in Buffalo, the eighth game of the season. The Bills, with O.J. Simpson rolling, built up a quick 28-7 lead. But, guard Elmer Collett confided afterwards, "we still knew we were going to win." The Colts have that much confidence in Jones' direction.

Zingo, an 89-yard touchdown pass to Roger Carr! Flit, a scramble out of trouble for a first down. Zip, zip, zip, three quick passes to Lydell Mitchell. Final score: Baltimore 42, Buffalo 35.

"Jonesey can crank up and hit one for 70 yards, on a dime, any time he likes," says Carr.

That's not much of an overstatement.

Another thing about Bert. He can play with pain. He suffered three cracked ribs in that Buffalo game in '75 and played the rest of the season in pain—and without losing.

"It made me a little more careful when I take off on the run, though," he admits. "I like to run, but you have to wonder about the risks. You do it when you have to do it."

He did tone himself down a bit. In '75 he led NFL quarterbacks in rushing, with 321 yards and three touchdowns. Last year he ran just 38 times for 214 yards and two touchdowns.

His passing stats didn't flag, however.

He broke the Colt completion percentage record again, compiling a 60.3 figure. His interception percentage was low again, 2.6. His touchdown passes inflated from 18 the previous year to 24 and his yardage went from 2483 to 3104, highest in the NFL for the season.

But what will make Bert Jones a quarterback to deal with for the next NFL decade is the way he leads a team. "He's heady, he's tough, he's wild," says offensive tackle George Kunz. "It kind of rubs off on the rest of us."

THE ROOKIE CROP

Team	Player	Pos.	College
	First Round		
Tampa Bay	BELL, Ricky	RB	So. California
Dallas	DORSETT, Tony	RB	Pittsburgh
from Seattle			
Cincinnati	EDWARDS, Eddie	DT	Miami
from Buffalo			
New York Jets	POWELL, Marvin	T	So. California
New York Giants	JETER, Gary	DT	So. California
Atlanta	BRYANT, Warren	T	Kentucky
New Orleans	CAMPBELL, Joe	DE	Maryland
Cincinnati	WHITLEY, Wilson	DT	Houston
from Philadelphia			
Green Bay	BUTLER, Mike	DE	Kansas
Kansas City	GREEN, Gary	DB	Baylor
Houston	TOWNS, Morris	T	Missouri
Buffalo	DOKES, Phil	DT	Oklahoma State
from Detroit			
Miami	DUHE, A. J.	DT	Louisiana State
Seattle	AUGUST, Steve	G	Tulsa
from San Diego			
thru Dallas			
Chicago	ALBRECHT, Ted	T	California
New England	CLAYBORN, Raymond	DB	Texas
from San Francisco			
Cleveland	JACKSON, Robert	LB	Texas A&M
Denver	SCHINDLER, Steve	G	Boston College
St. Louis	PISARKIEWICZ, Steve	QB	Missouri
from Washington			
Atlanta	FAUMUINA, Wilson	DT	San Jose State
from St. Louis			
Pittsburgh	COLE, Robin	LB	New Mexico
Cincinnati	COBB, Mike	TE	Michigan State
Los Angeles	BRUDZINSKI, Bob	LB	Ohio State
San Diego	RUSH, Bob	C	Memphis State
from Dallas			

254

Team	Player	Pos.	College
New England	MORGAN, Stanley	WR	Tennessee
Baltimore	BURKE, Randy	WR	Kentucky
Minnesota	KRAMER, Tommy	QB	Rice
Green Bay	JOHNSON, Ezra	DE	Morris Brown
from Oakland			

Second Round

Team	Player	Pos.	College
Tampa Bay	LEWIS, Dave	LB	So. California
Seattle	LYNCH, Tom	T	Boston College
from Buffalo thru Dallas			
Los Angeles	CROMWELL, Nolan	DB	Kansas
from Seattle			
New York Giants	PERKINS, Johnny	WR	Abilene Christian
New York Jets	WALKER, Wesley	WR	California
New Orleans	FULTZ, Mike	DT	Nebraska
Oakland	DAVIS, Mike	DB	Colorado
from Philadelphia			
Atlanta	THIELEMANN, R. C.	G	Arkansas
Kansas City	REED, Tony	RB	Colorado
Houston	REIHNER, George	G	Penn State
Green Bay	KOCH, Greg	DT	Arkansas
Miami	BAUMHOWER, Bob	DT	Alabama
Seattle	BEESON, Terry	LB	Kansas
from San Diego thru Dallas			
Detroit	WILLIAMS, Walt	DB	New Mexico State
Chicago	SPIVEY, Mike	DB	Colorado
New England	IVORY, Horace	RB	Oklahoma
from San Francisco			
Denver	LYTLE, Rob	RB	Michigan
Cleveland	SKLADANY, Tom	P-K	Ohio State
St. Louis	FRANKLIN, George	RB	Texas A&I
Pittsburgh	THORNTON, Sidney	RB	N. W. Louisiana
Cincinnati	JOHNSON, Pete	RB	Ohio State
Los Angeles	WADDY, Billy	RB-WR	Colorado
from Washington thru San Diego			
Seattle	CRONAN, Pete	LB	Boston College
from Los Angeles			
New England	HASSELBECK, Don	TE	Colorado
Baltimore	OZDOWSKI, Mike	DE	Virginia
Dallas	CARANO, Glen	QB	Nevada-Las Vegas
Minnesota	SWILLEY, Dennis	G	Texas A&M
Oakland*	McKNIGHT, Ted	RB	Minn.-Duluth

* Oakland selected after Tampa Bay, which selected first in the third round.

Team	Player	Pos.	College

Third Round

Team	Player	Pos.	College
Tampa Bay*	HANNAH, Charles	DE	Alabama
Seattle	BOYD, Dennis	DE	Oregon State
Buffalo	BROWN, Curtis	RB	Missouri
Pittsburgh from New York Jets	BEASLEY, Tom	DT	Virginia Tech
Chicago from New York Giants	EARL, Robin	RB	Washington
Dallas from Philadelphia	HILL, Tony	WR	Stanford
Atlanta	FIELDS, Edgar	DT	Texas A&M
New Orleans	WATTS, Bob	LB	Boston College
San Francisco from Houston	BOYD, Elmo	WR	Eastern Kentucky
Houston from Green Bay	WILSON, Tim	RB	Maryland
Kansas City	HOWARD, Thomas	LB	Texas Tech
Los Angeles from San Diego	FULTON, Ed	G	Maryland
Detroit	KANE, Rick	RB	San Jose State
Houston from Miami	GILES, Jimmy	TE	Alcorn State
Miami from Chicago	WATSON, Mike	T	Miami, Ohio
New York Jets from San Francisco	MARSHALL, Tank	DE	Texas A&M
Buffalo from Cleveland	KIMBROUGH, John	WR	St. Cloud, Minn.
Green Bay from Denver	SCRIBNER, Rick	G	Idaho State
Pittsburgh	SMITH, Jim	WR	Michigan
Cincinnati	VOIGHT, Mike	RB	North Carolina
San Diego from Washington	KING, Keith	DB	Colorado State
St. Louis	ALLERMAN, Kurt	LB	Penn State
Los Angeles	TYLER, Wendell	RB	UCLA
St. Louis from Baltimore	MIDDLETON, Terdell	RB	Memphis State
Dallas	BELCHER, Val	G	Houston
New England	BROWN, Sidney	DB	Oklahoma
Minnesota	HANNON, Tom	DB	Michigan State
Houston from Oakland thru Buffalo	CARPENTER, Rob	RB	Miami, Ohio

* Tampa Bay selected ahead of Oakland, which passed at the end of Round 2.

Team	Player	Pos.	College

Fourth Round

Team	Player	Pos.	College
Cincinnati from Tampa Bay	WALKER, Rick	TE	UCLA
Buffalo	DEAN, Jimmy	DT	Texas A&M
Seattle	YARNO, John	C	Idaho
New York Giants	VAUGHAN, Mike	T	Oklahoma
New York Jets	DIERKING, Scott	RB	Purdue
Atlanta*	LEAVITT, Allan	K	Georgia
Los Angeles from New Orleans	FERRAGAMO, Vince	QB	Nebraska
Kansas City from Philadelphia	BAILEY, Mark	RB	Cal State-LB
Pittsburgh from Green Bay	PETERSEN, Ted	C	Eastern Illinois
Kansas City	SAMUELS, Andre	TE	Bethune-Cookman
Kansas City from Houston	HELTON, Darius	G	N. C. Central
Detroit	BLUE, Luther	WR	Iowa State
Washington from Miami	MC COLL, Duncan	DE	Stanford
Houston from San Diego thru Miami	ANDERSON, Warren	WR	West Virginia St.
Pittsburgh from Chicago	SMITH, Laverne	RB	Kansas
San Francisco	BLACK, Stan	DB	Mississippi State
Denver	BRYAN, Billy	C	Duke
Cleveland	DAVIS, Oliver	DB	Tennessee State
Cincinnati	WILSON, Mike	T	Georgia
Kansas City from Washington	HARRIS, Eric	DB	Memphis State
Cincinnati from St. Louis	ANDERSON, Jerry	DB	Oklahoma
Pittsburgh	AUDICK, Dan	G	Hawaii
Los Angeles	JONES, Eary	DE	Memphis State
Dallas	BROWN, Guy	LB	Houston
New England	SKINNER, Gerald	T	Arkansas
Cleveland from Baltimore thru Washington, Miami and Chicago	SIMS, Robert	DT	South Carolina St.
Seattle from Minnesota	SEIVERS, Larry	WR	Tennessee
Oakland	MARVIN, Mickey	G	Tennessee

* Atlanta selected ahead of the New York Jets, which passed.

Team	Player	Pos.	College

Fifth Round

Team	Player	Pos.	College
Miami	MICHEL, Mike	K	Stanford
from Tampa Bay			
Detroit	CROSBY, Ron	LB	Penn State
from Seattle			
Buffalo	BESANA, Fred	QB	California
New York Jets	GRIGGS, Perry	WR	Troy State
New York Giants	DEAN, Randy	QB	Northwestern
New Orleans	LAFARY, Dave	T	Purdue
Philadelphia	SHARP, Skip	DB	Kansas
Atlanta	DIGGS, Shelton	WR	So. California
Pittsburgh	STOUDT, Cliff	QB	Youngstown
from Kansas City			
Houston			
choice forfeited			
Green Bay	SIMPSON, Nathan	RB	Tennessee State
Miami	HARRIS, Leroy	RB	Arkansas State
San Diego	WILLIAMS, Clarence	RB	South Carolina
Pittsburgh	COURSON, Steve	G	South Carolina
from Detroit			
Oakland	HAYES, Lester	RB	Texas A&M
from Chicago			
Buffalo	O'DONOGHUE, Neil	K	Auburn
from San Francisco			
San Diego	OLANDER, Cliff	QB	New Mexico State
from Cleveland			
New York Jets	GREGORY, Gary	T	Baylor
from Denver			
Los Angeles	HICKMAN, Donnie	G	So. California
from Washington			
St. Louis	LEE, Ernest	DT	Texas
Pittsburgh	WINSTON, Dennis	LB	Arkansas
Cincinnati	PHILLIPS, Ray	LB	Nebraska
Los Angeles	WILLIAMS, Jeff	G	Rhode Island
St. Louis	SPIVA, Andy	LB	Tennessee
from New England			
New Orleans	HUBBARD, Dave	T	Brigham Young
from Baltimore			
Dallas	FREDERICK, Andy	DT	New Mexico
Minnesota	MOORE, Ken	TE	Northern Illinois
Oakland	BARNES, Jeff	LB	California

Sixth Round

Team	Player	Pos.	College
Chicago	EVANS, Vince	QB	So. California
from Tampa Bay			
San Francisco	BURNS, Mike	DB	So. California
from Buffalo			
Seattle	BENJAMIN, Tony	RB	Duke

Team	Player	Pos.	College
New York Giants	JORDAN, Bob	T	Memphis State
New York Jets	KLECKO, Joe	DT	Temple
Philadelphia	RUSSELL, Kevin	DB	Tennessee State
San Diego from Atlanta	LINDSTROM, Dave	DE	Boston University
New Orleans	PARSLEY, Cliff	P	Oklahoma State
Houston	WOOLFORD, Gary	DB	Florida State
Green Bay	MORESCO, Tim	DB	Syracuse
Kansas City	BURLESON, Rick	DE	Texas
San Diego	BARNES, Lawrence	RB	Tennessee State
San Diego from Detroit	SHAW, Pete	DB	Northwestern
New York Giants from Miami	MOOREHEAD, Emery	WR-RB	Colorado
Philadelphia from Chicago	MONTGOMERY, Wilbert	RB	Abilene Christian
San Francisco	HARLAN, Jim	C	Howard Payne
Los Angeles from Denver	BEST, Art	RB	Kent State
Buffalo from Cleveland	PRUITT, Ron	DE	Nebraska
Philadelphia from St. Louis thru Washington	MITCHELL, Martin	DB	Tulane
Pittsburgh	HARRIS, Paul	LB	Alabama
Cincinnati	DUNIVEN, Tommy	QB	Texas Tech
Atlanta from Washington	JENKINS, Keith	DB	Cincinnati
New Orleans from Los Angeles	SCHICK, Tom	G	Maryland
Baltimore	O'NEAL, Calvin	LB	Michigan
Dallas	COOPER, Jim	T	Temple
Houston from New England	CARTER, David	C	Western Kentucky
Detroit from Minnesota thru New England	PINKNEY, Reggie	DB	East Carolina
Kansas City from Oakland thru Tampa Bay and Chicago	HERRERA, Andre	RB	Southern Illinois

Seventh Round

Team	Player	Pos.	College
New York Jets from Tampa Bay	WHITE, Charlie	RB	Bethune-Cookman
Seattle	SIMS, David	RB	Georgia Tech
Buffalo	NELMS, Mike	DB	Baylor
New York Jets	GRUPP, Bob	DB	Duke

Team	Player	Pos.	College
Green Bay from New York Giants	GOFOURTH, Derrel	C	Oklahoma State
Cleveland from Atlanta	RANDLE, Kenny	WR	So. California
New Orleans	BOYKIN, Greg	RB	Northwestern
Philadelphia	JOHNSON, Charles	DT	Colorado
Green Bay	TIPTON, Rell	G	Baylor
Kansas City	GOLUB, Chris	DB	Kansas
New York Giants from Houston	DIXON, Al	TE	Iowa State
Detroit	BLACK, Tim	LB	Baylor
Miami	HERRON, Bruce	LB	New Mexico
San Diego	BUSH, Ron	DB	So. California
Chicago	BUTLER, Gerald	WR	Nicholls State
San Francisco	VAN WAGNER, Jim	RB	Michigan Tech
Cleveland	SMITH, Blane	TE	Purdue
Denver	SWIDER, Larry	P	Pittsburgh
Pittsburgh	FRISCH, Randy	DT	Missouri
Cincinnati	BREEDEN, Louis	DB	N. C. Central
Oakland from Washington thru Houston and New York Giants	MARTINI, Rich	WR	Cal-Davis
Cleveland* from St. Louis	LINGENFELTER, Bob	T	Nebraska
Washington* from Los Angeles	HAYNES, Reggie	TE	Nevada-Las Vegas
Dallas	STALLS, David	DE	Northern Colorado
New England	SMITH, Ken	WR	Ark.-Pine Bluff
Baltimore	CARTER, Blanchard	T	Nevada-Las Vegas
Cincinnati from Minnesota	CORBETT, Jim	TE	Pittsburgh
New York Jets from Oakland	LONG, Kevin	RB	South Carolina

Eighth Round

Team	Player	Pos.	College
Tampa Bay	HEDBERG, Randy	QB	Minot State
Buffalo	MORTON, Greg	DT	Michigan
Houston from Seattle	DAVIS, Steve	WR	Georgia
New York Giants	RICE, Bill	DT	Brigham Young
New York Jets	ALEXANDER, Dan	DT	Louisiana State
New Orleans	STEWART, Jim	DB	Tulsa
Philadelphia	FRANKLIN, Cleveland	RB	Baylor
Atlanta	PACKER, Walter	WR	Mississippi State
Kansas City	OLSONOSKI, Ron	LB	St. Thomas, Minn.

* Cleveland and Washington selected ahead of Oakland, which passed.

Team	Player	Pos.	College
Houston	FOSTER, Eddie	WR	Houston
Green Bay	WHITEHURST, David	QB	Furman
Miami	PERKINS, Horace	DB	Colorado
Dallas	CLEVELAND, Al	DE	Pacific
from San Diego			
Detroit	GRIFFIN, Mark	T	North Carolina
New York Jets	THOMPSON, Ed	LB	Ohio State
from Chicago			
New York Giants	RODGERS, Otis	LB	Iowa State
from San Francisco			
Denver	CULLIVER, Calvin	RB	Alabama
Cleveland	ARMSTRONG, Bill	DB	Wake Forest
Cincinnati	ST. VICTOR, Jose	G	Syracuse
Kansas City	SMITH, Waddell	WR	Kansas
from Washington			
St. Louis	WILLIAMS, Eric	LB	So. California
Pittsburgh	AUGUST, Phil	WR	Miami
Los Angeles	BOCKWOLDT, Rod	DB	Weber State
New England	BENSON, Brad	G	Penn State
Baltimore	HELMS, Ken	T-C	Georgia
Dallas	WILLIAMS, Fred	RB	Arizona State
Minnesota	STROZIER, Clint	DB	So. California
Oakland	ROBISKIE, Terry	RB	Louisiana State

Ninth Round

Team	Player	Pos.	College
Tampa Bay	HEMINGWAY, Byron	LB	Boston College
Seattle	ADZICK, George	DB	Minnesota
Kansas City	GLANTON, Derrick	DE	Bishop
from Buffalo			
New York Jets	ROBINSON, Matt	QB	Georgia
New York Giants	MULLINS, Ken	DE	Florida A&M
Philadelphia	HUMPHREYS, T. J.	G	Arkansas State
Atlanta	MAXWELL, John	T	Boston College
New Orleans	KNOWLES, Dave	T	Indiana
Houston	CURRIER, Bill	DB	South Carolina
Green Bay	MULLINS, Joel	T	Arkansas State
Kansas City	GREEN, Dave	T	New Mexico
San Diego*	WASHINGTON, Gene	WR	Georgia
Detroit	MATHIESON, Steve	QB	Florida State
Miami	TURNER, Robert	RB	Oklahoma State
Chicago	BUONAMICI, Nick	DT	Ohio State
San Francisco	POSEY, David	K	Florida
Cleveland	BROWN, Daryl	DB	Tufts
Denver	JACKSON, Charles	DT	Washington
Atlanta	SPEER, Robert	DE	Arkansas State
from Washington			
St. Louis	JACKSON, Johnny	DT	Southern
Pittsburgh	KELLY, Roosevelt	TE	Eastern Kentucky

* San Diego selected ahead of Kansas City, which passed.

Team	Player	Pos.	College
Cincinnati	ZACHERY, Willie	WR	Central St., Ohio
Washington	NORTHINGTON, Mike	RB	Purdue
from Los Angeles			
Baltimore	CAPRIOLA, Glen	RB	Boston College
Dallas	CANTRELL, Mark	C	North Carolina
New England	VOGELE, Jerry	LB	Michigan
Minnesota	STUDWELL, Scott	LB	Illinois
Tampa Bay	MUCKER, Larry	WR	Arizona State
from Oakland			

Tenth Round

Team	Player	Pos.	College
Tampa Bay	MORGAN, Robert	RB	Florida
Pittsburgh	COWANS, Alvin	DB	Florida
from Buffalo			
Seattle	ADKINS, Sam	QB	Wichita State
New York Giants	JONES, Mike	WR	Minnesota
New York Jets	HENNESSY, John	DE	Michigan
Atlanta	RYCKMAN, Billy	WR	Louisiana Tech
New Orleans	SEPTIEN, Rafael	K	S. W. Louisiana
Philadelphia	MASTRONARDO, John	WR	Villanova
Green Bay	CULBREATH, Jimmy	RB	Oklahoma
Kansas City	VITALI, Mark	QB	Purdue
Houston	HULL, Harvey	LB	Mississippi State
Detroit	ANDERSON, Gary	G	Stanford
Miami	CARTER, Mark	T	Eastern Michigan
San Diego	TOWNSEND, Curtis	LB	Arkansas
Chicago	BRECKNER, Dennis	DE	Miami
Tampa Bay	BALL, Aaron	LB	Cal St.-Fullerton
from San Francisco			
Denver	MIDDLEBROOK, Orna	WR	Arkansas State
Cleveland	BURKETT, Tom	T	North Carolina
St. Louis	LE JAY, Jim	WR	San Jose State
Pittsburgh	LA CROSSE, Dave	LB	Wake Forest
Cincinnati	BIALIK, Bob	P	Hillsdale, Mich.
Washington	SYKES, James	RB	Rice
Los Angeles	PETERSEN, Don	TE	Boston College
Dallas	DE BERG, Steve	QB	San Jose State
New England	RASMUSSEN, John	T	Wisconsin
Baltimore	BAKER, Ron	G	Oklahoma State
Minnesota	BEAVER, Dan	K	Illinois
New England	ALEXANDER, Giles	DE	Tulsa
from Oakland			

Eleventh Round

Team	Player	Pos.	College
Tampa Bay	RODGERS, Chuck	DB	North Dakota St.
Seattle	WESTBELD, Bill	T	Dayton
Buffalo	JACKSON, Nate	RB	Tennessee State
Philadelphia	MOORE, Rocco	T	Western Michigan
from New York Jets			

Team	Player	Pos.	College
New York Giants	HELMS, Bill	TE	San Diego State
New Orleans	BLAIN, John	T	San Jose State
Philadelphia	CORDOVA, Mike	QB	Stanford
Atlanta	FARMER, Dave	RB	So. California
Kansas City	MITCHELL, Maurice	WR	Northern Michigan
Houston	ROMANO, Al	LB	Pittsburgh
Green Bay	RANDOLPH, Terry	DB	American Int.
Miami	ALEXANDER, John	DE	Rutgers
Cincinnati	PARRISH, Joel	G	Georgia
from San Diego			
Detroit	DAYKIN, Tony	LB	Georgia Tech
Chicago	ZELENCIK, Connie	C	Purdue
San Francisco	BILLICK, Brian	TE	Brigham Young
Cleveland	NASH, Charles	WR	Arizona
Denver	HECK, Phil	LB	California
Pittsburgh	WEST, Lou	DB	Cincinnati
Cincinnati	ALLEN, Carl	DB	So. Mississippi
Washington	HARRIS, Don	DB	Rutgers
St. Louis	LEE, Greg	DB	Western Illinois
Los Angeles	LONG, Carson	K	Pittsburgh
New England	COSTICT, Ray	LB	Mississippi State
Baltimore	RUFF, Brian	LB	Citadel
Dallas	WARDLOW, Don	TE	Washington
Minnesota	HARTWIG, Keith	WR	Arizona
New York Jets	BUTTERFIELD, Dave	DB	Nebraska
from Oakland			

Twelfth Round

Team	Player	Pos.	College
Tampa Bay	SHEFFIELD, Chip	WR	Lenoir Rhyne
Buffalo	ROMES, Charles	DB	N. C. Central
Pittsburgh	STEPHENS, Jimmy	TE	Florida
from Seattle			
New York Giants	SIMMONS, Elmo	RB	Texas-Arlington
New York Jets	GARGIS, Phil	RB-DB	Auburn
New York Jets	CONRAD, Dave	T	Maryland
from Philadelphia			
Atlanta	PARRISH, Don	DE	Pittsburgh
New Orleans	DALTON, Oakley	DE	Jackson State
Houston	JOHANSSON, Ove	K	Abilene Christian
Oakland	MARTIN, Rod	LB	So. California
from Green Bay			
Kansas City	BURKS, Ray	LB	UCLA
San Diego	STANSIK, Jim	TE	Eastern Michigan
Detroit	GREENWOOD, Dave	G-C	Iowa State
Miami	ANDERSON, Terry	WR	Bethune-Cookman
Chicago	IRVIN, Terry	DB	Jackson State
San Francisco	MARTIN, Scott	G	North Dakota
Denver	LEVENHAGEN, Scott	TE	Western Illinois
Cleveland	TIERNEY, Leo	C	Georgia Tech

Team	Player	Pos.	College
Cincinnati	PERCIVAL, Alex	WR	Morehouse
Washington	KIRKLAND, Curtis	DE	Missouri
St. Louis	FENLAW, Rick	LB	Texas
Seattle	WILSON, I. V.	DT	Tulsa
from Pittsburgh			
Los Angeles	CAUDILL, Barry	C	So. Mississippi
Baltimore	DEUTSCH, Bill	RB	North Dakota
Dallas	PETERS, Greg	G	California
New England	PRESTON, Dave	RB	Bowling Green
Minnesota	KELLEHER, Jim	RB	Colorado
Oakland*	BENIRSHKE, Rolf	K	Cal-Davis

* Oakland selected ahead of Minnesota, which passed.

HALL OF RECORDS

NFC INDIVIDUAL LEADERS, YEARLY
Scoring

Year	Player	Team	TD	PAT	FG	Pts.
1976	Moseley, Mark	Wash	0	31	22	97
1975	Foreman, Chuck	Vikings	22	0	0	132
1974	Marcol, Chester	GB	0	19	25	94
1973	Ray, David	LA	0	40	30	130
1972	Marcol, Chester	GB	0	29	33	128
1971	Knight, Curt	Wash	0	27	29	114
1970	Cox, Fred	Vikings	0	35	30	125
1969	Cox, Fred	Vikings	0	43	26	121
1968	Kelly, Leroy	Browns	20	0	0	120
1967	Bakken, Jim	Cards	0	36	27	117
1966	Gossett, Bruce	LA	0	29	28	113
1965	Sayers, Gale	Bears	22	0	0	132
1964	Moore, Lenny	Balt	20	0	0	120
1963	Chandler, Don	NY	0	52	18	106
1962	Taylor, Jim	GB	19	0	0	114
1961	Hornung, Paul	GB	10	41	15	146
1960	Hornung, Paul	GB	15	41	15	176
1959	Hornung, Paul	GB	7	31	7	94
1958	Brown, Jimmy	Cleve	18	0	0	108
1957	Baker, Sam	Wash	1	29	14	77
1957	Groza, Lou	Cleve	0	32	15	77
1956	Layne, Bobby	Det	5	33	12	99
1955	Walker, Doak	Det	7	27	9	96
1954	Walston, Bobby	Phil	11	36	4	114
1953	Soltau, Gordie	SF	6	48	10	114
1952	Soltau, Gordie	SF	7	34	6	94
1951	Hirsch, Elroy	LA	17	0	0	102
1950	Walker, Doak	Det	11	38	8	128
1949	Harder, Pat	Cards	8	45	3	102
1949	Roberts, Gene	NY	17	0	0	102
1948	Harder, Pat	Cards	6	53	7	110
1947	Harder, Pat	Cards	7	39	7	102
1946	Fritsch, Ted	GB	10	13	9	100
1945	Van Buren, Steve	Phil	18	2	0	110
1944	Hutson, Don	GB	9	31	0	85

Scoring (Contd.)

Year	Player	Team	TD	PAT	FG	Pts.
1943	Hutson, Don	GB	12	36	3	117
1942	Hutson, Don	GB	17	33	1	138
1941	Hutson, Don	GB	12	20	0	95
1940	Hutson, Don	GB	7	15	0	57
1939	Farkas, Andy	Wash	11	2	0	68
1938	Hinkle, Clark	GB	7	7	3	58
1937	Manders, Jack	Bears	5	15	8	69
1936	Clark, Earl	Det	7	19	4	73
1935	Clark, Earl	Det	6	16	1	55
1934	Manders, Jack	Bears	3	31	10	79
1933	Strong, Ken	NY	6	13	5	64
	Pressnell, Glenn	Port	6	10	6	64
1932	Clark, Earl	Det	4	6	3	39

Rushing

Year	Player	Team	YG	Atts.	Ave. G. Per Att.
1976	Payton, Walter	Bears	1390	311	4.5
1975	Otis, Jim	Cards	1076	269	4.0
1974	McCutcheon, Lawr.	LA	1109	236	4.7
1973	Brockington, John	GB	1144	265	4.3
1972	Brown, Larry	Redskins	1216	285	4.3
1971	Brockington, John	GB	1105	216	5.1
1970	Brown, Larry	Redskins	1125	237	4.7
1969	Sayers, Gale	Bears	1032	236	4.4
1968	Kelly, Leroy	Cleve	1239	248	5.0
1967	Kelly, Leroy	Cleve	1205	235	5.1
1966	Sayers, Gale	Bears	1231	229	5.4
1965	Brown, Jimmy	Cleve	1544	289	5.3
1964	Brown, Jimmy	Cleve	1446	280	5.2
1963	Brown, Jimmy	Cleve	1863	291	6.4
1962	Taylor, Jim	GB	1474	272	5.4
1961	Brown, Jimmy	Cleve	1408	305	4.6
1960	Brown, Jimmy	Cleve	1257	215	5.8
1959	Brown, Jimmy	Cleve	1329	290	4.6
1958	Brown, Jimmy	Cleve	1527	257	5.9
1957	Brown, Jimmy	Cleve	942	202	4.7
1956	Casares, Rick	Bears	1126	234	4.8
1955	Ameche, Alan	Balt	961	213	4.5
1954	Perry, Joe	SF	1049	173	6.1
1953	Perry, Joe	SF	1018	192	5.3
1952	Towler, Dan	LA	894	156	5.7
1951	Price, Eddie	NY	971	271	3.2
1950	Motley, Marion	Cleve	810	140	5.8
1949	Van Buren, Steve	Phil	1146	263	4.4

Rushing (Contd.)

Year	Player	Team	YG	Atts.	Ave. G. Per Att.
1948	Van Buren, Steve	Phil	845	201	4.7
1947	Van Buren, Steve	Phil	1008	217	4.6
1946	Dudley, Bill	Pitt	604	146	4.1
1945	Van Buren, Steve	Phil	832	143	5.8
1944	Paschal, Bill	NY	737	196	3.8
1943	Paschal, Bill	NY	572	147	3.9
1942	Dudley, Bill	Pitt	696	162	4.3
1941	Manders, Clarence	Brook	486	111	4.4
1940	White, Whizzer	Det	514	146	3.5
1939	Osmanski, Bill	Bears	699	121	5.8
1938	White, Whizzer	Det	567	152	3.7
1937	Battles, Cliff	Wash	874	216	4.1
1936	Leemans, Tuffy	NY	830	206	4.1
1935	Russell, Doug	Cards	499	140	3.6
1934	Feathers, Beattie	Bears	1004	101	9.9
1933	Battles, Cliff	Bos	737	146	5.1
1932	Campiglio, Bob	Stapleton	504	104	4.8

Pass Receiving

Year	Player	Team	Caught	YG	TDS
1976	Pearson, Drew	Dall	58	806	6
1975	Foreman, Chuck	Vikings	73	691	9
1974	Young, Charles	Phil	63	696	3
1973	Carmichael, Harold	Phil	67	1116	9
1972	Jackson, Harold	Phil	62	1048	4
1971	Tucker, Bob	NY	59	791	4
1970	Gordon, Dick	Bears	71	1026	13
1969	Abramowicz, Dan	NO	73	1015	7
1968	McNeil, Clifton	SF	71	994	7
1967	Taylor, Charley	Wash	70	990	9
1966	Taylor, Charley	Wash	72	1119	12
1965	Parks, Dave	SF	80	1344	12
1964	Morris, Johnny	Bears	93	1200	10
1963	Conrad, Bobby Joe	St. L	73	967	10
1962	Mitchell, Bobby	Wash	72	1384	11
1961	Phillips, Jim	LA	78	1092	5
1960	Berry, Ray	Balt	74	1298	10
1959	Berry, Ray	Balt	66	959	14
1958	Berry, Ray	Balt	56	794	9
1958	Retzlaff, Pete	Phil	56	766	2
1957	Wilson, Billy	SF	52	757	6
1956	Wilson, Billy	SF	60	889	5
1955	Pihos, Pete	Phil	62	864	7
1954	Pihos, Pete	Phil	60	872	10
1954	Wilson, Billy	SF	60	830	5

Pass Receiving (Contd.)

Year	Player	Team	Caught	YG	TDS
1953	Pihos, Pete	Phil	63	1049	10
1952	Speedie, Mac	Cleve	62	911	5
1951	Hirsch, Elroy	LA	66	1495	17
1950	Fears, Tom	LA	84	1116	7
1949	Fears, Tom	LA	77	1013	9
1948	Fears, Tom	LA	51	698	4
1947	Keane, Jim	Bears	64	910	10
1946	Benton, Jim	LA	63	981	6
1945	Hutson, Don	GB	47	834	9
1944	Hutson, Don	GB	58	866	9
1943	Hutson, Don	GB	47	776	11
1942	Hutson, Don	GB	74	1211	17
1941	Hutson, Don	GB	58	738	10
1940	Looney, Don	Phil	58	707	4
1939	Hutson, Don	GB	34	846	6
1938	Tinsley, Gaynell	Cards	41	516	1
1937	Hutson, Don	GB	41	552	7
1936	Hutson, Don	GB	34	526	9
1935	Goodwin, Tod	NY	26	432	4
1934	Carter, Joe	Phil	16	237	3
1933	Kelley, John	Brook	21	219	3
1932	Johnsos, Luke	Bears	24	321	2

Passing

Year	Player	Team	YG Per Att.	Atts.	Com.	Avg. Pct. Com.	YG	TDS
1976	Harris, James	LA	9.2	158	91	57.6	1460	8
1975	Tarkenton, Fran	Vikings	7.0	425	273	64.2	2994	25
1974	Jurgensen, Sonny	Wash	7.1	167	107	64.1	1185	11
1973	Staubach, Roger	Dall	8.4	286	179	62.6	2428	23
1972	Snead, Norm	NY	7.1	325	196	60.3	2307	17
1971	Staubach, Roger	Dall	8.9	211	126	59.7	1882	15
1970	Brodie, John	SF	7.8	378	223	59.0	2941	24
1969	Jurgensen, Sonny	Wash	7.0	442	274	62.0	3102	22
1968	Morrall, Earl	Balt	9.1	317	182	57.4	2909	26
1967	Jurgensen, Sonny	Wash	7.4	508	288	56.7	3747	31
1966	Starr, Bart	GB	8.9	251	156	62.2	2257	14
1965	Bukich, Rudy	Bears	8.5	312	176	56.4	2641	20
1964	Starr, Bart	GB	7.8	272	163	59.9	2144	15
1963	Tittle, Y. A.	NY	8.6	367	221	60	3145	36
1962	Starr, Bart	GB	8.6	285	178	63	2438	12
1961	Plum, Milt	Cleve	8.0	302	177	59	2416	18
1960	Plum, Milt	Cleve	9.2	250	151	60	2297	21
1959	Conerly, Charley	NY	8.8	194	113	58	1706	14
1958	LeBaron, Eddie	Wash	9.4	145	79	54	1365	11

Passing (Contd.)

Year	Player	Team	YG Per Att.	Atts.	Com.	Avg. Pct. Com.	YG	TDS
1957	O'Connell, Tom	Cleve	12.1	110	63	57	1229	9
1956	Brown, Ed	Bears	9.9	168	96	57	1667	11
1955	Graham, Otto	Cleve	9.3	185	98	53	1721	15
1954	Van Brocklin, Norm	LA	10.1	260	139	53	2637	13
1953	Graham, Otto	Cleve	10.5	258	167	65	2722	11
1952	Van Brocklin, Norm	LA	8.5	205	113	55	1736	14
1951	Waterfield, Bob	LA	8.8	176	88	50	1556	13
1950	Van Brocklin, Norm	LA	8.8	233	127	55	2061	18
1949	Baugh, Sammy	Wash	7.5	255	145	57	1903	18
1948	Thompson, Tommy	Phil	8.0	246	141	57	1965	25
1947	Baugh, Sammy	Wash	8.4	354	210	59	2938	25
1946	Waterfield, Bob	LA	7.0	251	127	51	1747	18
1945	Baugh, Sammy	Wash	9.2	182	128	70	1669	11
1944	Filchock, Frank	Wash	7.8	147	84	57	1139	13
1943	Baugh, Sammy	Wash	7.3	239	133	56	1754	23
1942	Isbell, Cecil	GB	7.5	268	146	55	2021	24
1941	Isbell, Cecil	GB	7.2	206	117	57	1479	15
1940	Baugh, Sammy	Wash	7.7	177	111	63	1367	12
1939	Hall, Parker	Cleve R	5.9	208	106	51	1227	9
1938	Danowski, Ed	NY	6.6	129	70	53	848	8
1937	Baugh, Sammy	Wash	6.6	171	81	47	1127	7
1936	Herber, Arnie	GB	7.2	173	77	45	1239	9
1935	Danowski, Ed	NY	7.1	113	57	50	795	9
1934	Herber, Arnie	GB	6.9	115	42	37	799	8
1933	Newman, Harry	NY	7.3	132	53	41	963	8
1932	Herber, Arnie	GB	6.3	101	37	37	639	9

NFC TEAM LEADERS, YEARLY

Points Scored

Year	Team	Total	Year	Team	Total
1976	Los Angeles	351	1965	San Francisco	421
1975	Minnesota	377	1964	Baltimore	428
1974	Washington	320	1963	NY Giants	448
1973	Los Angeles	388	1962	Green Bay	415
1972	San Francisco	353	1961	Green Bay	391
1971	Dallas	406	1960	Cleveland	362
1970	San Francisco	352	1959	Baltimore	374
1969	Minnesota	379	1958	Baltimore	381
1968	Dallas	431	1957	Los Angeles	307
1967	Los Angeles	398	1956	Chi. Bears	363
1966	Dallas	445	1955	Cleve. Browns	349

Points Scored (Contd.)

Year	Team	Total	Year	Team	Total
1954	Detroit	337	1942	Chi. Bears	376
1953	San Francisco	372	1941	Chi. Bears	396
1952	Los Angeles	349	1940	Washington	245
1951	Los Angeles	392	1939	Chi. Bears	298
1950	Los Angeles	466	1938	Green Bay	223
1949	Philadelphia	364	1937	Green Bay	220
1948	Chi. Bears	395	1936	Green Bay	248
1947	Chi. Bears	363	1935	Chi. Bears	192
1946	Chi. Bears	289	1934	Chi. Bears	286
1945	Philadelphia	272	1933	NY Giants	244
1944	Philadelphia	267	1932	Green Bay	152
1943	Chi. Bears	303			

Total Yards Gained

Year	Team	Total	Year	Team	Total
1976	St. Louis	5136	1952	Cleve. Browns	4352
1975	Dallas	5025	1951	Los Angeles	5506
1974	Dallas	4983	1950	Los Angeles	5420
1973	Los Angeles	4906	1949	Chi. Bears	4873
1972	NY Giants	4483	1948	*Chi. Cards	4694
1971	San Francisco	4706	1947	Chi. Bears	5053
1970	San Francisco	4503	1946	Los Angeles	3763
1969	Dallas	5122	1945	**Cleve. Rams	3571
1968	Dallas	5117	1944	Chi. Bears	3239
1967	Baltimore	5008	1943	Chi. Bears	4045
1966	Dallas	5145	1942	Chi. Bears	3900
1965	San Francisco	5270	1941	Chi. Bears	4265
1964	Baltimore	4779	1940	Green Bay	3400
1963	NY Giants	5024	1939	Chi. Bears	3988
1962	NY Giants	5005	1938	Green Bay	3037
1961	Philadelphia	5112	1937	Green Bay	3201
1960	Baltimore	4245	1936	Detroit	3703
1959	Baltimore	4458	1935	Chi. Bears	3454
1958	Baltimore	4539	1934	Chi. Bears	3750
1957	Los Angeles	4143	1933	NY Giants	2970
1956	Chi. Bears	4537	1932	Chi. Bears	2755
1955	Chi. Bears	4316			
1954	Los Angeles	5187	* Became St. Louis Cardinals.		
1953	Philadelphia	4811	** Became Los Angeles Rams.		

Yards Passing

Year	Team	Total	Year	Team	Total
1976	Minnesota	2855	1952	Cleve. Browns	2566
1975	Washington	2917	1951	Los Angeles	3296
1974	Washington	2802	1950	Los Angeles	3709
1973	Philadelphia	2998	1949	Chi. Bears	3055
1972	NY Giants	2461	1948	Washington	2861
1971	Dallas	2786	1947	Washington	3336
1970	San Francisco	2923	1946	Los Angeles	2080
1969	Dallas	2846	1945	°Cleve. Rams	1857
1968	Cleveland	2858	1944	Washington	2021
1967	Washington	3730	1943	Chi. Bears	2310
1966	Green Bay	2602	1942	Green Bay	2407
1965	San Francisco	3487	1941	Chi. Bears	2002
1964	Washington	2721	1940	Washington	1887
1963	Baltimore	3296	1939	Chi. Bears	1965
1962	Philadelphia	3632	1938	Washington	1536
1961	Philadelphia	3605	1937	Green Bay	1398
1960	Baltimore	2956	1936	Green Bay	1629
1959	Baltimore	2753	1935	Green Bay	1416
1958	Pittsburgh	2752	1934	Green Bay	1165
1957	Baltimore	2388	1933	NY Giants	1335
1956	Los Angeles	2419	1932	Chi. Bears	1013
1955	Philadelphia	2472			
1954	Chi. Bears	3104			
1953	Philadelphia	3089		° Became Los Angeles Rams.	

Yards Rushing

Year	Team	Total	Year	Team	Total
1976	Los Angeles	2528	1956	Chi. Bears	2468
1975	Dallas	2432	1955	Chi. Bears	2388
1974	Dallas	2454	1954	San Francisco	2498
1973	Los Angeles	2925	1953	San Francisco	2230
1972	Chicago	2360	1952	San Francisco	1905
1971	Detroit	2376	1951	Chi. Bears	2408
1970	Dallas	2300	1950	NY Giants	2336
1969	Dallas	2276	1949	Philadelphia	2607
1968	Chicago	2337	1948	°Chi. Cards	2560
1967	Cleve. Browns	2139	1947	Los Angeles	2171
1966	Cleve. Browns	2166	1946	Green Bay	1765
1965	Cleve. Browns	2331	1945	°°Cleve. Rams	1714
1964	Green Bay	2276	1944	Philadelphia	1663
1963	Cleve. Browns	2639	1943	†Philadelphia-Pittsburgh	1730
1962	Green Bay	2460	1942	Chi. Bears	1881
1961	Green Bay	2350			
1960	St. Louis	2356		° Became St. Louis Cardinals.	
1959	Cleve. Browns	2149		°° Became Los Angeles Rams.	
1958	Cleve. Browns	2526		† Philadelphia and Pittsburgh played as one unit.	
1957	Los Angeles	2142			

Yards Rushing (Contd.)

Year	Team	Total	Year	Team	Total
1941	Chi. Bears	2156	1935	Chi. Bears	2096
1940	Chi. Bears	1818	1934	Detroit	2763
1939	Chi. Bears	2043	1933	‡Bos. Redskins	2367
1938	Detroit	1893	1932	Chi. Bears	1770
1937	Detroit	2074			
1936	Detroit	2885	‡ Became Washington Redskins.		

Season Winners

Year	Winning Teams	Season Records W	L	T	Pct.	Team Coaches
1976	*Dallas (E)	11	3	0	.786	Tom Landry
	Minnesota (C)	11	2	1	.821	Bud Grant
	Los Angeles (W)	10	3	1	.750	Chuck Knox
1975	*St. Louis Cardinals (E)	11	3	0	.786	Don Coryell
	Minnesota Vikings (C)	12	2	0	.857	Bud Grant
	Los Angeles Rams (W)	12	2	0	.857	Chuck Knox
1974	*St. Louis Cardinals (E)	10	4	0	.714	Don Coryell
	Minnesota Vikings (C)	10	4	0	.714	Bud Grant
	Los Angeles Rams (W)	10	4	0	.714	Chuck Knox
1973	*Dallas Cowboys (E)	10	4	0	.714	Tom Landry
	Minnesota Vikings (C)	12	2	0	.857	Bud Grant
	Los Angeles Rams (W)	12	2	0	.857	Chuck Knox
1972	*Washington Redskins (E)	11	3	0	.786	George Allen
	Green Bay Packers (C)	10	4	0	.714	Dan Devine
	San Francisco 49ers (W)	8	5	1	.607	Dick Nolan
1971	*Dallas Cowboys (E)	11	3	0	.786	Tom Landry
	Minnesota Vikings (C)	11	3	0	.786	Bud Grant
	San Francisco 49ers (W)	9	5	0	.643	Dick Nolan
1970	*Dallas Cowboys (E)	10	4	0	.714	Tom Landry
	Minnesota Vikings (C)	12	2	0	.857	Bud Grant
	San Francisco 49ers (W)	10	3	1	.769	Dick Nolan
1969	Minnesota Vikings (W)	12	2	0	.857	Bud Grant
	Cleveland Browns (E)	10	3	1	.769	Blanton Collier

(1976)—* The Washington Redskins earned a playoff berth as the second-place team with the best won-lost percentage in the conference, .714.

(1975)—* The Dallas Cowboys earned a playoff berth as the second-place team with the best won-lost percentage in the conference, .714.

(1974)—* The Washington Redskins earned a playoff berth as the second-place team with the best won-lost percentage in the conference, .714.

(1973)—* The Washington Redskins earned a playoff berth as the second-place team with the best won-lost percentage in the conference, .714.

(1972)—* The Dallas Cowboys earned a playoff berth as the second-place team with the best won-lost percentage in the conference, .714.

(1971)—* The Washington Redskins earned a playoff berth as the second-place team with the best won-lost percentage in the conference, .692.

(1970)—* The Detroit Lions earned a playoff berth as the second-place team with the best won-lost percentage in the conference, .714.

Season Winners (Contd.)

Year	Winning Teams	Season Records W L T	Pct.	Team Coaches
1968	Baltimore Colts (W)	13—1—0	.929	Don Shula
	Cleveland Browns (E)	10—4—0	.714	Blanton Collier
1967	Green Bay Packers (W)	9—4—1	.692	Vince Lombardi
	Dallas Cowboys (E)	9—5—0	.643	Tom Landry
1966	Green Bay Packers (W)	12—2—0	.857	Vince Lombardi
	Dallas Cowboys (E)	10—3—1	.769	Tom Landry
1965	•Green Bay Packers (W)	10—3—1	.769	Vince Lombardi
	Cleveland Browns (E)	11—3—0	.786	Blanton Collier
1964	Cleveland Browns (E)	10—3—1	.769	Blanton Collier
	Baltimore Colts (W)	12—2—0	.857	Don Shula
1963	Chicago Bears (W)	11—1—2	.917	George Halas
	New York Giants (E)	11—3—0	.786	Al Sherman
1962	Green Bay Packers (W)	13—1—0	.929	Vince Lombardi
	New York Giants (E)	12—2—0	.857	Al Sherman
1961	Green Bay Packers (W)	11—3—0	.786	Vince Lombardi
	New York Giants (E)	10—3—1	.769	Al Sherman
1960	Philadelphia Eagles (E)	10—2—0	.833	Buck Shaw
	Green Bay Packers (W)	8—4—0	.667	Vince Lombardi
1959	Baltimore Colts (W)	9—3—0	.750	Weeb Ewbank
	New York Giants (E)	10—2—0	.833	Jim Howell
1958	Baltimore Colts (W)	9—3—0	.750	Weeb Ewbank
	•New York Giants (E)	9—3—0	.750	Jim Howell
1957	•Detroit Lions (W)	8—4—0	.667	George Wilson
	Cleveland Browns (E)	9—2—1	.818	Paul Brown
1956	New York Giants (E)	8—3—1	.727	Jim Howell
	Chicago Bears (W)	9—2—1	.818	Paddy Driscoll
1955	Cleveland Browns (E)	9—2—1	.818	Paul Brown
	Los Angeles Rams (W)	8—3—1	.727	Sid Gillman
1954	Cleveland Browns (E)	9—3—0	.750	Paul Brown
	Detroit Lions (W)	9—2—1	.818	Buddy Parker
1953	Detroit Lions (N)	10—2—0	.833	Buddy Parker
	Cleveland Browns (A)	11—1—0	.917	Paul Brown
1952	•Detroit Lions (N)	9—3—0	.750	Buddy Parker
	Cleveland Browns (A)	8—4—0	.667	Paul Brown
1951	Los Angeles Rams (N)	8—4—0	.667	Joe Stydahar
	Cleveland Browns (A)	11—1—0	.917	Paul Brown
1950	•Cleveland Browns (A)	10—2—0	.833	Paul Brown
	†Los Angeles Rams (N)	9—3—0	.750	Joe Stydahar

(1965)—• Green Bay and Baltimore tied for conference title; Packers won playoff, 13—10, in sudden-death overtime.
(1958)—• Giants and Cleveland Browns tied for conference title; Giants won playoff, 10—0.
(1957)—• Lions and San Francisco 49ers tied for conference title; Lions won playoff, 31—27.
(1952)—• Lions and Los Angeles Rams tied for conference title; Lions won playoff, 31—21.
(1950)—• Browns and New York Giants tied for conference title; Browns won playoff, 8—3.
(1950)—† Rams and Chicago Bears tied for conference title; Rams won playoff, 24—14.

Season Winners (Contd.)

Year	Winning Teams	W	L	T	Pct.	Team Coaches
1949	Philadelphia Eagles (E)	11	1	0	.917	Greasy Neale
	Los Angeles Rams (W)	8	2	2	.800	Clark Shaughnessy
1948	Philadelphia Eagles (E)	9	2	1	.818	Greasy Neale
	Chicago Cardinals (W)	11	1	0	.917	Jimmy Conzleman
1947	Chicago Cardinals (W)	9	3	0	.750	Jimmy Conzleman
	°Philadelphia Eagles (E)	8	4	0	.667	Greasy Neale
1946	Chicago Bears (W)	8	2	1	.800	George Halas
	New York Giants (E)	7	3	1	.700	Steve Owen
1945	Cleveland Rams (W)	9	1	0	.900	Adam Walsh
	Washington Redskins (E)	8	2	0	.800	Dudley De Groot
1944	Green Bay Packers (W)	8	2	0	.800	Curly Lambeau
	New York Giants (E)	8	1	1	.889	Steve Owen
1943	Chicago Bears (W)	8	1	1	.889	George Halas
	°Washington Redskins (E)	6	3	1	.667	Arthur Bergman
1942	Washington Redskins (E)	10	1	0	.909	Ray Flaherty
	Chicago Bears (W)	11	0	0	1.000	George Halas
1941	°Chicago Bears (W)	10	1	0	.909	George Halas
	New York Giants (E)	8	3	0	.727	Steve Owen
1940	Chicago Bears (W)	8	3	0	.727	George Halas
	Washington Redskins (E)	9	2	0	.818	Ray Flaherty
1939	Green Bay Packers (W)	9	2	0	.818	Curly Lambeau
	New York Giants (E)	9	1	1	.900	Steve Owen
1938	New York Giants (E)	8	2	1	.800	Steve Owen
	Green Bay Packers (W)	8	3	0	.727	Curly Lambeau
1937	Washington Redskins (E)	8	3	0	.727	Ray Flaherty
	Chicago Bears (W)	9	1	1	.900	George Halas
1936	Green Bay Packers (W)	10	1	1	.909	Curly Lambeau
	Boston Redskins (E)	7	5	0	.583	Ray Flaherty
1935	Detroit Lions (W)	7	3	2	.700	Milo Creighton
	New York Giants (E)	9	3	0	.750	Steve Owen
1934	New York Giants (E)	8	5	0	.615	Steve Owen
	Chicago Bears (W)	13	0	0	1.000	George Halas
1933	Chicago Bears (W)	10	2	1	.833	George Halas
	New York Giants (E)	11	3	0	.786	Steve Owen

(1947)—* Eagles and Pittsburgh Steelers tied for conference title; Eagles
won playoff, 21—0.
(1943)—* Redskins and New York Giants tied for conference title; Redskins
won playoff, 28—0.
(1941)—* Bears and Green Bay Packers tied for conference title; Bears won
playoff, 33—14.

Championship Game Results

Year	Teams and Scores	Year	Teams and Scores
1976	Minnesota 24, Los Angeles 13	1950	Cleveland 30,
1975	Dallas 37, Los Angeles 7		Los Angeles 28
1974	Minnesota 14, Los Angeles 10	1949	Philadelphia 14,
1973	Minnesota 27, Dallas 10		Los Angeles 0
1972	Washington 26, Dallas 3	1948	Philadelphia 7,
1971	Dallas 14, San Francisco 3		Chicago (Cardinals) 0
1970	Dallas 17, San Francisco 10	1947	Chicago (Cardinals) 28,
1969	Minnesota 27, Cleveland 7		Philadelphia 21
1968	Baltimore 34, Cleveland 0	1946	Chicago 24, New York 14
1967	Green Bay 21, Dallas 17	1945	Cleveland (Rams) 15,
1966	Green Bay 34, Dallas 27		Washington 14
1965	Green Bay 23, Cleveland 12	1944	Green Bay 14, New York 7
1964	Cleveland 27, Baltimore 0	1943	Chicago 41, Washington 21
1963	Chicago 14, New York 10	1942	Washington 14, Chicago 6
1962	Green Bay 16, New York 7	1941	Chicago 37, New York 9
1961	Green Bay 37, New York 0	1940	Chicago 73, Washington 0
1960	Philadelphia 17, Green Bay 13	1939	Green Bay 27, New York 0
1959	Baltimore 31, New York 16	1938	New York 23, Green Bay 17
1958	Baltimore 23, New York 17	1937	Washington 28, Chicago 21
1957	Detroit 59, Cleveland 14	1936	Green Bay 21,
1956	New York 47, Chicago 7		Boston (Redskins) 6
1955	Cleveland 38, Los Angeles 14	1935	Detroit 26, New York 7
1954	Cleveland 56, Detroit 10	1934	New York 30, Chicago 13
1953	Detroit 17, Cleveland 16	1933	Chicago 23, New York 21
1952	Detroit 17, Cleveland 7		
1951	Los Angeles 24, Cleveland 17		

SUPER BOWL WINNERS

Year	Teams and Scores
1977	Oakland Raiders 32, Minnesota Vikings 14
1976	Pittsburgh Steelers 21, Dallas Cowboys 17
1975	Pittsburgh Steelers 16, Minnesota Vikings 6
1974	Miami Dolphins 24, Minnesota Vikings 7
1973	Miami Dolphins 14, Washington Redskins 7
1972	Dallas Cowboys 24, Miami Dolphins 3
1971	Baltimore Colts 16, Dallas Cowboys 13
1970	Kansas City Chiefs 23, Minnesota Vikings 7
1969	New York Jets 16, Baltimore Colts 7
1968	Green Bay Packers 33, Oakland Raiders 14
1967	Green Bay Packers 35, Kansas City Chiefs 10

AFC INDIVIDUAL LEADERS, YEARLY
Scoring

Year	Player	Team	TD	PAT	FG	Pts.
1976	Linhart, Toni	Baltimore	0	49	20	109
1975	Simpson, O.J.	Buffalo	23	0	0	138

Scoring (Contd.)

Year	Player	Team	TD	PAT	FG	Pts.
1974	Gerela, Roy	Pittsburgh	0	33	20	93
1973	Gerela, Roy	Pittsburgh	0	36	29	123
1972	Howfield, Bobby	NY	0	40	27	121
1971	Yepremian, Garo	Miami	0	33	28	117
1970	Stenerud, Jan	KC	0	26	30	116
1969	Turner, Jim	NY	0	33	32	129
1968	Turner, Jim	NY	0	43	34	145
1967	Blanda, George	Oakland	0	56	20	116
1966	Cappelletti, Gino	Boston	6	35	16	119
1965	Cappelletti, Gino	Boston	9	27	17	132
1964	Cappelletti, Gino	Boston	7	38	25	155
1963	Cappelletti, Gino	Boston	0	35	22	113
1962	Mingo, Gene	Denver	4	32	27	137
1961	Cappelletti, Gino	Boston	8	48	17	147
1960	Mingo, Gene	Denver	6	33	18	123

Rushing

Year	Player	Team	YG	Atts.	Ave. G. Per Att.	TDS
1976	Simpson, O.J.	Buffalo	1503	290	5.2	8
1975	Simpson, O.J.	Buffalo	1817	329	5.5	16
1974	Armstrong, Otis	Denver	1407	263	5.3	9
1973	Simpson, O.J.	Buffalo	2003	332	6.0	12
1972	Simpson, O.J.	Buffalo	1251	292	4.3	6
1971	Little, Floyd	Denver	1133	284	4.0	6
1970	Little, Floyd	Denver	901	209	4.3	3
1969	Post, Dick	San Diego	873	182	4.8	6
1968	Robinson, Paul	Cincinnati	1023	238	4.3	8
1967	Nance, Jim	Boston	1216	269	4.5	7
1966	Nance, Jim	Boston	1458	299	4.9	11
1965	Lowe, Paul	San Diego	1121	222	5.0	7
1964	Gilchrist, Cookie	Buffalo	981	230	4.2	6
1963	Daniels, Clem	Oakland	1099	215	5.1	3
1962	Gilchrist, Cookie	Buffalo	1096	214	5.1	15
1961	Cannon, Billy	Houston	948	200	4.7	6
1960	Haynes, Abner	Dallas	875	156	5.6	9

Pass Receiving

Year	Player	Team	Caught	YG	TDS
1976	Lane, MacArthur	KC	66	686	1
1975	Rucker, Reggie	Cleveland	60	770	3
1975	Mitchell, Lydell	Baltimore	60	544	4
1974	Mitchell, Lydell	Baltimore	72	544	2
1973	Willis, Fred	Houston	57	371	1
1972	Biletnikoff, Fred	Oakland	58	802	7
1971	Biletnikoff, Fred	Oakland	61	929	9
1970	Briscoe, Marlin	Buffalo	57	1036	8

Pass Receiving (Contd.)

Year	Player	Team	Caught	YG	TDS
1969	Alworth, Lance	San Diego	64	1003	4
1968	Alworth, Lance	Oakland	68	1312	10
1967	Sauer, George	New York	75	1189	6
1966	Alworth, Lance	San Diego	73	1383	13
1965	Taylor, Lionel	Denver	85	1131	6
1964	Hennigan, Charley	Houston	101	1561	8
1963	Taylor, Lionel	Denver	78	1101	10
1962	Taylor, Lionel	Denver	77	908	4
1961	Taylor, Lionel	Denver	100	1176	4
1960	Groman, Bill	Houston	72	1473	12

Passing

Year	Player	Team	YG Per Att.	Atts.	Com.	Avg. Pct. Com.	YG	TDS
1976	Stabler, Ken	Oakland	9.41	291	194	66.7	2737	27
1975	Anderson, Ken	Cin	8.41	377	228	60.5	3169	21
1974	Anderson, Ken	Cin	8.13	328	213	64.9	2667	18
1973	Stabler, Ken	Oakland	7.68	260	163	62.7	1997	14
1972	Morrall, Earl	Miami	9.07	150	83	55.3	1360	11
1971	Griese, Bob	Miami	7.94	263	145	55.1	2089	19
1970	Lamonica, Daryle	Oakland	7.07	356	179	50.3	2516	22
1969	Cook, Greg	Cin	9.4	197	106	54	1854	15
1968	Dawson, Len	KC	9.4	224	131	58	2109	17
1967	Lamonica, Daryle	Oakland	7.6	425	220	52	3228	30
1966	Dawson, Len	KC	8.9	284	159	56	2527	26
1965	Hadl, John	SD	8.1	348	174	50	2798	20
1964	Dawson, Len	KC	8.1	354	199	56	2879	30
1963	Rote, Tobin	SD	8.7	287	170	59	2510	20
1962	Dawson, Len	Dallas	8.9	310	189	61	2759	29
1961	Blanda, George	Houston	9.2	362	187	52	3330	36
1960	Kemp, Jack	LA	7.4	406	211	52	3018	20

AFC TEAM LEADERS, YEARLY
Points Scored

Year	Team	Total	Year	Team	Total
1976	Baltimore	417	1967	Oakland	468
1975	Buffalo	420	1966	Kansas City	448
1974	Oakland	355	1965	San Diego	340
1973	Denver	354	1964	Buffalo	400
1972	Miami	385	1963	San Diego	399
1971	Oakland	344	1962	*Dallas	382
1970	Baltimore	321	1961	San Diego	399
1969	Oakland	377	1960	New York	386
1968	Oakland	453			

* Became Kansas City Chiefs.

Total Yards Gained

Year	Team	Total	Year	Team	Total
1976	Baltimore	5236	1967	New York	5155
1975	Buffalo	5467	1966	Kansas City	5114
1974	Oakland	4718	1965	San Diego	5101
1973	Oakland	4773	1964	Buffalo	5205
1972	Miami	5027	1963	San Diego	5160
1971	San Diego	4738	1962	Houston	4971
1970	Oakland	4829	1961	Houston	6288
1969	Oakland	5036	1960	Houston	4936
1968	Kansas City	4503			

Yards Passing / Yards Rushing

Year	Team	Total	Year	Team	Total
1976	Baltimore	2933	1976	Pittsburgh	2971
1975	Cincinnati	3241	1975	Buffalo	2974
1974	Cincinnati	2511	1974	Pittsburgh	2417
1973	Denver	2519	1973	Buffalo	3088
1972	Miami	2076	1972	Miami	2960
1971	San Diego	3134	1971	Miami	2429
1970	Oakland	2865	1970	Miami	2082
1969	Oakland	3271	1969	Kansas City	2220
1968	Kansas City	2276	1968	Kansas City	2227
1967	New York	3845	1967	Houston	2122
1966	New York	3464	1966	Kansas City	2274
1965	San Diego	3103	1965	San Diego	1998
1964	Houston	3527	1964	Buffalo	2039
1963	Houston	3210	1963	San Diego	2203
1962	Denver	3404	1962	Buffalo	2437
1961	Houston	4392	1961	*Dallas	2183
1960	Houston	3371	1960	*Dallas	1814

* Became Kansas City Chiefs.

Season Winners

Year	Winning Teams	W	L	T	Pct.	Team Coaches
1976	*Baltimore (E)	11	3	0	.786	Ted Marchibroda
	Pittsburgh (C)	10	4	0	.714	Chuck Noll
	Oakland (W)	13	1	0	.929	John Madden
1975	*Baltimore Colts (E)	10	4	0	.714	Ted Marchibroda
	Pittsburgh Steelers (C)	12	2	0	.857	Chuck Noll
	Oakland Raiders (W)	11	3	0	.786	John Madden

(1976)—* The New England Patriots earned a playoff berth as the second-place team with the best won-lost percentage in the conference, .786.

(1975)—* The Cincinnati Bengals earned a playoff berth as the second-place team with the best won-lost percentage in the conference, .786.

Season Winners (Contd.)

Year	Winning Teams	W	L	T	Pct.	Team Coaches
1974	*Miami Dolphins (E)	11	3	0	.786	Don Shula
	Pittsburgh Steelers (C)	10	3	1	.750	Chuck Noll
	Oakland Raiders (W)	12	2	0	.857	John Madden
1973	*Miami Dolphins (E)	12	2	0	.857	Don Shula
	Cincinnati Bengals (C)	10	4	0	.714	Paul Brown
	Oakland Raiders (W)	9	4	1	.679	John Madden
1972	*Miami Dolphins (E)	14	0	0	1.000	Don Shula
	Pittsburgh Steelers (C)	11	3	0	.786	Chuck Noll
	Oakland Raiders (W)	10	3	1	.750	John Madden
1971	*Miami Dolphins (E)	10	3	1	.769	Don Shula
	Cleveland Browns (C)	9	5	0	.643	Nick Skorich
	Kansas City Chiefs (W)	10	3	1	.769	Hank Stram
1970	*Baltimore Colts (E)	11	2	1	.846	Don McCafferty
	Cincinnati Bengals (C)	8	6	0	.571	Paul Brown
	Oakland Raiders (W)	8	4	2	.667	John Madden
1969	Kansas City Chiefs (W)	11	3	0	.786	Hank Stram
	Oakland Raiders (W)	12	1	1	.923	John Madden
1968	Oakland Raiders (W)	12	2	0	.857	Johnny Rauch
	New York Jets (E)	11	3	0	.786	Weeb Ewbank
1967	Oakland Raiders (W)	13	1	0	.929	Johnny Rauch
	Houston Oilers (E)	9	4	1	.692	Wally Lemm
1966	Kansas City Chiefs (W)	11	2	1	.846	Hank Stram
	Buffalo Bills (E)	9	4	1	.692	Joel Collier
1965	Buffalo Bills (E)	10	3	1	.769	Lou Saban
	San Diego Chargers (W)	9	2	3	.819	Sid Gillman
1964	Buffalo Bills (E)	12	2	0	.857	Lou Saban
	San Diego Chargers (W)	8	5	1	.615	Sid Gillman
1963	San Diego Chargers (W)	11	3	0	.786	Sid Gillman
	*Boston Patriots (E)	7	6	1	.538	Mike Holovak
1962	Dallas Texans (W)	11	3	0	.786	Hank Stram
	Houston Oilers (E)	11	3	0	.786	Pop Ivy
1961	San Diego Chargers (W)	12	2	0	.857	Sid Gillman
	Houston Oilers (E)	10	3	1	.769	Wally Lemm
1960	Los Angeles Chargers (W)	10	4	0	.714	Sid Gillman
	Houston Oilers (E)	10	4	0	.714	Lou Rykmus

(1974)—* The Buffalo Bills earned a playoff berth as the second-place team with the best won-lost percentage in the conference, .643.

(1973)—* The Pittsburgh Steelers earned a playoff berth as the second-place team with the best won-lost percentage in the conference, .714.

(1972)—* The Cleveland Browns earned a playoff berth as the second-place team with the best won-lost percentage in the conference, .714.

(1971)—* The Baltimore Colts earned a playoff berth as the second-place team with the best won-lost percentage in the conference, .714.

(1970)—* The Miami Dolphins earned a playoff berth as the second-place team with the best won-lost percentage in the conference, .714.

(1963)—* Patriots and Buffalo Bills tied for division title; Patriots won play-off, 26—8.

Championship Game Results

Year	Teams and Scores	Year	Teams and Scores
1976	Oakland 24, Pittsburgh 7	1966	Kansas City 31, Buffalo 7
1975	Pittsburgh 16, Oakland 10	1965	Buffalo 23, San Diego 0
1974	Pittsburgh 24, Oakland 13	1964	Buffalo 20, San Diego 7
1973	Miami 27, Oakland 10	1963	San Diego 51,
1972	Miami 21, Pittsburgh 17		Boston (Patriots) 10
1971	Miami 21, Baltimore 0	1962	Dallas (Texans) 20,
1970	Baltimore 27, Oakland 17		Houston 17
1969	Kansas City 17, Oakland 7	1961	Houston 10, San Diego 3
1968	New York 27, Oakland 23	1960	Houston 24,
1967	Oakland 40, Houston 7		Los Angeles (Chargers) 16